Is a truly race-neutral society possible? Can the United States wipe the slate clean and surmount the racism of its past? Or is color blindness just another name for denial? Ellis Cose, author of *The Rage of a Privileged Class*, now probes the murky depths of the American mind and exposes the contradictions, fears, hopes, and illusions embedded in our complicated perceptions of race.

As he investigates whether Martin Luther King's dream of a society in which people would be judged not by color but by character is realizable, Cose explains, in his pointed and provocative style, how the ongoing race debate—one side claiming that discrimination is at the root of all of America's racial problems, the other maintaining that prejudice has practically disappeared—has failed to paint a complete picture of reality.

Drawing on the experiences of South Africa and Latin America, Cose illustrates why it has been impossible for the United States to move directly from race relations hell (where discrimination is sanctioned and animosity flows freely) to race relations utopia (where discrimination is condemned and a race-neutral society prevails) without passing through a purgatory where legal barriers have been dropped but racial misunderstandings and ingrained prejudices persist. With the concrete solutions of a true visionary, Cose concludes by offering twelve steps toward the society of Dr. King's dream, presenting America with a powerful challenge to achieve its true potential.

Anecdotally rich, analytically powerful, and completely original in approach, *Color-Blind* is Ellis Cose's most penetrating and thought-provoking book to date.

Color-
Blind

Other Books by Ellis Cose

The Press
A Nation of Strangers
The Rage of a Privileged Class
A Man's World

Color-Blind

SEEING BEYOND RACE IN A RACE-OBSESSED WORLD

ELLIS COSE

HarperCollins*Publishers*

HarperCollins books may be purchased for educational, business, or sales promotional use. For information please write: Special Markets Department, HarperCollins Publishers, Inc., 10 East 53rd Street, New York, NY 10022.

FIRST EDITION

Designed by Alma Orenstein

Library of Congress Cataloging-in-Publication Data

Cose, Ellis.
Color-blind : seeing beyond race in a race-obsessed world / Ellis Cose.—1st ed.
p. cm.
Includes bibliographical references (p.) and index.
ISBN 0-06-017497-8
1. Race discrimination—United States. 2. Affirmative action programs—United States. 3. United States—Race relations. 4. Racism—United States. 5. Afro-Americans—Civil rights.
I. Title.
E185.615.C68 1997
305.8'00973—dc20 96-34433

---

97 98 99 00 01 ❖/RRD 10 9 8 7 6 5

For
Lee, Nelson, Elsa, and Wanda

CONTENTS

ACKNOWLEDGMENTS

I am grateful to many people who contributed to the making of this book, and none more so than Paul Rogers, my researcher, who anticipated questions well before they were asked and came up with many materials long before I realized they would be needed. He was a valuable partner who has moved on to what I am sure will be a distinguished career as a journalist.

I am indebted as well to Michael Congdon, my agent, who provided not only guidance but calm reassurance that wrestling with such a contentious subject would have a constructive result; to Diane Reverand, HarperCollins editor-in-chief, whose enthusiasm for the project was contagious and essential; and to Peternelle van Arsdale, an editor who has a knack for asking the questions that take the text to a higher level.

Bill Lynch, Milton Morris, Eve Thompson, Dumisani Kumalo, Ulric Haynes, Mondli waka Makhanya, and Joe Contreras ensured, through their counsel and contacts, that my travels in South Africa would be both enjoyable and productive. Emilio Pantojas and Marya Muñoz Vázquez were of invaluable help in Puerto Rico.

Dolores Prida, Maite Junco, and Raúl Cotto Serrano provided wise and invaluable advice.

Alexis Gelber, Maynard Parker, Aric Press, and Mark Whitaker of *Newsweek* have been consistently supportive colleagues. Oliver Cromwell and Youtha Hardman have been steadfast in their feedback and their friendship. Finally, Lee, my wife, has served so many roles—as researcher, interviewer, proofreader, occasionally even transcriptionist, and always as a source of boundless faith and love.

INTRODUCTION

Trapped in the dominant dialogue

"The white race deems itself to be the dominant race in this country. And so it is, in prestige, in achievement, in education, in wealth, and in power. So, I doubt not, it will continue to be for all time, if it remains true to its great heritage and holds fast to the principles of constitutional liberty. But in view of the constitution, in the eyes of the law, there is in this country no superior, dominant, ruling class of citizens. There is no caste here. Our constitution is color-blind, and neither knows nor tolerates classes among citizens. . . . The destinies of the two races, in this country, are indissolubly linked together, and the interests of both require that the common government of all shall not permit the seeds of race hate to be planted under the sanction of law."

—JUSTICE JOHN MARSHALL HARLAN
DISSENTING IN *PLESSY V. FERGUSON*, 1896

"Freedom is about having a dream. And maybe I feel that particularly because the greatest Georgian of this century, Martin Luther King, went to the Lincoln Memorial and said in his extraordinary speech, 'I have a dream.' And the dream he outlined is a dream for every American of every background to participate in creating an America that is better for our children and our grandchildren."

—HOUSE SPEAKER NEWT GINGRICH
AT THE 1996 REPUBLICAN NATIONAL CONVENTION

"This just says we've got to be color-blind. I do not believe I have any prejudice—never had in my opinion. I don't look at color . . . Dr. King dedicated his life to the pursuit of equality and opportunity for all Americans. He believed all men should be judged by their character, not by the color of their skin."

—LOUISIANA GOVERNOR MIKE FOSTER, JANUARY 1996, ON SIGNING AN ORDER BANNING AFFIRMATIVE ACTION IN AGENCIES UNDER HIS CONTROL AND, ON THE SAME DAY, SIGNING A BILL DECLARING THE BIRTHDAY OF MARTIN LUTHER KING, JR., A STATE HOLIDAY

Martin Luther King, Jr., would probably be more astonished than anyone to hear that conservatives now claim him as one of their own, that they have embraced his dream of a color-blind world and invoke it as proof of the immorality of gender and racial "preferences." But even if he had a bit of trouble accepting his status as a general in the war against affirmative action, he would appreciate the joke. And he would realize that it is the fate of the dead to be reborn as angels to the living.

King no doubt would be pleased to have new friends in his fight for justice, but he would approach them with caution, for he would recall, as he did for readers of *Where Do We Go From Here: Chaos or Community?*, that friendship has its limits. "With Selma and the Voting Rights Act one phase of development in the civil rights revolution came to an end," he wrote.

> A new phase opened, but few observers realized it or were prepared for its implications. For the vast majority of white Americans, the past decade—the first phase—had been a struggle to treat the Negro with a degree of decency, not of equality. White America was ready to demand that the Negro should be spared the lash of brutality and coarse degradation, but it had never been truly committed to helping him out of poverty, exploitation or all forms of discrimination. . . . When Negroes looked for the second phase, the realization of equality, they found that many of their white allies had quietly disappeared.

After sharing his disappointment over past alliances with people whose commitment to change did not match his own, King would address his new associates bluntly. "All right," he might say, "I understand why you oppose affirmative action. But tell me: What is *your* plan? What is your plan to crush the tragic walls separating the wealth and comfort of the outer city from the despair of the inner city? What is *your* plan to cast the slums of our cities on the junk heaps of history? What is *your* program to transform the dark yesterdays of segregated education into the bright tomorrows of high-quality, integrated education. What is *your* strategy to smash separatism, to destroy discrimination, to make justice roll down like water and righteousness flow like a mighty stream from every city hall and statehouse in this great and blessed nation?" He might then pause for a reply, his countenance making it unmistakably clear that he would accept neither silence nor sweet nothings as an answer.

That King is now a hero to those on both sides of the anti–affirmative-action aisle is arguably a sign of progress. It is also a simple reflection of the fact that the ways in which we remember people often have more to do with our needs than with the actual focus of their existence—even when those people are not nearly as famous as Martin Luther King, Jr.

Ada Lois Sipuel Fisher, for instance, is hardly a household name. Yet the *New York Times* presented her October 1995 obituary ("Ada Fisher, 71; Broke a Law School Color Barrier") as a glorious parable of triumph and hope.

Mrs. Fisher was black, and that fact was paramount in her life or, at least, it was back in 1946, when, as an honors graduate of Langston College, she applied to the University of Oklahoma Law School. She was rejected but not deterred. Backed by the NAACP, she appealed her case to the Supreme Court, which ordered the state to provide her with a legal (though not necessarily an integrated) education. It took time, and there were setbacks, even an attempt by the state to accommodate Ada by setting up a separate black law school just for her. In the end, the state caved, but not exactly with grace. The school admitted her in 1949 but insisted that she sit in a raised chair behind a sign reading Colored—separated in status and by space, chain, and a uniformed guard from the law school's white students. But those students were better than their elders. Whenever the guard took a break, they would climb under the chain and offer encouragement. "Come on, Ada," they would say, "we've been waiting for you."

Mrs. Fisher persevered, going on to earn her law degree and later a master's degree in history. In April 1992 she got her sweet reward: She joined the board of regents of the very university that had once rejected her.

The obituary was only thirteen short paragraphs, but it was beautifully written. Moreover, it was a perfect example of the kind of racial news America loves to hear: a story that acknowledges that racism was once a serious problem, deep in our country's past, but recognizes that even then, there were good white people around, particularly the young, who were too pure to be tainted by bigotry. With the encouragement of such sweet souls and the help of her own people, a forgiving and talented African American rose eventually to be included in the ranks of those who so foolishly had abhorred her. If only all the stories of America could be so sweet.

The problem, of course, is that most are not, particularly most that deal with race. Though Americans prefer to dwell on parables of white virtue and black advancement—culminating in the flowering of goodwill all around—events periodically force us to widen our gaze and to focus on terrain we would rather not see. The 1992 Los Angeles riots did that, and so did the O. J. Simpson trial, just as the riots of the 1960s forced America to wring its hands, ponder—however briefly—its racial hypocrisy, and hope that the crisis would soon pass.

Racial crises, unfortunately, have a way of reprising themselves, if not precisely with the same notes. It is, perhaps, inevitable that they do, given that we seem to be singularly uncreative when it comes to talking about—much less dealing with—race.

For several decades, America has waged an ongoing argument. On one side have sounded the voices of protest, claiming that discrimination is at the root of America's racial problems. On the other side have sounded the voices of conservatism, maintaining that discrimination is nowhere near as pervasive as minority groups believe and that the discrimination that does exist is largely the fault of minorities themselves. Because many of the more brazen exponents of the latter view were never receptive to the goals of civil rights and because their analysis often rests on an acceptance of the notion of the intellectual or cultural inferiority of blacks, their ideas are about as credible among most blacks as a former SS officer's critique of Judaism would be among Jews. For those of us who strongly reject the idea that blacks are fundamentally flawed, these conservatives are extremely easy to tune out.

Yet, though the dialogue remains largely unchanged, American reality does not. The high and low notes modulate. Occasionally, scholars and others, realizing that fact, have tried to shift the racial discussion—to find a middle range or merely to acknowledge the complexity of the harmonics. In *The Declining Significance of Race,* published in 1978, sociologist William Julius Wilson argued that economic class has more do with blacks' lack of opportunities than does outright racial discrimination. Basic changes in the economy, he said, had become larger barriers to success for certain segments of the black population than was old-fashioned white racism.

Such middle-range positions, as Wilson quickly discovered, can be politically precarious. Wilson's basic insight, that racism *alone* cannot explain the condition of blacks in American society, was rejected by those who saw Wilson as little more than an Uncle Tom, presumably currying favor with whites by denying the discrimination that most blacks knew to be all too real, and it was distorted beyond recognition by conservatives who took his argument as an admission that racism no longer existed or, perhaps, just no longer mattered. Dinesh D'Souza, author of *The End of Racism,* is one of many who carried Wilson's point to absurd conclusions. D'Souza, an East Indian immigrant, claimed that his own minority status provided a certain "ethnic immunity," meaning that he was allowed more frankness than a white person would be in discussing sensitive racial issues. D'Souza was certainly frank. In fact, some of his black colleagues at the American Enterprise Institute found his language so insulting that they publicly denounced him. D'Souza's basic point was that antiblack racism has largely disappeared. What sometimes is taken for racism, he concluded, is nothing more than "rational discrimination"—which, not to put too fine a point on it, is discrimination against those who ought to be discriminated against. The statistical fact that black men are more likely than white men to be involved in violent crime, for instance, means that potential crime victims are justified in treating all black men with suspicion. Such discrimination is not a result of racism, D'Souza argued, but of a rational recognition of "black cultural pathology" and of its toxicity to American life.

A similar point was made, in a much milder form, by political scientist James Q. Wilson in a 1992 *Wall Street Journal* article. "The best way to reduce racism real or imagined is to reduce the black crime rate to equal the white crime rate," Wilson wrote. But whereas Wilson acknowledged the reality of racism, D'Souza essentially denied its existence. Both, however, excused one evil (discrimination against innocent people) by pointing to another evil (crimes committed by blacks). They also suggested, implicitly, that blacks are still on probation in America and therefore have to earn the right (in this case by making lawbreaking blacks behave themselves) to be treated with the same respect as whites. That message, of course, is not new. And it engenders resentment even among politically moderate blacks, who assume that African Americans as a group (whatever some members of the group may have done) deserve (no less than any other Americans) to be treated with decency and fairness, but who sometimes despair that blacks in the United States will ever be permitted to feel as welcome and as optimistic as do whites.

Not long ago, I came upon an essay by novelist Trey Ellis entitled (in homage to W. E. B. Du Bois's famous formulation) "How Does It Feel to Be a Problem?" Ellis was taking strong issue with what he termed Shelby Steele's theory of "individual liberation through assimilation." "It is irrefutable that if we African Americans abandoned our culture, stopped griping, and joined the melting pot, we would be better off," wrote Ellis. "The catch is the very real limit to our ambition. If we play by Steele's rules—work hard, scrimp, save and study—then one day one of us just might become vice president of the United States. Therein lies the rub. In this land of opportunity, we are promised riches, a degree of respect, and respectability, but we know we are still barred from the highest corridors of power. It's a crippling message. How can you expect someone to dedicate his entire life to training for the Olympics if all he can hope for is a silver medal?"

It was not evident, from the 1995 collection (entitled *Speak My*

Name) in which this piece was included, at just what point Ellis first set down that thought. I suspect that it was some time before America became caught up in Powellmania. For what if blacks are no longer limited to playing second fiddle? How does it change things if at least some blacks can break through the previously impregnable roadblocks? Colin Powell, after all, seemed poised to do so. Untold millions had convinced themselves that if only he would run, the country would be healed, America would work efficiently again, and people would regain the strut in their stride. Exactly how Powell would work his magic was never clear. His very presence in the White House, it seemed, would do the trick.

There have been many moments in the past when a military hero—a Washington, an Eisenhower—stood taller than anyone else in sight. Powell's moment, however, was different. His ascension in America's estimation was fueled not just by an eternal hunger for heroes, but for a black hero, for a healer. Though he always made it clear that if he ran, he would not just be a "black" president, many fans saw him as an undeniable symbol of racial progress. And partly because he made such a good advertisement for race relations, support for him was generally much stronger among whites than among blacks.

Ironically, blacks were uncertain what to make of the Powell phenomenon. When I brought up the subject of Powell's strong showing in the polls among whites during a discussion with a black social scientist in California, the professor shook his head skeptically and asked: "Do they [whites] really mean it? . . . I don't think they are ready to go all the way." When I raised the same subject with a group of black scholars in the South, they reminded me of Tom Bradley's 1982 experience in California. Bradley, opting to become the first elected black governor in America's history, had been comfortably ahead of his white opponent in the polls. Nonetheless, he lost the race. Seven years later, Douglas Wilder also watched his supposed lead in Virginia's race for governor mysteriously evaporate. Though he was as much as 15 percentage points ahead in certain polls, he ended up in a cliffhanger, which, happily for him, he won by a fraction of a percent of the vote. The moral, many pollsters concluded, was that whites were not necessarily honest when asked about their support for black candidates.

At a time when the polls showed whites preferring Powell to Bill Clinton, Bob Dole, or Ross Perot (even as they showed blacks preferring Clinton to Powell), Bradley's and Wilder's experiences were highly relevant. Yet even if one assumes that white support for Powell was not as strong as it seemed or would fade as the election season wore on, the enthusiasm behind his possible candidacy was undeniably genuine. It was evident to anyone who had the experience of talking to voters when Powell's name was in play. Clearly, Powell's American journey was not necessarily predestined to end with a silver medal.

Powell himself made the point at the crowded press conference in November 1995, at which he made public his decision not to run. "In one generation," he said, "we have moved from denying a black man service at a lunch counter to elevating one to the highest military office in the nation and to being a serious contender for the presidency. This is a magnificent country, and I am proud to be one of its sons." When a reporter followed up by asking when a black candidate's time would come, he replied: "I think it will happen at some point. . . . But I think the important point is that the nation has arrived at a point in our national life where such a possibility exists, and that's the realization of a great dream, even though I may not be the one to fill it."

Powell did not specify whose dream he had in mind, though his words naturally evoked memories of Martin Luther King, Jr.—and his vision of a society in which people would be judged not by color but by character. Where the sons of slaves and the sons of slaveholders would sit together in brotherhood. Where "little black boys and black girls will be able to join hands with little white boys and white girls and walk together as brothers and sisters."

In the years since King spoke those words, they have found an audience much broader than the throng gathered on the Washington mall in August 1963—including, as I noted earlier, among partisans of the political Right. In explaining his opposition to affirmative action, for instance, Louisiana Governor Mike Foster remarked, "I can't find anywhere in his writings that he [King] wanted reverse discrimination. He just wanted an end to all discrimination based on color."

A self-declared black conservative, who was one of the leaders of the so-called California Civil Rights Initiative (CCRI), passionately invoked King's name over dinner one night when I asked him why he had jumped on the anti–affirmative action bandwagon. Erroll Smith, an entrepreneur who was then serving as cochair of the CCRI campaign, replied, "I couldn't believe we had abandoned the mission of striving toward a color-blind society. I couldn't believe that somehow the talk about race neutrality, a color-blind society [had shifted]. . . . I thought that was the essence of King's movement. When did the game change? Who changed the rules? Who checked with me? Who checked with any of us?"

When King made his most fondly remembered speech, he was not so much describing a plausible future (he did not, after all, proclaim, "I have a prophecy") as voicing a fantasy. Yet today, though King's vision is far from realized, the very possibility of a Powell presidency raises the question of whether that fantasy is in the process of becoming a fact in some segments of American society. Have race relations truly changed all that much since the summer when the world heard King declaim his famous dream?

In July 1963 (a month before King delivered his stirring address), *Newsweek* magazine published the results of a pioneering Louis Harris poll. It was, as the cover story boasted, the "first definitive national survey" of "The Negro in America." For this unprecedented project, the magazine adopted the tone of an explorer investigating an alien race, promising to reveal "who he [the Negro] is, what he wants, what he fears, what he hates, how he lives, how he votes, why he is fighting . . . and why now."

Discrimination, *Newsweek* concluded, was the "central fact" of black life in America; it was also the cause of the "Revolution of 1963." The magazine went on to spell out, in poignant detail, how sharply blacks felt the sting of discrimination and how it had undermined their faith in whites.

Poor blacks, *Newsweek* noted, were generally distrustful of whites and of their motives: "Only one in four rank-and-file Negroes thinks the white man sincerely wants to see him get a better break. Forty-one percent think the white man wants to keep the Negro in his place, and 17 percent say the whites simply don't care."

Though more affluent blacks were more trusting of whites than were poor blacks, they were far from unanimous in the belief that whites meant them no harm. Thirty-three percent of middle- and upper-income blacks in the North and 45 percent of those in the South reported having favorable impressions of whites.

Whites themselves were ambivalent to blacks' demands for equal treatment, observed *Newsweek*.

> For the future, the crisis point will come if and when the irresistible force of Negro protest meets the immovable object of white intractability. In polls for the *Washington Post*, Louis Harris found majorities of white Americans in favor—at least in principle—of taking Federal action to secure the Negro's rights. But the white man's commitment thins in practice. Three in five don't think the Negro is ready to hold a better job or to live in a better neighborhood, and nearly three in four feel Negroes are moving faster than whites will accept them. The white man's resistance is particularly strong at the prospect of a Negro moving into the house next door to his.

The same October, the Gallup Organization canvassed reactions of American adults to a hypothetical black presidential candidacy and found that whites were not particularly keen on the idea. The interviewers started by stating, "There is always much discussion about the qualifications of presidential candidates—their education, age, race, religion, and the like"—and then asked, "If your party nominated a generally well-qualified man for president and he happened to be Negro, would you vote for him?" Forty–eight percent said yes, 45 percent said no, and 7 percent claimed to have no opinion. Putting aside the question of whether race and religion reveal anything about the "qualifications of presidential candidates," nearly half the voters in America (and more than half the whites if one assumes that blacks in the sample were generally willing to vote for a black candidate) were comfortable admitting in 1963 (even as King challenged the nation with his vision of a color-blind society) that they would reject a candidate simply because he was a Negro.

Five years later—following King's assassination and a series of violent outbreaks in urban, predominantly black, areas—the National Advisory Commission on Civil Disorders (popularly called the Kerner Commission) followed up some of Harris's work.

Angus Campbell and Howard Schuman, the social scientists responsible for the new surveys, concluded that things had not changed much. "The majority of Negroes expect little from whites other than hostility, opposition, or at best indifference," they wrote in a special supplemental report to the Kerner Commission study. The "psychological distance between the races," they observed, "makes it easy for each to develop misunderstandings, apprehension and mistrust." They also noted that although a majority of whites acknowledged the existence of some discrimination, most believed that discrimination had little to do with the Negroes' fate. Fifty–six percent of whites thought that Negroes, on average, had worse jobs, education, and housing than did whites "mainly due to something about Negroes themselves." Blacks, as Harris had already discovered, generally held the opposite view.

On the basis of these interpretations of the early polls, one could have forecast much of the racial dialogue of the next several decades, as well as the chronically divergent white-black perceptions of racial prejudice and of racially charged public events. As reactions to the O. J. Simpson trial demonstrated, the "psychological distance between the races" remains large.

Yet the trial also showed that even the most sensationalized and racially ticklish case cannot always be reduced purely to questions of race. For one thing, although practically from the beginning most whites concluded that Simpson was guilty and most blacks thought he was not, a substantial number of those of both races refused to split along racial lines. If their views did not exactly transcend race, they were not always dominated by it.

Much of the early news coverage of the case deemphasized race precisely because it was the celebrity of the accused perpetrator, not his race, that gave the case such a prominent profile. For many, the case was primarily a soap opera about the downfall of the rich and famous, of beautiful people (the most prominent one of whom happened to be black) caught up in a tangle of pathology. Race, though always present, was often peripheral.

The coverage reflected society's struggle to balance two competing realities: that though race mattered, it was far from all that mattered. The public fascination with the prospect of Powell's candidacy likewise reflected, in an altogether different context, the same struggle, as well as an attempt to come to terms with a broader question: What is the proper and future role of race in America?

For many of Powell's supporters, the answer seemed self–evident. The very fact that they could support Powell was evidence that Americans were closer than ever to achieving King's fabled dream. That answer, however, is far too facile, for it was not as if Powell's supporters somehow didn't notice that he was black; they simply decided—for various reasons—that his race was not a drawback, that perhaps (at that time and for that position) it was an advantage, if only in that it would allow the country to make a positive statement about race. Indeed, Powell's standing among many whites as something of a black messiah—as someone larger than race and yet, in some respects, reassuring precisely because of his race (and because of the patriotic, nonthreatening way in which he wore his racial pride)—can just as easily be cited as evidence that Americans are not really embracing King's dream at all—if that dream is defined as the creation of a color-blind state. Instead, we may simply have become more accepting of positive black stereotypes to counteract the disparaging ones that have always existed.

In a world in which opportunities, positions, and even wealth are often dispensed largely on the basis of connections, family ties, and physical appearance (not to mention race and ethnicity), King's celebrated dream may be hopelessly naive. But its improbability does not detract from its power. Americans cherish fairness. We like to believe that people, for the most part, are neither penalized nor unduly rewarded without justifiable cause.

And certainly, when looked at logically, racial difference is not a justifiable reason to penalize people. Race, after all, defines a relatively small part of who we are—at least from a strictly scientific perspective. As geneticist Christopher Wills noted in the November 1994 issue of *Discover* magazine: "We have known for decades that variation in skin color is caused by rather small genetic differences, and it seems *highly* [italics in the original] unlikely that these differences have anything to do with intelligence, personality, or ability."

Yet, weak as its scientific foundation may be, race is an essential part of who we are (and of how we see others) that is no more easily shed than unpleasant memories. Few of us would choose to be rendered raceless—to be suddenly without a tribe. Even something as prosaic as television-viewing habits is heavily influenced by race. A special analysis of the Nielsen ratings for the 1994–95 season by the advertising agency BBDO found that blacks and whites generally watched totally different prime-time shows. Of the top twenty shows in America, only two were in the top twenty among blacks—*NFL Monday Night Football* and the *NBC Monday Night Movie*. Many of the differences in ratings were extreme. *Living Single*, a comedy centered on a group of young black singles, for instance, came in first among blacks and 110th among whites. *New York Undercover*, a police drama featuring a black and a Latino lead, was second among blacks and 114th among whites. *Home Improvement*, *Grace Under Fire*, and *Seinfeld*, all comedies featuring whites, were the top three shows overall but none ranked high among blacks; *Seinfeld* came in at 109th place.

The ratings numbers reflect a simple fact: that even in our least political moments, when relaxing in the privacy of our homes, we are much more likely than not to gravitate toward those whom we perceive as our own kind (racially). That inclination—along with the tendency by jurists, politicians, and others to confuse color blindness with blindness to discrimination (and the continuing effects of past discrimination)—gives the lie to any literal notion of color blindness. Yet it does not change a basic reality: that while discrimination for most blacks is an unfortunate fact of life, it is no longer, as *Newsweek* previously put it, the central fact of life. As William Julius Wilson, among others, convincingly argued: Education and access to decent jobs may be more important variables in many black and brown lives than anything directly connected to race.

The attempt to think through where we may be heading led me to spend most of February 1996 in various parts of South Africa, which is how I came to be in the office of George Bizos, Nelson Mandela's longtime attorney, confidant, and sometime emissary and a lifelong opponent of apartheid. The morning we spoke, Bizos, working with South Africa's Legal Resources Centre, was engaged in planning the defense of a group of three hundred indigents who were in danger of being evicted from a squatters' camp outside Johannesburg. Bizos, a rotund man with the courtly, commanding air of a born barrister, made the tongue-in-cheek observation, "It's very difficult to find anyone who was in favor of apartheid."

Did it matter, I asked him, whether people were for apartheid as long as they acted as if they believed in equality. "I believe that the attitude of many whites is cosmetic," he replied, "but, you know, very often, you become the person whose role you are playing." After a brief pause, he added, "The majority of whites in South Africa, I think, are pleasantly surprised that the horror stories they were fed during the apartheid years and the stereotypes that were painted then, the stereotypes of blacks, have been proved wrong."

When I asked him to compare America's experience with South Africa's, he focused not on a similarity but on a difference: "Black people in South Africa—with all the insults they have suffered, and in some instances still suffer, and all the deprivation—feel that the future is theirs. They are the majority. They have their own president, their own local commissioner of the police force, their own shop stewards. . . . [There is] a confidence that . . . sooner or later, their unhappy lot will improve."

The United States, of course, has never been under black rule. Martin Luther King, Jr., was, after all, assassinated, not made president. And even if he had become president, he would not have had a majority black government with, say, Andrew Young as his vice president and Jesse Jackson as his secretary of health, education, and welfare. Yet, in both countries, the language of "nonracialism" is now accepted; the idea that race should not be an excuse for racism has been endorsed as an ideal. Neither nation, however, has yet shown that the words and the sentiment necessarily lead to the reality. In Latin America, where the language of nonracialism is older than in either the United States or South Africa, color blindness is still more a fable than a fact. Indeed, the experiences of South Africa and South America may go a long way toward disproving an enduring American fable: that it is possible to move directly from race-relations hell (where discrimination is officially sanctioned and animosity flows freely) to race-relations utopia (where discrimination is condemned and a color-blind society has risen) without passing through and ultimately surmounting race-relations purgatory (where the legal apparatus of discrimination is dead, but the ugly legacy lingers). In fact, the larger question raised by the experiences of those societies (and by American history as well) is whether color blindness is truly an achievable goal, for though it has become obligatory throughout the world to condemn racism and celebrate equality, racial distinctions continue to matter—not only as physical descriptors (such as eye color), but as presumed indications of individual worth. Indeed, the American civil rights movement has not so much been about attempting to blind people to color as about trying to strip race of the ugly connotations that gives racism the power to wound. That effort has been far from a resounding success—causing many people to wonder whether some of the strategies employed in pursuit of racial fairness were somehow fundamentally flawed.

For much of the past three decades, much of liberal America believed that racial progress would come about through the use of race-conscious policies. Justice Harry Blackmun spelled out the basic assumption in 1978 in commenting on the case of *Regents of University of California v. Bakke:* "In order to get beyond racism, we must first take account of race. There is no other way. And in order to treat some persons equally, we must treat them differently." Today's opponents of affirmative action argue from the opposite premise: that treating people differently can never result in treating them equally, that racially targeted programs merely compound one evil with another. Even most people who support such programs agree that affirmative action alone can never create equality, that at best it can guarantee relatively few people access to a relatively small number of opportunities. So where do Americans go from here? Is it realistic to envision an America where race and extreme disadvantage do not go hand in hand? If color blindness is an impossible dream, what of color neutrality? If color neutrality is a possibility, how do we get there? At a time when liberal guilt has become as unfashionable as love beads and polyester leisure suits, do we even have the will to try? Are we serious when we proclaim our desire for a color-blind state? Or are we merely saying we are tired of thinking about the problems associated with race?

In 1897, the year after Supreme Court Justice John Marshall Harlan famously failed to convince his colleagues that the U.S. Constitution was "color-blind," W. E. B. Du Bois wrestled with questions very much like those above. "No Negro who has given earnest thought to the situation of his people in America has failed, at some time in life, to find himself at these crossroads; has failed to ask himself at some time: what, after all, am I? Am I an American or am I a Negro? Can I be both? Or is it my duty to cease to be a Negro as soon as possible and be an American? If I strive as a Negro, am I not perpetuating the very cleft that threatens and separates black and white America? Is not my only possible practical aim the subduction of all that is Negro in me to the American? Does my black blood place upon me any more obligation to assert my nationality than German, or Irish, or Italian blood would?" asked Du Bois in a speech to the American Negro Academy.

Eliminating color consciousness, Du Bois ultimately concluded, was probably not possible and perhaps not even desirable; but he did not equate an absence of color-blindness with an inability of people of different races to live in harmony. As long as issues of law, language, economics, and religion could be resolved, there was no reason why people of different races might not strive together "in the same country and on the same street" to advance their common and particular goals: "Here, it seems to me, is the reading of the riddle that puzzles so many of us. We are Americans, not only by birth and by citizenship, but by our political ideas, our language, our religion. Farther than that, our Americanism does not go. At that point, we are Negroes, members of a vast historic race that from the very dawn of creation has slept, but half awakening in the dark forests of its African fatherland. We are the first fruits of this new nation, the harbinger of that black tomorrow which is yet destined to soften the whiteness of the Teutonic today."

Du Bois went on to celebrate black creativity ("We are that people whose subtle sense of song has given America its only American music, its only American fairy tales, its only touch of pathos and humor amid its mad money-getting plutocracy") and to urge that organizations not only advance the cause of the race but promote realization "of that broader humanity which freely recognizes differences in men, but sternly deprecates inequality in their opportunities of development." He also issued a somber admonition: "Let us not deceive ourselves at our situation in this country. Weighted with a heritage of moral iniquity from our past, hard pressed in the economic world by foreign immigrants and native prejudice, hated here, despised there and pitied everywhere; our only haven of refuge is ourselves, and but one means of advance, our own belief in our great destiny, our own implicit trust in our ability and worth."

Obviously, a great deal has changed since Du Bois's era. Opportunity has expanded, racial definitions are shifting. Still, much in his century-old speech remains relevant today. That is both a sign of Du Bois's enduring genius and of the glacial pace of change in some basic American attitudes. It is a reminder of just how deep is the well-worn rut into which racial reflections and conversations commonly fall.

For over a hundred years America's ostensible commitment to racial equality has faltered over our inability to see beyond race. The scary thought is, that may be equally true of the next hundred, unless, as we approach the millennium, we can learn to stop using the misbegotten assumptions of America's past as our template for the future.

CHAPTER 1

Can a new race surmount old prejudices?

Americans are accustomed to infinite shades of ebony, but the South African journalist Mzimkulu Malunga found the notion hilarious. So he named one celebrity after another—Tina Turner, Vanessa Williams, Mariah Carey—tickled at the thought that anyone might consider them all black. The impromptu racial-identity game soon had the small group in Soweto in stitches. It seemed an appropriately absurd end to an evening spent, for the most part, in more serious conversation in a country whose governing principle once had been: "Tell me your race, and I'll tell you your place." As his guests finished a dinner of beer, beans, beef, and a grits-like delicacy called pap, Malunga, business editor of *The Sowetan*, finally shrugged as if to say: Race is a strange and flexible concept, with an endless capacity to confound.

That evening took me back to an encounter, some years earlier, on a bus several miles outside Caracas, Venezuela. Upon learning I was from the United States, the dark-skinned woman beside me had peppered me with questions. Did I find Venezuelans to be prejudiced? Was there racism in the United States? Were Canadians less biased than their neighbors to the south? Finally, she focused on her son, seated directly in front of us. He was the color of caramel and about seven years old. His father, she told me, was "white," and the son, despite his dusky appearance and faintly African features, had decided that he was white, too. At first, the idea struck me as ridiculous, but, by and by, I found myself thinking, "Why the hell not?" By any logical calculus, he was probably more "white" than "black" (not that, in most of Latin America, he would be considered either). And from the perspective of a child who was old enough to know that whiteness means status but too young to realize how whiteness is defined, wanting to be white was just as natural as wanting to be a quarterback instead of a cheerleader. I wondered, however, if the boy had been American, whether he would have thought he had the option to choose his color. For most of us, race is simply accepted as a given and on faith, no more subject to questioning than the reality of our existence.

Even before the civil rights movement erupted and Jim Crow died, racial definitions in the United States were somewhat different from those in South Africa (and Latin America), and specific policies varied as well. But these countries shared the conceit that the concept of race was reasonably precise and that it told us something important. In fact, those assumptions never really made sense.

Earlier in this century, for instance, Italians, Jews, and Rumanians were widely considered to be of different (and inferior) racial stock compared to the English, Germans, and Swedes. Just a few decades later, those groups were fully accepted into the community of whites. In an essay entitled, "How Did Jews Become White Folks?" Karen Brodkin Sacks asked, "Did Jews and other Euroethnics become white because they became middle class? That is, did money whiten? Or did being incorporated in an expanded version of whiteness open up the economic doors to middle-class status?" The answer, she concluded, is both. The question, nonetheless, illustrates the absurdity of the premise that racial classifications are fixed.

That supposition, at long last, is under serious challenge—from intellectuals who doubt that the concept of race has much meaning; from immigrants who have a different and more elastic view of racial classifications; and, perhaps most interestingly, from those who refuse to consider themselves members of any currently accepted racial category but refer to themselves as multiracial and demand the recognition of a new melded race.

Success in that endeavor, some advocates believe, would be a huge step in the direction of a color-blind society, for by embracing those who are multiracial, the United States would be recognizing, if only implicitly, that the ugly racial lines etched in the nation's soul will, sooner or later, disappear. Alternatively, goes the argument, the nation's failure to recognize formally the existence of multiracial Americans would be a tragedy, not only for mixed-race people but for American society, and would perhaps be a fatal blow to the dream of racial harmony and egalitarianism.

In 1992, in Bethesda, Maryland, several hundred multiracialists came together for the "first national gathering of the multiracial community," as described by Bijan Gilanshah, in the December 1993 issue of the journal *Law and Inequality.* The "Loving Conference" was named in honor of the Supreme Court's decision in the case of *Loving v. Virginia,* which outlawed antimiscegenation statutes in 1967. But the meeting was not simply a celebration of the right to reproduce across racial lines; it would mark—or so its organizers hoped—the public launching of a new and potent political movement.

At stake, in Gilanshah's eyes, was nothing less than the prevention of "cultural genocide." Instead of leaving mixed-race people in a vulnerable and nebulous state of official nowhereness, the government, he thought, was obliged to give them full recognition "as a distinct, powerful social unit with idiosyncratic cultural, social and legal interests." Much the same point was made by Charles Byrd, who organized a rally at the Washington Mall in July 1996 to allow mixed-raced Americans, like himself, an opportunity to collectively and "proudly affirm a self-determined identity" while attempting to persuade the federal government to sanction the multiracial category.

Multiracial people with a heritage that is, to some degree, black have a special interest in how mixed-race people are to be defined. "In physical as well as cultural terms every Negro is a little bit colored and a little bit white," observed Martin Luther King, Jr. in

Where Do We Go From Here: Chaos or Community? Yet it is only the "colored" part that has generally been acknowledged. Unlike Americans of other races, blacks have largely been defined by the so-called one-drop rule: the presumption that even a small percentage of black ancestry effectively cancels out any other racial stock. It is a rule that some biracial people believe compels them either to deny a big part of who they are or to explain constantly to a rigid, "monoracial" world why they reject a patently illogical designation. Why, they ask, should they renounce the ancestry of a nonblack parent or grandparent? What's the point, they ask, in forcing people into narrow boxes that cannot possibly accommodate America's growing racial diversity?—particularly when the black box is fundamentally different from the others, carries the full baggage of slavery, and defies all common sense. As Lawrence Hirschfeld, author of *Race in the Making*, observed: "The absurdity of the biological reading of the one-drop rule is obvious. . . . How reasonable is it to say that a white woman can give birth to a Black baby, but a Black woman can't give birth to a white baby?"

Lise Funderburg, author of *Black, White, Other*, which profiles several children of black-white interracial unions, extracted the following comment from one of the persons she interviewed: "A lot of Blacks get upset if they ask you exactly what you are and you come back and say, 'Biracial.' One response is, 'What? Are you too good to identify with Blacks?' I say, 'It's not that I'm too good at all, but I'm composed of two different races and I choose to value each of those.' It's not as though I'm going to write off my mother's race for the convenience of pleasing somebody else's view of what I should or should not be doing." The one-drop rule, however, demands that biracial children do just that. As novelist Gish Jen noted in an essay in the *New York Times Magazine*, "a mulatto is not a kind of white person, but a kind of black person." Yet there is nothing in biology—indeed, nothing in science at all—that says "black" should trump "white" when it comes to assigning racial categories.

The argument against such an illogical racial-classification scheme ultimately takes you down one of two roads: rejection of the idea of race altogether or acceptance of the possibility of an endless proliferation of new races. In recent years, the debate has focused on the census for the year 2000—specifically on an edict known as

"Statistical Policy Directive Number 15." That directive, conjured up by the Office of Management and Budget (OMB) in the late 1970s, sets out the minimum categories that governmental agencies can use when collecting racial and ethnic data. It provides for four racial clusters (white, black, Asian and Pacific Islander, and American Indian and Alaska Native) and one distinct ethnic group (Hispanic). If someone doesn't quite fit, they are squeezed into the pigeonhole that "most closely reflects the individual's recognition in his community." If that doesn't work, they can always be lumped into "other."

These particular groups are not arbitrary. They reflect OMB's best attempt to capture the American consensus on race. They also reflect the needs of an array of governmental agencies that enforce civil rights laws, run American Indian programs, fight poverty, and calculate health and other statistics—agencies, in short, that need to know something about America's racial makeup to do their jobs. The problem is that America's racial composition is quite different now from the way it was in the 1970s. It is less "monoracial," less black and white, more intermarried, and a hell of a lot more confusing.

At the time of the 1970 census, America had few shades of gray. Whites (at 87.5 percent) and blacks (at 11.1 percent) accounted for more than 98 percent of the total U.S. population. Other racial minorities added up to just over 1 percent. Hispanics, who could be of any race, stood at 4.5 percent. Twenty years later, the nation was spinning from a demographic whirlwind. Newcomers were pouring in from Mexico, the Philippines, Korea, Cuba, India, mainland China, and other non-European countries, while Europeans—no longer favored by U.S. immigration laws—had dwindled to a trickle. America, in short, was no longer nearly so black and white. By 1990, whites and blacks stood at roughly 80 percent and 12 percent, respectively, and Hispanics at 9 percent.

Meanwhile, interracial families were forming apace. In 1960, according to the U.S. census, fewer than half of 1 percent of married couples were interracial. By 1990, the number had risen to about 3 percent—the majority comprised of mixtures other than black and white.

After reanalyzing U.S. Bureau of the Census's survey data for

1985 and 1990, scholars Douglas Besharov and Timothy Sullivan concluded that even black-white marriages were growing faster than had previously been thought. In 1990, they estimated, nearly 10 percent of black grooms married whites brides. Although the sample of the Current Population Survey was too small to allow a good estimate for marriages between black brides and white grooms, Besharov and Sullivan conjectured that their number was also rising rapidly. The children of such unions, they declared (in the July–August 1996 issue of *The New Democrat*), "may be the best hope for the future of American race relations."

To multiracialists, America's approximately 3 million multiracial children are a forceful argument for the recognition of a new race and a new racial reality—and perhaps, as Besharov and Sullivan suggested, even a way out of America's racial quagmire.

Susan Graham, a white woman married to a black man in Roswell, Georgia, tried to explain the rationale for the new racial category at congressional hearings in 1993. Accompanied by her young son, she related the frustrations of trying to find a comfortable racial niche for biracial children. When she had asked a census official how to identify her two biracial children, the official insulted her. "In cases like these, we always know who the mother is and not always the father," the official said, in explaining why the child should take the mother's race. Her experience, Graham pointed out, was far from unique. A multiracial teenager in North Carolina, she said, had been humiliated by a teacher blurting out in class: "You're so light. Are you sure your mother knows who your father is?" Graham expressed gratitude for a new state policy that had allowed her to identify her five-year-old daughter as "multiracial" when she had enrolled the child in kindergarten. Thanks to Georgia's legislators, her child "was not made to choose between her parents." She urged Congress to protect other children from having to make that painful decision.

"I'm not a scholar, attorney, or lawmaker," Graham continued. "I'm just a mother, a mother who cares about children; and whether I like it or not, I realize that self-esteem is directly tied to accurate racial identity. More and more parents all over our country are instilling new pride in our multiracial children. Can we say we have succeeded if our children leave home only to be denied an equal place in our society?" In closing, she invoked the ever-handy memory of Martin Luther King, Jr.: "I believe Doctor King was speaking thirty years ago for multiracial children too. With your help, their time has finally come."

Carlos Fernández, president of the Association of Multiethnic Americans, was equally impassioned. Governmental administrators' refusal to recognize multiracial children, he suggested, could put them in violation of the U.S. Constitution: "When government compels the multiracial, multiethnic family to signify a factually false identity for their child, it invades their fundamental right of privacy." Fernández made clear, however, that he was primarily concerned not with constitutional issues but with the well-being of multiracial youngsters. The status quo, he intimated, amounted to a form of child abuse. It denied multiracial offspring their "distinctive identity," damaged their self-esteem, and forced them to "favor one parent over the other." Meanwhile, it did nothing to protect them from—or even document—the special form of bigotry aimed at people of mixed race.

Julie C. Lythcott-Haimes made a similar argument in the *Harvard Civil Rights–Civil Liberties Law Review*. "The Multiracial person can hardly advocate the superiority or inferiority of one race without touching off a potentially damaging identity struggle within herself," wrote Lythcott-Haimes. And even if a person's psyche could put up with such turmoil, Lythcott-Haimes saw no reason why anyone should have to. The one-drop rule is not only absurd, she contended, it is blatantly racist, grounded in the central premise "that 'Black blood' is a contaminant while 'White blood' is pure."

Clearly, the multiracialists have flagged a nettlesome problem. Forcing multiracial children into prefabricated "monoracial" boxes is illogical. It is preposterous—not to mention cruel—to ask any child of mixed race to choose one race (and symbolically one parent) arbitrarily over the other. As Gish Jen, a Chinese American married to a man of Irish descent, acknowledged, there is pain in seeing her child stripped of what he considers to be an essential part of his identity. Yet many Americans insist on seeing multiracial children through monochromatic eyes. Some spiteful schoolmates gave her son a taste of what his future might hold when they taunted him for being "Chinese"—even as he futilely insisted that he was not. Though Jen and her husband originally had hoped their son would "grow up embracing his whole complex ethnic heritage," they have had to accept a harsher reality and recognize that their son "is considered a kind of Asian person."

It's unclear whether the federal government's official adoption of a multiracial category would lead to broader public acceptance of multiracialism and eventually make things easier for children such as Jen's son or for families such as Graham's. It is even less clear what effect a multiracial box would have on statistical analyses of America's racial stock. "Multiracial," after all, is not a particularly precise description. It simply means that a person theoretically fits into more than one category. It's a fancy way, in short, of saying "other." Consequently, a multiracial designation conceivably could end up being less accurate (in the sense of grouping people together who are deemed to be phenotypically similar) than the groupings we have now, depending on how it is defined and who decides who belongs to it.

Even if a multiracial designation is taken (as many proponents would like) to apply only to those with two parents of recognizably different racial stocks, it's unclear how useful the descriptor would be. Unless the census spelled out specifically what racial heritages were subsumed by the designation, it would put the offspring of a white person and an American Indian in the same pigeonhole as the child of a black person and a Chinese American or of a black person and a white person. Although the offspring of all the couples would certainly be multiracial, not many Americans would consider them to be of the same race. Many would still consider the black-Asian and black-white children to be black (or perhaps mixed) and the white–American Indian child to be white. The children, in any number of circumstances, would be treated differently, as would be the unions of their parents.

A *New York Times* poll in 1991 found that 66 percent of whites were opposed to a relative marrying a black person, whereas 45 percent were opposed to a relative marrying a Hispanic or Asian person. (The survey did not attempt to ascertain whether responses would differ depending on whether the prospective Hispanic spouse was black, white, or something else.) Clearly, in the eyes of many of those respondents, all multiracial families are not created equal. And if part of the purpose of such classifications is to permit researchers to determine how various groups are treated, aggregating groups whose only common denominator is that their parents are racially different would not do much to advance that purpose. One is thus faced with the option of creating at least two multiracial categories—one perhaps labeled "multiracial-dark" and the other called "multiracial-light." But it's unlikely that anyone would see those categories as an improvement over the current system—least of all those who think that the multiracial category is a form of defense against America's obsession with rigid racial categories.

And what about those people who don't care for the multiracial designation? What about the children of black-and-white unions, for instance, who insist on calling themselves black? Providing them with a multiracial box is no guarantee that they will climb into it. And what about the children of "multiracial" parents. If the designation applies only to the first generation, will these children (like many light-skinned "blacks") become monoracial by the second generation? Or will their children, twenty years from now, be fighting for yet another redefinition of race?—for, perhaps, a new box labeled "old multiracial" as opposed to "new multiracial" or even "part multiracial" (which, of course, raises the question of how much multiracial one has to be to be considered truly multiracial).

And what about Latin Americans? Obviously, many Latinos find the current categories lacking. In the 1990 census, 43 percent of Latinos apparently thought of themselves as neither black, white, American Indian, nor Asian. They were "other." In fact, of all American residents who put themselves in the "other" category and indicated an ethnicity, the overwhelming majority (86 percent, according to the census bureau) were Hispanic.

A preliminary test of the multiracial option by the Bureau of Labor Statistics provided only a hazy idea of who might check it. When the option was offered to half of the 60,000 households polled in the May 1995 *Current Population Survey,* it got the biggest response from people in the white, Hispanic, and American Indian–Eskimo–Aleut categories. When Hispanic was offered as a racial (and not just an ethnic) option, the number of Hispanics claiming to be multiracial dropped considerably. Some of the whites who chose to describe themselves as multiracial apparently did so on the basis of belonging to various European ethnic groups. "Multiracial" respondents who did belong to more than one racial group were most likely to be from the American Indian–Eskimo–Aleut cluster. Different ways of asking the question elicited different responses, but it seems likely, on the basis of the results of the 1995 survey (which were essentially replicated in another governmental survey in 1996), that a significant portion of those who choose to be listed as multiracial will not be the children of "mixed"-race unions but either people from traditionally mestizo groups or whites with ancestors whom they consider to be exotic.

Assuming that the technical and definitional issues can be resolved, what will certifying a multirace accomplish? And at what cost? For all the heartfelt concern expressed by the parents of mixed-race children, it's unclear that the U.S. Bureau of the Census's recognition of that category would help. Could a new census category really protect children from crude, callous remarks? Or build self-esteem in those who lack it? Or serve as an effective shield against prejudice? And what influence would it have on the enforcement of laws dealing with housing discrimination and employment discrimination? Or on those private concerns that sell ads, conduct public-opinion research, and do other business based largely on current racial categories? As writer Lawrence Wright asked in the *New Yorker*: "Suppose a court orders a city to hire additional black police officers to make up for past discrimination. Will mixed-race officers count? Will they count wholly or partly?" And as has already been suggested, a new racial category would not even unfailingly provide a reliable anchor for racial identity, since the label is infinitely elastic.

Indeed, many critics would argue—some for scientific and others for sociopolitical reasons—that the creation of more racial pigeonholes is precisely what America doesn't need. The bigger problem, in short, may not be that the current groupings are insufficient, but that they foster a belief that there is something logical, necessary, scientific, or wise about dividing people into groups called races.

Certainly, when it comes to racial "science," not much has changed since 1942, the year anthropologist Ashley Montagu published the first edition of *Man's Most Dangerous Myth: The Fallacy of*

Race. "In earlier days we believed in magic, possession, and exorcism, in good and evil supernatural powers, and until recently we believed in witchcraft. Today many of us believe in 'race.' 'Race' is the witchcraft of our time. The means by which we exorcise demons. It is the contemporary myth. Man's most dangerous myth," wrote Montagu.

Montagu acknowledged that racial groups were real. He rejected the notion, however, that the categories amounted to anything important. Racial groups were merely people with geographic origins in common who, to certain European taxonomists, looked somewhat alike. "No one ever asks whether there are mental and temperamental differences between white, black, or brown horses—such a question would seem rather silly," he pointed out, suggesting that the question was no less silly when applied to humans. Having rejected the idea that race represents different evolutionary paths taken en route to becoming Homo sapiens or is linked to fundamentally different capabilities or traits or indicates the existence of any "hard and fast genetic boundaries," Montagu concluded that it is little more than an excuse for prejudice.

Americans are no closer than we were half a century ago to coming up with a sound scientific rationale for the myriad ways we regard race. Certainly, as Montagu admitted, different races exist—if only because we have decided that they do. We can theoretically create races at will. If Americans agreed, for instance, that people with red hair constitute a separate race, these people would be one. And if we proceeded to treat all people with red hair differently from everyone else, they would soon take on all the attributes we associate with "real" races. If, for instance, they were allowed only to do menial labor, refused an education, compelled to intermarry, forced to live in predominantly redhead communities, and told that their only real gifts were drinking and song, they would eventually develop a culture that embodied the new redhead stereotype. But all we would have proved is that human beings have the power to define (and thereby create) races—not that the classification has any value or makes any sense.

Race, in and of itself, is a harmless concept. It is the attributes and meaning we ascribe to race that make it potentially pernicious. And, unfortunately, race began as a value-loaded conceit. As paleontologist Stephen Jay Gould noted, eighteenth-century German naturalist Johann Friedrich Blumenbach created the modern system of racial classification as a "hierarchy of worth, oddly based upon perceived beauty, and fanning out in two directions from a Caucasian ideal." Blumenbach's racial pyramid had Africans and Asians on the bottom, Malays and American Indians in the middle, and whites at the top. That history and the uses to which race was subsequently put go a long way toward explaining why the movement to create a new multirace makes some people uncomfortable.

The Reverend Jesse Jackson, for instance, sees the multiracial category as a disconcertingly close analog to the South African classification of "colored." Indeed, many South Africans with whom I discussed the multiracial issue responded with horror, amusement, or astonishment. One black South African economist with a Ph.D., who is married to a white woman and has two interracial children, laughed heartily at the idea of a special multiracial group. Finally, he gained control of himself and sputtered, "Wouldn't that be a regression?"

Antonio Hercules, himself a so-called Cape Colored and head of a Cape Town–based nonprofit organization called ERASE (for End Racism and Sexism), pronounced the notion "crazy." In South Africa, he observed, the creation of a colored class had led to disunity and conflict between blacks and coloreds over housing, schools, facilities, and even implementation of affirmative action policies. Madoda Hlatshwayo, administrative secretary for the South African Ministry of Trade, dismissed the idea as "redundant." "We are all multiracial," he pointed out. "There is no pure race. Hitler tried. He failed." Joseph Thloloe, deputy editor-in-chief of the South African Broadcasting Corporation, shook his head in befuddlement and said, "I don't understand if blacks are oppressed, why somebody who is slightly black would be better off."

Wilmot James, executive director of the Institute for Democracy in South Africa, is considered "colored" by South African standards, and he has witnessed close up the polarizing effect of subdividing people into separate racial categories. Following the governmental changeover in South Africa, James was invited by Cape Town residents, worried about black rule, to "open up a dialogue" within the colored community there. The meeting was also an occasion to explore issues of colored identity, to "give people an opportunity to articulate their feelings as to who they are," he said. One of his goals was to let the audience know that it was all right to value their colored identity but "don't be racist about it." The very fact that he found it necessary to make such a statement says much about the distance between blacks and coloreds in South Africa, about the barriers that racial subclassification and stratification—under the worst circumstances—can put in the way of brotherhood.

The December 1995 newsletter of the Institute for Multi-Party Democracy, an independent South African organization that promotes national reconciliation, reported on a debate at the University of the Western Cape on the issue of colored ethnicity. Some participants argued for an end to the colored classification, viewing it as a racially divisive remnant of apartheid. Others, just as impassioned, contended that they were, in fact, a separate group, neither black nor white, and should continue to be recognized as such. Florina Serfontein, a local politician and a member of the newly formed "Coloured Forum," declared: "Among the people out there, millions of them, there is support for the idea of 'coloured people.' They are motivated by a desire to protect their language, culture, religion, and physical assets, such as land. . . . There was a time when we were not white enough, and now we are not black enough. We are being discriminated against."

The feeling of being trapped between two races is widespread among South Africa's colored population. During a performance in a Cape Town cabaret called Over the Top, a colored singer echoed Serfontein's concerns. In between belting out servings of American soul music, vocalist Sophia Foster turned to her mixed white-and-colored audience and voiced her disappointment with the new programming on the South African Broadcasting Corporation. "Have you seen a colored person on the new SABC?" she asked rhetorically, before dryly answering her own question. "They're [presumably meaning the whites and blacks who control the SABC] *not* interested."

A middle-aged black South African acquaintance underscored the breadth of the colored-black racial schism when he observed, in a moment of idle chatter, that many coloreds feel threatened by black majority rule. The coloreds, he said, are "trying to make us forget that they used to call us kaffirs," in a tone that made it clear that he had no intention of forgetting.

In fact, there is no real reason why America's experience with a mixed-race category should mirror South Africa's. No one in the United States is seriously proposing, for instance, that the government ensure that access to jobs, housing, and education is allocated along rigid racial parameters favoring those with lighter skin, straighter hair, and other evidence of non-African ancestry—as was the case in South Africa under apartheid. Nonetheless, given their own experience, it's hardly surprising that many South Africans would find America's experimentation with new racial groupings to be a bit bizarre.

Those who have watched the creation of intermediate races in South America and the Caribbean are equally wary. Anani Dzidzienyo, professor of Afro-American Studies and Portuguese and Brazilian Studies at Brown University, said he thought that the creation of an American multiracial category would be a "disaster." By one count, Brazil has some 150 racial categories, partly because "given a chance [to choose something else], nobody wants to be called black," he observed. One result is that people of darker hue in Brazil and elsewhere south of America's border find it difficult to organize to fight discrimination. "I know of no Latin American country where there is the equivalent of the NAACP. I know no part of the Americas whose hierarchy is not white at the top and black at the bottom," Dzidzienyo commented.

Panamanian performer Rubén Blades acknowledged the existence of such a hierarchy in "Plástico," a song about status-climbing parents who direct their child not to play with children of a "different color." In another song, "Ligia Elena," Blades related the tale of a young woman who astonishes and shames her white, high-society family by eloping with a neighborhood trumpet player, who evidently is dark. In response to an inquiry from my researcher in 1995, Blades noted that both "Plástico" and "Ligia Elena" were written during the 1970s. "The fact that I can still play them underscores the sad reality of a society which has changed very little in two decades," he said.

Among certain Latin Americans and West Indians, marrying a lighter person is considered a step up. In the Caribbean, the practice is known as *mejorando la raza* (bettering the race)—the idea being that the children, who will presumably turn out lighter than the darker parent, will represent an improvement. In writing about his West Indian roots in the *New Yorker*, Malcolm Gladwell observed: "It was the infusion of white blood that gave the colored class its status in the Caribbean, and the members of this class have never forgotten that, nor have they failed, in a thousand subtle ways, to distance themselves from those around them who experienced a darker and less privileged past." He went on to confide that in his mother's house, "the family often passed around a pencilled drawing of two of my great grandparents; she was part Jewish, and he was part Scottish. The other side—the African side—was never mentioned."

Puerto Rican poet Fortunate Vizcarrondo has written about the shame some Puerto Ricans feel about the dark side of the family tree. In one poem, written in vernacular Spanish (the title of which translates as "An' Yo' Granma' Where She Be"), Vizcarrondo recorded the riposte of a black Puerto Rican fed up with being teased by a light-skinned acquaintance. The kinky-haired protagonist is angry at the straight-haired tormentor who had accused him of being a black with big lips. He wonders aloud why his nemesis—who is so happy to show off his white-skinned baby and his "good haired" father—never trots out his grandmother. Where is she? he demands to know, as he gives voice to his own suspicion. The grandmother, he concludes, is black and therefore is hidden away in the kitchen. His antagonist, in other words, is nothing more than a "white-plated" man, a part-black man trying to move up in society.

Piri Thomas, a writer who was born in Spanish Harlem of Puerto Rican parents, touched on the same theme in his autobiography, *Down These Mean Streets*. In the book, a discussion between the author and his brother José quickly turns ugly when Thomas insists that they both are "black." "I ain't black, damn you!" his brother replies. "Look at my hair. It's almost blond. My eyes are blue, my nose is straight. My motherfuckin' lips are not like a baboon's ass. My skin is white. White, goddamit! White! Maybe Poppa's a little dark, but that's the Indian blood in him."

When Thomas accuses his brother of being "sold on that white kick," the brother, growing more agitated by the moment, spits out, "I ain't no nigger! You can be one if you want to be. You can go South and grow cotton, or pick it, or whatever the fuck they do. You can bow and kiss and clean shit bowls. But—I—am *white*! And you can go to hell!"

Sandra García, a poet of Puerto Rican extraction born in the Dominican Republic, recalled a conversation she had a few years ago with the superintendent of the building where she was staying in Santo Domingo. The man, apparently pleased with the comfortable racial climate on the island, turned to García and observed: *"Mira como son las cosas, nosotros aquí sentados—tu blanca y yo indio"* ("Look how things are today, here we are seated together, you a white woman and me an Indian man").

García was surprised at the observation, since the man was quite obviously black and she considered herself to be *trigueña* (or wheat colored). So she responded good-naturedly: "Look, sir, I'm not white, nor are you Indian. You're black." The man moved back, stunned, and avoided her for the rest of her visit. She realized she had unwittingly drawn blood, that she had thrust a knife into an important part of the man's self-image, puncturing—if only briefly—his facade of racial denial.

That denial, of course, did not blossom in a vacuum. It is a direct result of what Dzidzienyo described as a New World racial hierarchy that has whites at the top and blacks at the bottom. And as Thomas's writings attest, that sense of hierarchy does not necessarily vanish when Latinos come to the United States; instead, it may be heightened in some cases.

In *Empowering Hispanic Families: A Critical Issue for the '90s*, Frank Montalvo observed: "At the heart of the Hispanic experience in the United States is a form of racism that both binds light and dark Latinos to each other and divides them into separate groups. Race may prove to be a more pernicious element in their lives than are linguistic, cultural and socioeconomic differences."

Given the United States' own longtime preoccupation with color and the real—if informal—hierarchy of complexion that preoccupation has fostered, Montalvo's concern is well justified. Indeed, it's impossible to understand much of the resentment of the prospect of a mixed-race governmental category without taking into account

America's legacy of colorism. The multiracial category, after all, is not new. The rise of the mulatto class during colonial times was an acknowledgment that the offspring of black-white unions were not necessarily either black or white. But as blacks edged toward freedom, the in-between status of mulattoes posed a growing threat to those who were determined to keep the races (and racial privileges) separate. Though it is not often remembered that way, the landmark 1896 case of *Plessy v. Ferguson,* which gave the Supreme Court imprimatur to the practice of separate (and supposedly equal) public accommodations, was, in part, a case about racial classifications—and whether the privileges of white skin were to be accorded those who were only partially black. As a test of Louisiana's Separate Car Act, Homer Adolph Plessy provoked a prearranged confrontation by sitting in the first-class "white" section of a train on the East Louisiana Railway. Plessy's blood was, by his own reckoning, only one-eighth "African." And as the Court noted in its decision, "the mixture of colored blood was not discernible in him." Plessy argued, among other things, that the reputation of belonging to the white race was a property right and that by denying him a seat in the white section, the statute deprived the white part of him the use of his property.

Still, the Court saw no reason to grant Plessy's demand for "every right, privilege, and immunity secured to citizens . . . of the white race," though Justice Henry B. Brown, writing for the majority, did concede that Louisiana might need to determine whether or not Plessy was white. But Plessy had the last laugh by apparently making the determination on his own. In later years, historian Charles O'Neill reported, Plessy registered to vote as a white man.

In his 1991 book, *Who Is Black?* F. James Davis noted that acceptance of the idea that mulattoes were something other than black diminished during the 1850s as the antislavery debate heated up. Even as many of America's mulattoes struggled to hold on to their in-between racial status, white American society—especially white southern society—closed ranks against them. "The one-drop rule received more solid support than ever throughout the South, for the simple reason that it helped defend slavery," Davis wrote. As southern whites "guardedly rejected the lighter mulattoes whom they had previously half–accepted, the latter sought alliances where they could find them," meaning increasingly with blacks, Davis observed.

Multiracial advocate Gilanshah obviously does not equate the new multiracial group with the privileged mulattoes of yesteryear. But, in many respects, the language of the multiracial lobby invites such a comparison. Many advocates of the new designation see multiracial individuals as ambassadors between groups. Gilanshah, for instance, argues that society would benefit from having multiracial people who are uniquely positioned to be "sensitive, objective negotiators of inter-group racial conflict." But to assume that only designated multiracial people can be a bridge between races is to assume that others lack that capacity. It is also to reawaken recollections of the middleman role of South African coloreds, American mulattoes, and Latin American mestizos, groups who were assigned a status that was lower than that of whites but higher than that of those with whom the whites had propagated. It is, in short, to invite questions, such as those posed by an *Ebony* magazine story in 1995 entitled, "Am I Black, White or In Between? Is There a Plot to Create a 'Colored' Buffer Race in America?"

In the article, writer Lynn Norment concluded that "some of the desire for alternative racial classification is due to individuals wanting to retreat from their Blackness." And she quoted with approval singer Lenny Kravitz's advice to his fellow part-black Americans: "Accept the blessing of having the advantage of two cultures, but understand that you are Black. In this world, if you have one spot of Black blood, you are Black. So get over it."

In congressional testimony, Ramona Davis, a woman of black, Sicilian, and America Indian extraction and a spokesperson for the Association of Multiethnic Americans, acknowledged the divisive potential of the multiracial issue: "In a society which continues to cripple itself with racial obsession, and rejection, it is understandable that there might be some suspicion that our motive to have a multiracial/multi-ethnic category is masking a more deep-seated desire to dissociates ourselves from those parts of our heritage that have been ill-favored, or depreciated by the stigma of racism." She insisted, however, that she and her colleagues are not trying to dissociate themselves from other minority groups: "What we are asking is that we also be recognized for our unique identity, special circumstances, and the discrimination we have had to endure, above and beyond what we've experienced when randomly lumped with one monoracial/mono-ethnic group or another, depending on how we are perceived, where we are perceived, and by whom we are perceived."

It is certainly true that people of unclear race or ethnicity often have particular concerns. Adrian Piper, an artist and philosopher who is light enough to "pass" for white but considers herself black, at one point took to handing out cards that read:

> Dear Friend,
>
> I am black. I am sure you did not realize this when you made/laughed at/agreed with that racist remark. In the past, I have attempted to alert white people to my racial identity in advance. Unfortunately, this invariably causes them to react to me as pushy, manipulative, or socially inappropriate. Therefore, my policy is to assume that white people do not make these remarks, even when they believe there are no black people present, and to distribute this card when they do. I regret any discomfort my presence is causing you, just as I am sure you regret the discomfort your racism is causing me.
>
> Sincerely yours,
> Adrian Margaret Smith Piper

She stopped giving out the cards, Piper told a *Washington Post* reporter, "after a man I met at a party said he was trying to think of a racial slur so he could get one of my cards."

In recent years, a host of writers have attempted to illuminate the special situation of being racially ambiguous. In an essay "High Yellow White Trash" (in *Skin Deep,* a collection of essays by both black and white women), Lisa Page, whose father is black and mother is white, wrote: "There are a lot of names for people like me. Bright-skinned, mixed, café au lait, high yellow white trash. The last one I made up myself. It sums up for me what it is to be black yet aware of a white heritage. You get a double consciousness that never goes away. You are forever light-skinned, no matter how black you feel on the inside." Page noted that when she was born in Chicago in 1956, her mother was situated in the white section of the hospital, but Page's arrival forced her mom into the colored section:

"My mother lost a piece of her identity that day: her status as a white woman, something she'd taken for granted all her life." Even her mother's family felt compromised. When Page and her siblings would visit relatives in Michigan, the family would explain the children's skin color by claiming that their father was East Indian. "During one family reunion the pictures weren't taken until my sister, brother, and I were out of the room."

In *Notes of a Black White Woman*, Judy Scales-Trent, a law professor at the State University of New York at Buffalo and a "black" woman who often is assumed to be white, discussed the problem of "coming out": "When do I tell someone that I am black? And how? And how will they respond? And if I don't tell people (the apartment rental agent, the cab driver), aren't I 'passing'?" Piper wrote on the subject of passing: "Once you realize what is denied you as an African-American simply because of your race, your sense of the unfairness of it may be so overwhelming that you may simply be incapable of accepting it. And if you are not inclined toward any form of overt political advocacy, passing in order to get the benefits you know you deserve may seem the only way to defy the system."

Shirlee Taylor Haizlip's *The Sweeter the Juice* is, among other things, the saga of her search for relations who had cut off all contact with her family and passed into the white world. With the help of a detective agency, she found a long-lost aunt. The woman was then eighty-eight years old and living in Anaheim, California. Initially, when the detective called, she claimed no relationship to the family who was looking for her, but eventually she owned up. Haizlip, in detailing her first encounter with her newly found aunt, wrote that she ended up asking herself, "Was it my responsibility to remind Grace who she was, to dredge up a past she had buried? Despite all the years of longing and conjecture, despite the fact that race was the central issue, I could not bring myself to broach it."

In the end, Haizlip managed to get the "white sister" and the "black sister" (Haizlip's mother) together for a visit. "Watching the sisters sit side by side in the restaurant booth, I sensed a budding comfort," she noted. "But I also thought it was just as well that after this visit they would be three thousand miles apart. Race still separated them. I understood now in ways I had not that Grace was indeed white. She could not give up being white, nor could she tear down the alabaster walls she had built around her life. She would be content to see us as often as we might like to visit, as long as no one in her circle knew who or what we were. In other words, she would be satisfied to continue the pattern of the past."

When I talked to Haizlip in 1995, her research on the newly found branch of her family tree had led her to a number of "white" cousins. She had taken on the task of establishing contact with them and, coincidentally, informing them they were not quite as white as they may have thought. Haizlip would call and identify herself as a long-lost relative and, during the course of the conversation, would reveal that she knew a "family secret." Only after that news had been absorbed would she reveal, "Our great grandfather was a former slave." Invariably, Haizlip said, the person on the other end would blurt out: "A black slave?"

She had recently had that discussion with a forty-four-year-old assistant professor who lived in a town near Cleveland and was married to a conservative Republican whose ancestors were among the town's founders. In a subsequent conversation, the woman described her initial reactions to Haizlip: "The first thing I did was I went to look in the mirror. I wanted to see if I looked any different. And the second thing I did was to look at my fingernails." (Apparently, she had heard that black people had more bluish "moons" on their fingernails.) "Then I thought for about thirty minutes. I sat in a chair and had a cup of tea and I wondered whether I was going to keep this a secret." She soon resolved that she could not keep the news to herself: "It had been a secret too long; but I had to figure out how I was going to tell my husband." She decided to tell him one evening after dinner and dessert. Her husband, who had a sense of humor, took the news in stride, replying, "Well, I got a black cat. I got a black dog. Now I got a black wife."

The process of reconnecting the various offshoots of the family tree, Haizlip told me, caused her to rethink her own racial identity. Previously, she had accepted the fact that she was black without so much as a second thought: "I had rejected the white part of my family. I didn't know them and I rejected them. . . . My father was a very active black minister. I grew up in a black church. So, for me, blackness was my grounding and frame of reference." She now has a more complicated view: "I call myself black politically, socially and culturally, but I say I have roots in many gardens and genetically I'm mixed. I'm more convinced than ever now that all of us are mixed people. As geneticists now know, none of us [is] pure. So I have broadened my vision of myself. I haven't diminished it." As for what identifiably multiracial people should be called, she was unsure, but if forced, she would "push for mixed race for everybody, white and black. In other words, one label, which effectively is no label."

Haizlip believes that people are growing weary of racial polarization. "I think we have come to the end of our rope, and we want to say, 'God, what is the answer? We've tried everything, and *what* is the answer?'" The question, she suspects, may ultimately lead people to accept the notion that one racial label for everyone is the only course that makes sense. Once we recognize that everyone is mixed, that we all share genes from a common pool, perhaps "we can look at each other as extended family and distant cousins." If we begin to do that, Haizlip said, "we're going to be more tolerant of each other. We don't love everybody in our family, but we are more tolerant of them."

America, of course, has not quite gotten to that point; it insists not only on racial labels, but on treating people differently on the basis of perceived racial differences. Even under the so-called one-drop rule, as I noted earlier, not all shades of black are always seen as equal. In *The Color Complex*, authors Kathy Russell, Midge Wilson, and Ronald Hall pointed out, "For light-skinned Blacks, it simply remains easier to get ahead. Take a close look at Black urban professionals, or 'buppies,' with their corporate salaries, middle class values, and predominantly light-brown to medium-brown skin color. They benefit not only from their social contacts with other light-skinned Blacks but also from looks that, in a predominantly White society, are more mainstream."

Professors James Johnson and Walter Farrell attempted to quantify the color advantage. In their report of their study of two thousand male job seekers in the Los Angeles area in the *Chronicle of Higher Education* in 1995, they stated that color seemed to play a role in determining who worked and who did not; being African American and dark reduced the odds of working considerably: "In our sample, only 8.6 percent of white males were unemployed, compared with 23.1 percent of black males in general and 27 percent of dark-skinned black males," and among light-skinned black men, it was 20 percent. Even among those who were relatively well educated, Johnson and Farrell indicated, skin tone seemed to make a difference: "We found that only 10.3 percent of light-skinned African-American men with 13 or more years of schooling were unemployed, compared with 19.4 percent of their dark-skinned counterparts with similar education. Indeed, the unemployment rate for the light-skinned black males was only a little higher than the 9.5 percent rate for white males with comparable schooling." Johnson and Farrell's point was not that light skin ensures success or that dark skin guarantees failure, but that complexion is far from a neutral trait, that skin tone had a great deal to do with how warmly one is received by the world.

That a lighter complexion may be related to success is not news to many blacks, who have long acknowledged—if not always openly—that color sometimes matters nearly as much as does race. As Teresa Wiltz, a light-skinned black journalist, observed in the *Chicago Tribune*: "From the beginning black wealth and skin color have been inextricably linked. The lighter you were—and most likely, that meant you were the descendant of a wealthy white slaveowner—the more likely you were to be middle class." Precisely because that linkage has always been there, some blacks are suspicious of those with lighter complexions. Piper alluded to that suspicion when she wrote: "I have sometimes met blacks socially who, as a condition of social acceptance of me, require me to prove my blackness." The standard of proof is elusive and sometimes unachievable, and the test creates frustration and a sense of injustice among "light" blacks that are no less real than the feelings of "dark" blacks when they see that a light complexion and "good" hair bestow social, professional, and even romantic advantages.

Much of the uneasiness engendered by the multiracialists is rooted in such frustration, in unpleasant and ugly racial memories, in racial insecurities, in anxieties about race and rank, and in the knowledge that race has never been neutral in America but has inevitably forced people to take sides. The debate, in short, is really not so much about a multiracial box as it is about what race means—and what it will come to mean as the society approaches the millennium. Juliet Fairley, a New York–based journalist whose white mother was born in France and whose father is African American, recalled the difficulty growing up with a split identity and desperately wanting to fit in. She went through a phase when she wanted to be totally "black" and even sported an Afro pick in her straightish dark hair. Eventually, she decided that she could not ignore the part of herself that is also her mother, and she has come around to support a multiracial category—but only "if it has no consequences."

Some analysts have considered the issue as fundamentally a political one. Lawrence Wright, for instance, noted: "Those who are charged with enforcing civil-rights laws see the Multiracial box as a wrecking ball aimed at affirmative action, and they hold those in the mixed-race movement responsible." Yet, on the basis of early research, it seems unlikely that any huge proportion of the people specifically protected by those laws would opt suddenly to decamp to the multiracial zone. And even if they would, it's easy to envision a multiracial census option that would not undermine civil rights laws or create a special legal status for the multiracial "race." People could mark whatever box they thought appropriate, and if the questionnaire then asked people to designate in what ways they were mixed, the information could eventually be aggregated or massaged (albeit at some cost) in whatever way was useful.

In short, the purpose of the data collection process could be served even as people were allowed to make statements about their personal identities. Whether the census should be used as an occasion for such statements (or, for that matter, should be seen as a solution to feelings of low self-esteem or racial estrangement) is another subject altogether. Suffice it to say that those who go to the U.S. Bureau of the Census searching for psychological deliverance are looking in the wrong place and are bound to be greatly disappointed. Certainly, what we call ourselves is important and, therefore, people ought to have broad latitude to call themselves whatever they wish. But the more important issue is not whether multiracial is officially a racial category or whether Hispanic-Latino is a race, or even whether black and white are races. As historian Gary Okihiro pointed out in *Margins and Mainstreams*, racial classifications are not inherently stable, even among groups now considered to be racially unambiguous. In Louisiana, for instance, Chinese were classified as whites in 1860 but as Chinese in 1870. Ten years later, children of Chinese men and non-Chinese women were classified as Chinese, but twenty years after that, such children were reclassified as either blacks or whites. Virginia Easley Demarce, a historian with the Bureau of Indian Affairs, noted in a letter to the *Washington Post* that census takers used a form of multiracial classification during parts of the nineteenth century: "In 1870 in Washington Territory and Oregon Territory, for example, white males who had married American Indian women were enumerated on the standard population schedules, while their children were listed as 'half-breeds not otherwise counted' on separate pages. . . . In these two territories, enumerators also often identified native Hawaiians as 'SI' for 'Sandwich Islander.'" Demarce went on to observe that those whose heritage was mixed black and white were, at various times, also separately tallied. "The same family may, in four successive censuses, appear as 'free persons of color' in 1830, white in 1840, mulatto in 1850, and white again in 1860."

Tomorrow's multiracial people could just as easily become the next decade's something else. A name, in the end, is just a name. The problem is that we want those names to mean so much—even if the only result is a perpetuation of an ever-more-refined kind of racial madness.

On the one hand, it makes perfect sense for children of parents of identifiably different races to insist that all their heritages are "honored" in what they are called. Yet, the assumption runs aground of an inescapable reality: that the very function of groups within racial classification is to erase identity, to render us less individuals (whatever our constituent parts) than undifferentiated members of groups within a previously heterogeneous mass. By what logic, for instance, can one take countless African tribes—and the offspring of individuals comprised of any combination of those tribes—and make them all into one race called black? The reasoning is certainly no less specious than that which allows us to ignore the fact that a "black" American may also be Irish and Greek.

In the past, Americans (which is not to exclude much of the rest of the world) have made much more of racial labels than we should. We have seen race as a convenient way of sorting out who is entitled to which rewards, who is capable of what accomplishments, and who is fit to associate with whom. In light of that history, asking whether we should have a new racial category is a trivial question. The infinitely more important question is whether it is possible to divorce any system of racial classification from the practice of racial discrimination, whether a nation splintered along racial lines—a nation that feels compelled to rank people on the basis of race (aesthetically; professionally; socially; and, most insistently, intellectually)—is capable of changing that propensity any time soon.

CHAPTER 2

If destiny is not all in the genes, why do we keep looking there?

If the races are inherently unequal, why even bother to aim for racial equality? That was the question put squarely before the nation in 1994 in a blockbuster book, *The Bell Curve*. It was not the only question the book raised; it was not even the most important one, according to the authors. Yet, in one sense, it was the only question that mattered. For though the opus, strictly speaking, was not primarily about race, the fact that it spoke so brazenly about race—and racial differences—was the only reason it got much notice. And the book, by Richard Herrnstein and Charles Murray, was a bona fide publishing phenomenon, spawning saturation coverage from television and garnering the covers of the *New Republic*, *Newsweek*, the *New York Times Magazine*, the *New York Review of Books*, and a multitude of other mainstream publications. From the star treatment accorded the tome, one would have thought it was a treatise that explained a momentous scientific discovery or, at the least, constituted a brilliant intellectual breakthrough.

It was no such thing. The authors had no stunning scientific insights to offer. They merely regurgitated one side of a debate as old as the field of psychology, supplying voluminous data in support of a theory they themselves acknowledged they could not prove. To their credit, they were relatively careful polemicists, sharply qualifying their most controversial (and dubious) conclusions. But even though they bit their tongues, the book was a masterpiece of insinuation.

This is not to suggest that the authors had anything important to say. Indeed, the volume, on its own merits, was fundamentally unimportant. Its only significance lay in what we (broadly meaning society but, more specifically and most shamefully, my own community of journalists) decided to do with it. Given the attention and respect—in some quarters verging on acclaim—accorded the authors by the press, it is not remarkable that *The Bell Curve* became a national best-seller. We gave it one hell of a ride, taking it as seriously as a Delphic prophecy, when it deserved mostly to be ignored. Why did we do so? To answer that question is to say a lot about why we are in such a muddle over race. Suffice it for the moment to say that we were predisposed, for a variety of reasons—some discussed in the last chapter—to accept more than we should of what it had to say.

It is not my intention to write a book about *The Bell Curve*. That volume has already generated a cottage industry of books and articles by analysts who were dedicated to taking it apart. Nonetheless, I think it is useful to review the book's relevant points. The basic message is straightforward and easily stated: Intelligence is terribly important in the modern world. It determines, in large measure, who is successful, who is on welfare, who is law abiding, and who is happy with his or her lot in life. It is also a reasonably stable attribute and is highly correlated with whatever it is (let's call it *g*, for Charles Spearman's model of general intelligence) that IQ tests measure. It is also inherited, to a substantial degree (probably in the 40 to 80 percent range) and differs among various racial and ethnic groups—with East Asians and whites, on average, doing much better than blacks and Latinos, on average.

Herrnstein and Murray conscientiously pointed out that any

particular black or Latino can have a higher IQ than any particular white or East Asian and that no conclusion can be reached about any individual by knowing the group's average scores, but they also made quite clear their view that the racial differences are real, are probably genetically based, and are of great consequence. Furthermore, they dismissed those who hold a different view as intellectual lightweights or liberal apologists. "Races are by definition groups of people who differ in characteristic ways," they asserted. "Intellectual fashion has dictated that all differences must be denied except the absolutely undeniable differences in appearances, but nothing in biology says this should be so." At another point, they tackled the nature-nurture question directly and managed to come down firmly on both sides: "It seems highly likely to us that both genes and the environment have something to do with racial differences. What might the mix be? We are resolutely agnostics on that issue; as far as we can determine, the evidence does not yet justify an estimate."

Herrnstein and Murray acknowledged—even as they pounded home the idea that genes are destiny and that genes have a lot to do with IQ—that the IQs of blacks have been rising consistently over the years, that, in fact, the average IQ scores of blacks are now comparable to what those of whites were a generation or so ago. However, they dismissed the importance of the concession that intelligence may be malleable by noting that whites' scores are rising as well and suggesting that there is no evidence, given that fact, that the gap will ever be closed. ("The national averages have in fact changed by amounts that are comparable to the fifteen or so IQ points separating whites and blacks in America. . . . Couldn't the mean of blacks move 15 points as well through environmental changes? There seems no reason why not—but also no reason to believe that white and Asian means can be made to stand still.") As for programs, such as Head Start, that once seemed to raise IQs, they argued that the effects invariably fade over time and therefore are not significant.

The Head Start critique, in particular, has always struck me as intellectually bizarre. It seems a bit like saying, "Well, we fed this guy great meals until he was five years old and then we starved him for a decade. Now he's scrawny. That proves early attention to nutrition doesn't work." As William Julius Wilson observed in *When Work Disappears*, anyone who is familiar with the communities in which Head Start is provided would not be surprised to find that the intellectual gains fade over time. Once the children leave Head Start, they typically are thrust into an environment in which they must contend with unchallenging curricula, inadequate facilities, overcrowded rooms, and a host of other distractions to educational attainment. If Head Start–type programs were continued into middle school and beyond, Wilson contended, it is likely that the initial intellectual gains would be sustained.

For whatever reason, Herrnstein and Murray preferred not to entertain that possibility, though they left open the door to the possibility that many of their conclusions might be way off the mark. Indeed, if one reads *The Bell Curve* closely, one realizes that despite the impression Herrnstein and Murray leave that inherited intelligence is everything and that whites have a lot more of it than do blacks, integrity compelled them to do enough backpedaling to render such a conclusion unwarranted. For instance, Herrnstein and Murray admitted that they really don't know whether intelligence is inherited a little or a lot, that they know nothing about the cause of the racial differences on the test, that they don't understand why the IQs of blacks are rising (or whether the phenomenon is important), and that they haven't a ghost of an idea of how the genetic and environmental factors interact. What they have is a blizzard of statistics, mostly correlations of various sorts, and an avalanche of largely unsubstantiated opinions about genetics or, at least, about the link between genes and intelligence. It's important to note, moreover, that neither author has any credentials in genetics. Herrnstein, who died shortly before the book came out, was a psychologist, and Murray is a political scientist and polemicist. Both authors were essentially statisticians with an ideological agenda.

Let's imagine if their agenda had been different. Suppose they had started with the goal of investigating another "unitary mental factor" called *g*? Suppose they had noticed that *g* (otherwise known as greed) expressed itself early, that in kindergarten some children were more interested in accumulating toys and treats than were others. Suppose they had also noticed that this trait remained constant, that greedy children normally grew into greedy adults—even if teachers and other authority figures urged them to be altruistic. Our investigators might have interpreted the children's lack of response to the adult models of altruism as evidence that environmental factors have little effect on greed. Even if they were not certain how the trait is transmitted genetically, they might have felt justified in surmising that greed is, at least in part, an inherited characteristic. They might also have assumed that the acquisition of wealth is strongly correlated with greed.

They might then have looked at statistics on the income and wealth of several groups (say, Jews, Japanese Americans, and Italians) and performed a series of multiple regression analyses. These analyses might have told them that Jews and Japanese Americans earn considerably more than do Italians, even when the population samples are controlled for education and parental income. Thus, a poor Japanese American, they might have concluded, is not similar to a poor Italian American. They might have conjectured (and performed any number of sophisticated statistical tests in support of this conjecture) that the reason for this difference is that Japanese Americans have more of the gene for greed. They might also have looked at Jews, Japanese Americans, and Italians who lived in similar neighborhoods and went to similar schools. And on that basis, they could have concluded that even when Jews, Japanese Americans, and Italians come from virtually identical backgrounds, they end up with different levels of wealth. The reason, they would have surmised, has a lot to do (perhaps 50 to 90 percent) with the gene (or combination of genes) that causes greed.

They might even have looked at data on twins and found that when raised apart (which they would have assumed is pretty much the same as being raised by random strangers), twins are much more similar in their economic attainments than are non-twin siblings who are raised together. The twins, they might have found, are also more alike financially than are similar people from the same ethnic groups who are raised apart. That finding is further proof, they might have concluded, of the power of the genes for greed.

Now suppose, on the basis of such analysis, they wrote a hefty book that suggested that Jews and Japanese Americans seem to have particularly powerful genes for greed (at least when compared to Italians) and ran hundreds of tables showing correlation coefficients in support of their thesis—even as they acknowledged, when pressed, that they had never done any experiments with genes, that they had no idea what a greed gene was, how it functioned, or where it might be found. Just how many major magazine covers would they get? And how many invitations to prime-time news shows? Probably not many. Even the most demented daytime talk-show hosts would probably scoff at the analysis and dismiss it as nothing more than the nutty musings of bigoted, anti-Semitic and anti–Japanese American minds.

So why was Herrnstein and Murray's message, only marginally more credible, given such serious consideration? Why was it even regarded as science? Why didn't journalists assume their traditionally skeptical position and vigorously question whether Murray and Herrnstein could conceivably have the evidence to make the claims that they did?

In the Spring 1995 issue of *Forbes Media Critic,* Jude Wanniski raised that question. "Reading through several dozen articles in the course of my survey was not a pleasant experience," he confessed in analyzing coverage of *The Bell Curve.* "They are written mainly by white opinion leaders, who are arguing among themselves about how much smarter white people are at the beginning of life than black people. Liberals think whites are a little bit smarter, conservatives think whites are a lot smarter. I also have discovered that, like Herrnstein and Murray, many of my friends are benevolent racists, who simply accept the authors' quackery as fact."

Wanniski harshly criticized America's three major newsweeklies and other publications for not taking issue—whatever they thought of the book's ideology—with its spectacularly flimsy science. Instead, the journalists pretty much accepted the science as valid; all the magazines reported essentially as fact the supposition that the ability to do well on IQ tests is substantially inherited. As *Newsweek* put it at one point: "Whatever mental ability is made of—dense neural circuitry, highly charged synapses or sheer brain mass—we didn't all get equal shares."

The journalists' largely uncritical acceptance of the findings presented in *The Bell Curve*—even as they questioned the authors' motives—may or may not, as Wanniski contended, reveal their racism. It certainly reflects ignorance (of history, of statistics, of the difference between a political scientist and a geneticist) on a massive scale. It also reflects fear—of challenging apparent experts even when the experts are not really what they seem to be. And the authors certainly put on a good show of pretending that they knew precisely what they were writing about. They dressed up their argument in a cloak of statistics, and the journalists, who, for the most part, are not good with numbers, were cowed. The authors also wrapped themselves in the mantle of truth tellers, essentially taking the position that they were merely helping a reluctant and sensitive public to face some hard facts: "We are not indifferent to the ways in which this book, wrongly construed, might do harm. But there can be no real progress in solving America's social problems when they are as misperceived as they are today."

In *Denying the Holocaust*, author Deborah Lipstadt wrote about another group of loudmouths who have positioned themselves as truth tellers. "When I turned to the topic of Holocaust denial, I knew that I was dealing with extremist antisemites who have increasingly managed, under the guise of scholarship, to camouflage their hateful ideology," she stated. Such people, she pointed out, have the right to "stand on any street corner and spread their calumnies. They have the right to publish books, but not to be treated as the other side of a legitimate debate." Much the same could be said about Herrnstein and Murray.

The authors of *The Bell Curve* do not represent, to use Lipstadt's phrase, "the other side of a legitimate debate." They represent, in Wanniski's words, "quackery" cloaked in the guise of objective science. Yet few reporters, as Wanniski noted, went out of their way to talk to physical scientists or with people who actually work in genetics. If they had, they might have gotten an earful.

In a 1996 article entitled "Our Genes, Ourselves?" published in *BioScience*, Ari Berkowitz, a neurobiologist in the Division of Biology, California Institute of Technology, elegantly critiqued the "science" of *The Bell Curve* without once mentioning the book by name. Berkowitz began with an obvious point, that genes operate in complicated and myriad ways and that there is rarely, if ever, a one-to-one correspondence between any specific behavior and a gene (though one defective gene can, occasionally, have a large and detrimental impact). In other words, to speculate that genes have something to do with intelligence is different from saying that scientists understand what that relationship is.

How do genetic scientists go about trying to figure out the genetic contribution to a specific behavior? Typically, they try to locate a marker on an easily identifiable piece of DNA that is consistently identified with the trait. Such research resulted in the discovery of the cause for Huntington's disease, which had the virtue, from a scientific perspective, of being induced by a single gene. But Huntington's disease is not typical. Most behaviorally expressed ailments—depression, schizophrenia, and alcoholism, for example—seem to be caused by a combination of genes interacting with each other and with the environment. Certainly, Berkowitz noted, intelligence is not likely to be the result of a single gene. So even finding a gene or two that is crucial to intelligence would not necessarily tell you much. "As an analogy, one can break a transistor radio by removing one component, but no one would seriously argue that the missing component alone normally causes the radio to play a particular radio station," Berkowitz argued. Figuring out how intelligence works at a genetic level is infinitely more difficult than figuring out the workings of a radio, but doing so is crucial if one is to say much that is meaningful about the heritability of intelligence.

As Berkowitz put it:

> The less scientists know about the chain of events linking a gene to a behavior, the greater the likelihood that a correlation is established that does not indicate causation. Even if a correlation between a stretch of DNA and a well-defined, complex human characteristic can be firmly established, what does this correlation tell us? We would like to know what causative role a gene plays in the chain of events leading to a behavioral outcome. This chain of events should include: which gene is involved, which protein it codes for, what the function(s) of this protein is, and how this protein could produce changes in the nervous system that could underlie the mental characteristic.

The Bell Curve's authors, of course, had no such research to present; they only had statistical correlations.

To Berkowitz, the folly of such an approach is obvious. If people with a gene for pale skin, for instance, got more cancer from sitting in the sun than did people with dark skin, a statistician who knows nothing more than the numbers (and is ignorant of the connection between exposure to the sun and skin cancer) might erroneously conclude that pale-skinned people are genetically programmed for skin cancer. By the same token, if people with genes for tallness are disproportionately among the ranks of professional basketball players, a statistically minded (but obtuse) political scientist might conclude that they had a gene for the ability to play basketball.

Psychologists often cite various studies of twins in an attempt to get around some of the problems of correlation without causation. For instance, a researcher could theoretically determine the genetic component of intelligence or some other trait by comparing identical twins and fraternal twins. Since identical twins share all their genes and fraternal twins generally share about half, one could interpret the variances between the two groups as a measure of the genetic contribution to intelligence. Unfortunately, as Berkowitz pointed out, such an analysis implicitly assumes that the "environment" shared by identical twins is equally similar to that shared by fraternal twins. That supposition is extremely questionable, given the reality that people (including parents) tend to treat identical twins differently from siblings who are not identical and the fact that identical twins, with their singularly close bonds, often create their own private—and unique—shared environment. But even if the assumption about the similarity of environments is correct, the estimates of heritability—generally in the 40 to 70 percent range—may be way too high. The reason is that intelligence is likely to be affected by a combination of genes. And though identical twins share two times as many of the same genes as do fraternal twins (or other siblings), on average, they share *more* than twice as many equivalent gene combinations, given that, for purely statistical reasons, combining genes will multiply the magnitude of genetic variance. That fact generally is not sufficiently taken into account by social science statisticians who are trying to tease out the relative contribution of genes to intelligence. Even when one looks merely at identical twins raised apart, it may be impossible to determine just how similar and how different their environments were and therefore impossible to determine how much of any similarity in attributes was caused solely by genes. And, assuming one could determine the relative genetic component of intelligence for twins or any other population, that component would not tell us much about another population. As Berkowitz put it:

> Even if a trait has a high heritability within each of two groups of genotypes (e.g., African Americans and Caucasian Americans), the results say nothing about the source of any differences between these groups. If a trait has a high heritability in the environments tested, a major change in the environment (which might include improving education or health care) may dramatically alter not only the phenotypes but also the heritability. In short, heritability cannot be measured accurately in human studies and, even if it could be, it would not indicate the relative importance of genes and environments.

He chalked up some of the misunderstanding of heritability to "confusion of the statistical term heritability with the ordinary use of the word heritable."

Even if geneticists did agree on a number for the genetic component of intelligence, Berkowitz wondered what in God's name it would mean: "It is a bit like asking what percentage contribution George Washington made to the establishment of the United States." Let's say, for the sake of discussion, that Washington was between 40 and 80 percent responsible for the establishment of the United States. The figure, of course, is meaningless, for Washington was not some independent factor operating in isolation; he was part of a much larger picture. And part of the large picture in the biological world is recognizing that genes are not a template of inevitability. Destiny is not just a matter of genetics—not with green peas and certainly not with humans. To say that something is linked to a gene tells you relatively little. As Berkowitz made clear, "Some conditions known to be caused by genes alone can be prevented or reversed by nongenetic means, such as providing a phenylalanine-free diet to children who have the genetic disorder phenylketonuria. On the other hand, some environmental events, such as alcohol abuse by pregnant women, can often have permanent effects."

In a letter to *Science* magazine, Lori Andrews and Dorothy Nelkin, of the Human Genome Project, underscored Berkowitz's arguments, deploring *The Bell Curve*'s "misrepresentation of the state of genetic knowledge in this area." After pointedly rebutting some of the book's major arguments, they stated:

> The more scientists learn about human genes the more complexity is revealed. This complexity has become apparent as more genes correlated with human genetic diseases are discovered. We are only beginning to explore the intricate relationship between genes and environment and between individual genes and the rest of the human genome. If anything, the lack of predictability from genetic information has become the rule rather than the exception. Simplistic claims about the inheritance of such a complex trait as cognitive ability are unjustified; moreover, as the track record of eugenics shows, they are dangerous.

So why—other than promoting a political agenda—do the self-proclaimed intelligence "scientists" make the claims that they do? Ashley Montagu quoted with approval the words of the nineteenth-century English economist and writer Walter Bagehot: "When a philosopher cannot account for anything in any other manner, he boldly ascribes it to an occult quality in some race."

This sort of stuff, as Andrews and Nelkin suggested, has an extensive history. Long before the IQ test was invented, Americans were speculating on the link between intelligence and race. In 1858, as Thomas Ross, a professor of law at the University of Pittsburgh, recalled in *Just Stories*, a South Carolina senator made the following observation on the floor of the U.S. Senate: "In all social systems there must be a class to do the menial duties, to perform the drudgery of life. That is a class requiring but a low order of intellect, and but little skill. . . . Fortunately for the South we have found a race adapted to that purpose to be at hand. . . . Our slaves are black, of another, inferior race. The status in which we have placed them is an elevation."

In the nineteenth century, the development of psychometrics gave such arguments the backing of "science." *The Bell Curve*'s forerunner, by more than a century, was *Hereditary Genius*, written by

Francis Galton, Charles Darwin's cousin and the father of eugenics. In that 1869 classic, Galton complained, "Much more care is taken to select appropriate varieties of plants and animals for plantations in foreign settlements than to select appropriate types of men." The most appropriate types of men, Galton made clear, were the better-bred ones, in particular those who were English. Galton also revered the ancient Greeks, whom he estimated were as superior, on average, to nineteenth-century Europeans as "our race is above that of the African Negro." Galton's conclusions were not totally based on speculation. He studied the family trees of prominent and accomplished Englishmen, found that many of their forebears had been accomplished as well, and took that as scientific proof that genius is inherited.

His disciples and philosophical peers and progeny brought Galton's ideas to America and were prominent among early psychometricians. Even before the IQ test was developed, psychologists were trying to prove that their assumptions about race and intelligence were sound. An 1895 article in the *Psychological Review,* which reported on a study of the reaction times of whites and blacks, went so far as to conclude that blacks' seemingly faster reflexes proved they were more primitive. After Alfred Binet's intelligence test, invented in 1905, was adapted and brought to America, such efforts picked up steam. Indeed, much of the early history of psychometrics is the story of various attempts to prove that intelligence is inherited, that the upper classes have more of it than the lower classes, and that northern and western Europeans have more of it than do Mexicans, people from Mediterranean countries, and Africans.

These efforts continued into the twentieth century. In a 1978 article in the *Journal of the History of the Behavioral Sciences,* Franz Samelson notes that in 1923 one M. J. Mayo reported on a study comparing black and white children in New York schools. Mayo found that black children did not perform especially well and, in an analysis that foreshadows Herrnstein and Murray's, concluded that the difference must be due to heredity "in as much as everything in the power of educator, philanthropist, and law giver had been done for the equalization of opportunity." That psychometricians in the early 1920s could argue, presumably with a straight face, that blacks had equal educational opportunities is a sign of just how out of touch with reality such social scientists can be. It certainly should make anyone dubious of current attempts to minimize the effects of social conditions—including educational inequality—that continue to impede the intellectual performance of blacks.

Psychometricians, unfortunately, have a long history of not letting relevant facts get in the way of their personal biases, both in America and elsewhere around the world. As Elaine Mensh and Henry Mensh noted in *The IQ Mythology*: "The first mental tests on the African continent were administered in South Africa in 1915, when one A. L. Martin gave the Binet to African youths and children. He came to two conclusions: that the testees were deficient in the requirements for 'abstract thought,' and that the Binet should be revised for use on 'uncivilised children and adults.'" In the 1920s, they observed, "several testing projects were also conducted to support a biological-determinist thesis known as 'early arrest,' which holds that an African's mental development stops earlier than that of a white, making an African adult the mental equivalent of a white child." In the 1960s, as many African nations acquired or moved toward independence, American psychologist Arthur Cryns argued, in the *Journal of Psychology,* for widespread mental testing of indigenous Africans to determine whether they had the "potentialities to deal effectively" with the problems associated with liberation.

In 1974, when research linking race to IQ had again leaped into the public limelight, John Ebling, chairman of the department of zoology at the University of Sheffield, convened a conference on "racial variation in man" at the Royal Geographical Society in London. At that conference, two decades before *The Bell Curve* exploded on the scene, Steven Rose, a biologist, made a point that remains relevant: "What is interesting is how, despite the distance in time and the advances in human genetics, we are now asked to return to the intellectual preoccupations of the eugenicists and mental testers of a past age. When 100 years after . . . *Hereditary Genius,* we are asked to reconsider the Nature/Nurture debate, it must surely be clear that we are not dealing with a scientific question at all, capable of scientific resolution; the issues . . . seem rather to be ideological."

The Bell Curve, without a doubt, reeks of ideology. But although personal and political biases may explain Herrnstein and Murray's motivation for writing the book, these biases do not explain Americans' continuing fascination with the authors' message. Why do theories of the genetic inferiority of blacks continue to resonate in so many circles? Why is research that is so fundamentally flawed taken so seriously? Some of the fault, as I argued earlier, rests with the press, but clearly, something more than journalistic incompetence is at work. While many Americans are repelled by the very notion that intelligence—or its absence—is a racial trait, others are eager to embrace the possibility, for it places the blame for inequality and for a host of other problems (from the joblessness of minority groups to the existence of the so-called underclass) in the genes, rather than in the hands of human beings. There is something comforting in the belief—even if it is rooted in fiction—that certain unfortunate realities are beyond our control, that certain unfortunate souls are destined to be losers. Such an outlook makes it easy for persons who are so inclined to accept, with a certain amount of equanimity and with no sense of culpability (or even irony), an unjust status quo—even as they, in the manner of Herrnstein and Murray, dolorously lament the plight of the cerebrally deprived. It also permits prejudice without guilt—what some wags might call rational prejudice. In an age of pretensions to color blindness, when old-fashioned racism is no longer chic, there is a psychological virtue in being able to attribute what might otherwise be deemed bigoted thoughts to a pseudo-scientifically documented deficiency in certain race-linked genes.

None of this is to imply that research on intelligence and learning is pointless. There are countless interesting and important questions that ought to be explored. People, after all, need all the help they can get in realizing their intellectual potential. No useful answers, however, are likely to be found by rooting around in the junk science of a century or so ago. And certainly nothing helpful will emerge from a mindset that implies that certain people (and certain ethnic groups) are mentally doomed at birth.

It is clear that ethnic and racial groups do vary in their performance on certain tests, and so, for that matter, do men and women. It is less clear, however, just what to make of that fact. Researchers have long known, for instance, that women tend to do less well than men on tests of advanced mathematical skills. One could take that fact to mean that men have better genes for mathematics and pronounce the puzzle solved, or one could look for more promising explanations.

Psychologists Steven Spencer (of Hope College), Claude Steele (of Stanford University), and Diane Quinn (of the University of Michigan) chose the second approach. They theorized that women's performance on difficult mathematical problems might be affected by a phenomenon they called "stereotype threat." In other words, society's stereotype of women as lousy mathematicians might be a source of anxiety for women who take mathematics tests. That anxiety, they hypothesized, might be unsettling enough to undermine the performance, even of those women who have a high aptitude for math.

Spencer, Steele, and Quinn tested the hypothesis by giving a series of tests under various conditions to male and female students, all of whom had decent mathematics backgrounds and were matched, as best as the researchers could determine, for ability. They did not, however, treat the groups equally. Some were told that women generally performed as well as men on the specific test they were preparing to take. Others were either told nothing about possible sex differences or were told that, in the past, performance on the text appeared to be related to gender. (They did not say precisely how it was related to gender but figured that most women would infer that females had done worse.)

In a paper entitled "Stereotype Threat and Women's Math Performance," the researchers reported their results. "When subjects were explicitly told that the test yielded gender differences, women greatly underperformed in relation to men, replicating the stereotype threat effects in the earlier experiments and suggesting that . . . women had assumed a male advantage on the test. But when the test was purported not to yield gender differences, women performed at the same level as equally-qualified men. This happened, of course, even though the test in these two conditions was the same."

In other words, simply telling the women that gender was not a factor was enough to raise their performance to the level of men's. Spencer and company reasoned that the phenomenon might not be peculiar to women, that other groups burdened by negative stereotypes might experience stereotype threat as well: "Our central proposition is this: when a stereotype about one's group indicts an important ability, one's performance in situations where that ability can be judged comes under an extra pressure—that of possibly being judged, or self-fulfilling the stereotype—and this extra pressure may interfere with performance through the anxiety, distraction or demotivation it causes."

Such anxiety, for example, could theoretically affect the ability of whites to play basketball (especially when competing with blacks) or of the elderly to function intellectually in situations in which senility may be assumed or, most obviously, of blacks or Puerto Ricans doing academic work.

When I spoke with Spencer (whose Ph.D. dissertation was the basis for the just-mentioned paper on gender) in 1996, he described some of his current research in which he is explicitly studying the issue of race and achievement. Investigators had given black and white students at the State University of New York at Buffalo a series of tests, much as the other team had done with women. The results had not yet been published, but the findings, said Spencer, were clear-cut: When black students were told the test was "culture free," they generally did as well as did whites. When they were told *nothing* about cultural correlations, they did worse. The researchers also looked at the blood-pressure readings of students who were taking the test and discovered that they were significantly lower when black students were told the test was culture free, in short, when they were not carrying the burden of negative racial expectations.

In an *Atlantic Monthly* article published in 1992, Claude Steele (who was Spencer's Ph.D. adviser) tackled the issue of race and academic anxiety. He described an encounter with a nineteen-year-old black student he had volunteered to mentor. When Steele arrived at their first meeting, however, he discovered that his commitment was futile: "My lunchtime companion was a statistic brought to life, a living example of one of the most disturbing facts of racial life in America today: the failure of so many black Americans to thrive in school. Before I could lift a hand to help this student, she had decided to do what 70 percent of all black Americans at four-year colleges do at some point in their academic careers—drop out."

Steele speculated on what might have happened to the young student to cause her to give up and conjectured that her problem began even before she arrived at the university. The recruitment process that brought her to the university had strongly focused on the fact that she was a minority student and had implied that simply because of her color, she was at academic risk. Once on campus, the university community had confirmed that assessment, steering her to largely segregated settings with others who were "under suspicion of intellectual inferiority." Laboring under such a heavy burden of perceived inadequacy, she dared not share news of any academic troubles with instructors, counselors, or peers. It is only a short step from that situation to a state of "disidentification," Steele argued. A person "disidentifies" by divesting any psychological and emotional investment made in academic excellence. High achievement becomes unimportant to one's sense of self-esteem. In short, one protects oneself emotionally by giving up on the goal of academic success—and thereby setting oneself up for failure. The stigma of academic inferiority undermines the achievement of black students, Steele concluded, "as effectively as a lock on a schoolhouse door."

Steele has since tested his theory of stereotype threat and black Americans and reported the results in a 1995 issue of the *Journal of Personality and Social Psychology*. In a manner similar to that employed in the experiments discussed earlier, Steele and an associate, Joshua Aronson, gave groups of black and white undergraduates at Stanford University a difficult examination under a variety of conditions. Some groups were told the test would diagnose their strengths and weaknesses in "problems requiring reading and verbal reasoning abilities." Others were told that it was not meant to evaluate their ability but merely would help researchers understand "psychological factors involved in solving verbal problems." Steele and Aronson hypothesized that presenting the test as "nondiagnostic" would remove much of the threat and therefore enhance the performance of black students. They discovered they were correct. The black students not only performed significantly better when they thought their ability was not being judged, but they were less anxious and expressed less self-doubt. The white students were not affected nearly as much.

Whatever "environmental or genetic endowments a person brings to the testing situation," Steele and Aronson concluded, "this research shows that this situation is not group-neutral—not even, quite possibly, when the tester and test content have been accommodated to the test-taker's background. The problem is that stereotypes afoot in the larger society establish a predicament in the testing situation—aside from test content—that still has the power to undermine standardized test performance, and, we suspect, contribute powerfully to the pattern of group differences that have characterized these tests since their inception."

John Ogbu, a Nigerian-born anthropologist at the University of California, Berkeley, has also pondered the question of academic inequality, looking not only at black and white Americans but at a host of other groups, including the Barakumin, a traditionally low-caste group in Japan. His research had shown that the IQs of the Barakumin are lower than those of other Japanese (though there are recent signs that the academic outlook for the Barakumin is finally improving). The gap in the IQs of the Barakumin and other Japanese was roughly the same as it is between blacks and whites in the United States. What intrigued Ogbu is that the gap seemed to disappear when Barakumin families immigrated to America.

What that finding said to Ogbu was that the cause of the gap could not possibly be genetic (especially given that the Barakumin come from the same racial stock as do other Japanese) but must be cultural. He has noticed similar gaps, Ogbu said, in low-caste groups in Africa, India, and elsewhere around the world, as well as among groups who are not of a lower caste but have different lifestyles or cultural orientations from those in the mainstream of their ethnic or racial groups: Hasidic Jews compared to other Jews, for instance, or Arabs in rural Lebanon versus those who live in cities. Ogbu has also noticed that the gaps are not always gender consistent, that American Indian boys in the Southwest tend to test higher than American Indian girls, whereas in Japan the pattern is reversed.

Ogbu is convinced that intelligence is extremely malleable. He sees the effect that schooling can have on a culture as evidence of that changeability: "Introduce school into any culture where they have had no school before and it helps people learn to think," he observed. He is also convinced that several factors in the culture explain why blacks, on average, do less well than do whites academically.

Ogbu has noticed, for instance, that some blacks (and certain American Indians) believe their culture is in conflict with academic achievement. They feel, as he puts it, that they must "denounce" part of who they are to be successful. He used as an example so-called black English, which most educators consider to be an inferior tongue. A student has the option of either unlearning black English and learning to speak standard English or being an academic failure. Ogbu compared the situation of the American-born black student to that of the Chinese immigrant. The immigrant also must learn standard English in order to succeed, but he does not have to unlearn his native tongue, and no one tells him that his first language or first culture is inferior. The same, Ogbu noted, is true of an immigrant from Africa: "I didn't go from Nigeria expecting Americans to teach me in Ibo. I came expecting to learn English. In fact, my first year at Princeton, I tried to take my notes in Ibo, and it did not work. Okay, so I had to learn English."

Such immigrants display what Ogbu calls a "tourist attitude." Much like a traveler in a foreign land, they adopt native practices without renouncing their own. They have no sense of conflict: "The difference however is that a black guy comes in with a feeling . . . that in order to learn standard English, he has to give up his black English" and therefore a part of his identity, and for that reason, he often resists. Such resistance applies not only to standard English. Many blacks also avoid mathematics and science.

Among the students Ogbu has studied in Oakland, only 21 percent of the blacks, compared to roughly two-thirds of the Chinese Americans, took mathematics and science courses that might prepare them for college. When he asked the black students why they were not taking these courses, the answer he got back, Ogbu said, is "because they think it's white. Or it's hard." In America, he noted, mathematics and science have never been regarded as areas of black expertise, and many black students are "scared of these areas that have been traditionally white."

Such research is obviously different from that undertaken by Herrnstein and Murray. For one thing, Ogbu deals with human beings, not merely numbers. The larger difference, however, is that he is looking for a way to help underachieving individuals get ahead. As an anthropologist, he has a professional bias, of course. He sees issues of culture, where Steele and Spencer see issues of attitude and cognition, but all three are essentially asking the same question: "Is there a way to help people improve?"

Mathematician Philip Uri Treisman faced that question in the mid-1970s, when he was at the University of California at Berkeley, working with teaching assistants in the mathematics department. He noticed that blacks were disproportionately represented among those doing poorly in freshmen calculus, while Chinese students, by and large, were doing much better than the norm.

Treisman decided to try to figure out why there were such differences and spent over a year closely observing both groups of students. He discovered that their approach to the university was quite different. "I was struck by the sharp separation that most black students maintained—regardless of class or educational background—between their school lives and their social lives," he wrote in a 1985 report. "Unlike the Chinese, black students rarely studied with classmates. Only two of the twenty students I interviewed reported that they regularly studied with other students." Those two, who studied with each other, married at the end of their freshman year and dropped out of school. The Chinese students generally studied in groups; they also studied longer, putting in nearly twice as many hours as the black students. With many blacks, he concluded, studying alone was essentially a matter of pride, reflecting their need to prove that they could do the work without help and that they were not inferior. They scorned the campus tutoring program, refused to ask graduate assistants for help, and ignored signs that they were in trouble. A large number of them failed, and Treisman decided to see if he could do something to change the situation.

He worked closely with a small group of black students, getting them, in effect, to adopt many of the practices of the Chinese students. The results were stunning. Of the 42 students he worked with, only one failed a calculus course and more than half got grades of B minus or better. Treisman eventually expanded the program with federal grants and got equally impressive results with a much larger group that was "ethnically diverse but predominantly black and Hispanic." By the time the program was cut back in the mid-1980s because funding was running out, he had gathered enough statistics to know that the approach worked. The black students who participated in the workshops got better grades in calculus (on average, a full grade higher) than those who did not; more than half passed with a B minus or above. Indeed, they performed better as a group than did their Asian and white peers. And a substantial proportion of those involved in the workshop—44 percent—went on to graduate with a mathematics-based major, compared to 10 percent of the black students who had not attended the workshops. In the process, Treisman reported, he learned some important principles: It is crucial to expect students to excel, not just to get by; it is important to stress collaboration and working in groups; and it is essential for the faculty to be deeply involved with and to support the students.

In 1989, Treisman moved to the University of Texas at Austin, where he designed an "emerging scholars" program based on his work at Berkeley. At that time, the school had only a handful of black and Hispanic mathematics majors—roughly 5, he recalled. When we spoke in 1996, he reported that the number had risen to 150—of whom approximately 110 were Latino and the remainder were black.

While working on this book, I visited Duke University, where I spoke with a group of fraternity brothers at the predominantly black Alpha Phi Alpha house. During the conversation, I mentioned Treisman's research on the importance of study groups. Thomas Martin, a twenty-year-old junior majoring in engineering, reacted as if a lightbulb had gone off in his head. When I gestured for him to speak, Martin replied, "The reason I'm quiet on the study group thing is that I didn't know that it was an issue, but I've only been in one study group in the two and a half years I've been here. I just realized that. I never thought about it. I always would study by myself. . . . Except in that one case, I've never been invited to participate in [a study group]."

The fact that he was not asked to join study groups, Martin said, stemmed from the tendency of Duke students to group themselves along racial lines, so it was often difficult to make real contact across those lines. He had noticed, he said, that some whites who had been in his classes since his freshman year barely acknowledged him. "And because there's not an incentive for them to talk to me or just work with me, they choose not to, to just ignore my presence." He wished, he said, that something would happen to make white students "see an incentive, or just have an incentive," to interact with nonwhites.

Wesley Brandon, Martin's fraternity brother, had similar frustrations: "If you're the only black student there, a lot of students are reluctant to talk to you. Maybe they just don't know you." His white classmates, he said, had a much easier time getting into groups and simply establishing lines of communication with their fellow students. Brandon noted that there were three other blacks in his department, and they made a point of not segregating themselves. Nonetheless, he said, whites were not, for the most part, embracing him: "If I chose not to speak to anyone, no one would speak to me. A lot of times, I have to make that first step to open up communications. Maybe it's because I'm the only black person they have come into contact with."

Peter Kuriloff, professor of education at the University of Pennsylvania, believes that such segregation on predominantly white campuses puts black and Latino students at a distinct academic disadvantage. "You need to be in study groups . . . to make friends, in order to learn and do well. And friends who do study groups do better than kids who do it on their own. . . . Self segregation means it's harder for black kids."

Psychologist Jeff Howard, president of the Efficacy Institute, a Massachusetts-based nonprofit educational consulting organization, thinks that another factor that has made it hard for black and Latino students is the persistence of the kind of thinking that undergirds *The Bell Curve*. "We operate from the self-fulfilling conviction that only a small percentage of children are intelligent enough to become well educated," and that assumption particularly hurts blacks and Latinos: "There is a rumor of inferiority that follows minority children to school, especially racially integrated schools. They enter the school environment under a general expectation that they have less intelligence, are severely overrepresented in slow, or special education classes and even more severely underrepresented in the upper end of the placement hierarchy, and are subject to a range of forces outside the school, including negative peer pressure, that oppose any commitment to intellectual development."

For all the research just cited, the fact is that relatively little is known about the ultimate effects of negative stereotypes. It is obvious, however, that they hurt, and hurt deeply—in ways researchers and teachers are only dimly beginning to understand. Giving credence to theories of racial hierarchy is not a neutral process. The dissemination of such claptrap poisons the atmosphere as surely as the release of a toxic gas.

Guessing about the genetic contribution to the distribution along a bell curve may be entertaining to some of those who fancy themselves to be "politically incorrect" independent thinkers. At this point, however, it is not a serious scientific pursuit, and until people who engage in such work can demonstrate, at a minimum, that they truly understand something useful about genetics, it is absurd to treat it as if it is. Their research merits no more respect than that given to astrologers or clairvoyants who, attired like mythical wizards, mumble mystical gibberish about the influence of the stars and the moon and invite us to squander our money on fortunetellers and psychic hot lines. Certainly, there will always be pundits who look at failure and call it fate. It takes no creativity or imagination or even any substantial amount of intelligence to do so. The more important challenge, it seems to me, is not in documenting human failure, but in figuring out how to help more people succeed.

CHAPTER 3

Achieving educational parity in six simple steps

Those who would encourage academic success must, at the outset, acknowledge a harsh reality: that the line separating success from failure—intellectual life from death—can be tissue thin, especially in places where academic aspirations are more often stifled than encouraged. There are many graveyards for intellectual dreams in black and brown America, places where no one needs to read *The Bell Curve* to understand how little is expected of him or her, places where achievement is considered unnatural and discouragement lurks at every turn—often in the guise of sympathetic condescension from educators who, certain that most of their pupils will never be scholars, don't dare to challenge the Fates.

I learned that fact early, growing up at a time when and in a Chicago neighborhood where a few vocal teachers made one thing clear: Black kids were naturally poor students. One teacher told the class (I believe I was in third grade at the time) that blacks had "lazy" tongues. Another informed us—when I complained that the books were insultingly undemanding—that we were lucky to have those, ragged and inadequate as they might be, since most of us probably couldn't read anyway. One announced that he didn't care whether we learned anything or not, since he would take his paycheck home whatever we did. And several were content to surrender the class to their charges, purposelessly wiling away the hours, as mayhem—penny pool competitions, card games, and random revelry—exploded all around them until the sound of the final bell.

Still, I consider myself fortunate, for I also had some teachers who cared and managed to get that feeling across and I had parents who made it clear that, whatever anyone else might say, *they* considered learning important. And I was lucky to have picked up the insight, from God knows where, that many people in authority—including teachers—are fools, or at least are incapable of seeing potential in unaccustomed places and therefore are not to be taken seriously.

Things obviously have changed since I was in elementary school, but in some places, things have not changed all that much or necessarily for the better. Many black and brown children are still being told that academic accomplishment is so much beyond them that there is no real purpose in trying. They are receiving that message not only from schools, but, in many cases, from virtually everyone around them. The very atmosphere, in large parts of America, is polluted with notions of intellectual inferiority.

More than a decade ago, when many Americans still believed in school desegregation, social psychologist Janet Ward Schofield spent several years studying a middle school in the Northeast that tried mightily to make it work. No expense was spared on the school's physical facilities. Teachers claimed they treated all children alike. Nonetheless, academic triumph and failure at the school immediately became color coded. Whiteness, as Schofield reported in *Black and White in School*, "became associated with success . . . in the school." Blackness, on the other hand, became linked to academic mediocrity, which left black students with a difficult choice: They could either try to make it as scholars, fully aware that they were expected (and likely) to fail, or they could opt out of academics and accept their designated roles as dunces and troublemakers.

In an adaptation of *The Bell Curve* prepared for the *New Republic*, Herrnstein and Murray pointed to the pervasiveness of presumptions of black mental mediocrity as a rationale for publishing their work.

> The private dialogue about race in America is far different from the public one, and we are not referring just to discussions among white rednecks. Our impression is that the private attitudes of white elites toward blacks is strained far beyond any public acknowledgment, that hostility is not uncommon and that a key part of the strain is a growing suspicion that fundamental racial differences are implicated in the social and economic gap that continues to separate blacks and whites, especially alleged genetic differences in intelligence. . . . We have been asked whether the question of racial genetic differences in intelligence should even be raised in polite society. We believe there's no alternative. A taboo issue, filled with potential for hurt and anger, lurks just beneath the surface of American life. It is essential that people begin to talk about this in the open.

That passage, like much in *The Bell Curve*, is disingenuous because it offers two rotten alternatives: continue to whisper about black intellectual inferiority in polite company, or shout such suspicions from the rooftop. All who are concerned, Herrnstein and Murray suggested, would be better off with the latter choice—particularly those poor black dimwits who, presumably, would be persuaded to come to terms with their sorry state. Either way, of course, we are left with a society that disparages the intelligence of blacks loudly or quietly and that demands that blacks either take on the daunting task of disproving the demeaning stereotype or accept the possibility that the insinuations are correct. There is another option, on which *The Bell Curve* authors didn't bother to dwell: to reject the mumblings of race-linked inferiority and to agree that since these insinuations have no sound basis and serve no useful purpose, we must treat people, whatever their color, as if they have unlimited intellectual potential.

For years, a relatively obscure, historically black Catholic university in a manifestly unfashionable New Orleans neighborhood has done just that, and the results, by virtually any standard, have been astounding. Xavier University, despite its small size (about 2,600 undergraduates) and meager resources, sends more black graduates to medical schools than any other college in the country, and the vast majority of those students (about 93 percent, according to a 1991 study) stay on track and successfully complete their professional training. Xavier is also the nation's leading producer of black pharmacists and has become such a reliable supplier of science talent overall that in 1995 the National Science Foundation named it one of six "Model Institutions for Excellence in Science."

Xavier's secret of success lies in its techniques and its philosophy. "From the very beginning, we always believed that every youngster could learn, that the mind was an unlimited facility, that if you gave the support, provided the environment and the teachers, young people would exceed even their own potential," observed Norman C. Francis, president of Xavier University. "Where others would say, 'They're not going to make it,' we say, 'We think they can.' And we will give them a chance. That's not saying we have open admissions. We don't. We make judgments, but we make judgments on a lot of factors. . . . And let me tell you, we win more than we lose."

Ability, the faculty of Xavier University has learned, can be found in the most unlikely places. Even for those who start out with little confidence and mediocre grades, failure is not a foregone conclusion, for, as university administrators have discovered, it is possible to raise confidence, aspirations, and even test scores. Along the way, the school has become a mecca of sorts for those who want to beat the odds—and a ringing refutation of the nonsense of *The Bell Curve*.

That was not always the case. In the early 1970s, Xavier's record in training students for the sciences was solidly second-rate. Biology and chemistry were taught in a dilapidated building that had served as a barracks during World War II, and the academic results were as uninspiring as the setting. Only a handful of students, four or five a year, were making the leap to medical school. Francis, who had been named president a few years earlier, decided things had to change. He turned to J. W. Carmichael, an energetic, young chemistry professor, and named him the premed adviser. Carmichael's charge was to increase the number of Xavier students who would get on the physician track, which he knew he could not accomplish without energizing the school's science programs overall.

Carmichael and his colleagues attacked the problem with zeal, picking up information and teaching hints wherever they could find them. They tested a range of methods in the classroom, searching for the special combination of elements that would work. As Carmichael acknowledged, "We didn't start from some theoretical base." The theory, however, came quickly, thanks, in large measure, to Arthur Whimbey, a psychologist and testing expert whose book *Intelligence Can Be Taught* was published in 1975 and who shortly thereafter became involved with the Xavier effort.

Whimbey's creed is summed up in his book's title. Intelligence ("skill at interpreting materials accurately and mentally reconstructing the relationships," as Whimbey defines it) can be taught much like skiing or playing the piano. By forcing students to think about every step in the problem-solving process and providing feedback as they go along, one can correct their bad reasoning habits, he insisted. One method is to pair students up and have one solve a mathematics problem aloud (a practice Whimbey calls "thinking-aloud problem solving") as the partner critiques the analysis. Whimbey does much the same with word problems. He will ask two students the same question, such as, "In how many days of the week does the third letter of the day's name immediately follow the first letter of the day's name in the alphabet?" and one student will talk it through as the other listens for errors. "For longer reading selections," he explained in the *Journal of Reading*, "both students read the selection and answer the questions silently. Then they compare answers. Where they differ, students must provide their partners with a detailed explanation of their answers, pinpointing facts or sections in the passage, and reconstructing their chain of reasoning." Whimbey also gives students scrambled sentences and has them arrange them in logical order. The object is to get the students thinking about thinking, not necessarily to have them learn the works of Shakespeare or Chaucer. In the scheme of things, Whimbey said, it's more important that students understand the reasoning process that undergirds clear writing than that they have read and savored good literature.

English teachers, Whimbey acknowledged, may find his approach repugnant and even heretical. "Teachers are saying, 'I love literature. I want students to love literature. I'm not going to stop teaching literature.'" All that is just fine, Whimbey believes, but teachers must also realize that assigning literature doesn't necessarily develop reading skills. "It does for a few," but not, he maintains, for most students.

Carmichael and his crew listened closely to Whimbey's advice, but they also recognized that poor abstract reasoning ability was not the only hurdle that many of their students had to overcome. It quickly became clear, Carmichael recalled, that a large part of the problem was that "they just had not read enough in their lives. They didn't know words that are common." The only way to change that situation quickly, Carmichael concluded, was with no-frills vocabulary-building exercises. Carmichael's message to students was direct: "We hope that you gain an appreciation for reading somewhere down the line, but we don't have time to . . . give you an appreciation for reading now. What we're trying to do is quick and dirty remediation. You've got to memorize a bunch of words."

The faculty at Xavier University realized that if their efforts were to have the maximum impact, they needed to start work even before students showed up for their freshmen classes. In 1977, the school launched a summer program called SOAR (for Stress on Analytical Reasoning). Aimed at students who had not yet started college, the program immediately became the foundation of Xavier's educational uplift efforts. Though the university has tinkered with SOAR throughout the years (it went from six weeks, for instance, to four), the basic approach remains much as it was in the beginning.

Participants (generally high school juniors and seniors who, not inconsequentially, given the poverty of many registrants, give up the opportunity to earn money during the summer) are put through what amounts to academic boot camp. "The only excused absence," Carmichael tells the students, "is if I see the Olympia brass band marching in front of your casket." Students are in class from eight in the morning until eight at night, with breaks for meals and required study sessions. They also have organized social activities, but the heart of the program is intense work: on reading skills, mathematics, vocabulary building, and exercises in abstract reasoning—many of which are from a book coauthored by Whimbey and J. Lochhead entitled *Problem-Solving and Comprehension*.

The faculty, comprised of Xavier professors, high school teachers, and high-performing Xavier juniors and seniors, turn the typical day into a whirlwind of activities. Teams compete constantly to solve mathematics or word problems. Each week ends with an intensively competitive "quiz bowl" and a social event. Deidre Labat, dean of the college of arts and sciences, sees the competition between groups as an integral part of the experience. "It moves them up a notch." She insists, however, on keeping the rivalry in check: "We never let a single student shine. It's always, 'How did your group do?' The idea of the group is to teach them, 'You can learn as well from one another as you can from the teacher. And when you find yourself being in [difficult] situations, reach out to someone.'"

The program drives home the point that academic achievement should be a source of pride. Once students are accepted in SOAR, their photographs are posted at the university, along with the names of their high schools. "We're highlighting their academic achievements. That's just never been done for our kids," said Labat. She recalls one young man who had been advised to go to a community college. Instead, he participated in SOAR and then went to Xavier. Now, he's a physician and an expert in spinal surgery. SOAR "told him how good he was," Labat boasted, smiling broadly.

The strong support given students in SOAR continues for those who attend Xavier University. During the first week of class, the school assigns each student an academic adviser with whom the student is expected to meet at least once a week. If problems arise, they are dealt with early. Long before a student is facing the prospect of academic probation, he or she can be given tutoring or whatever other help is necessary. "We say around here, we can't afford to have anybody fail," Francis noted.

Faculty members are required not only to keep long office hours, but to offer standardized content in lower-level courses: "With our kids coming in underprepared we want to be sure . . . they have a solid foundation," Labat explained. The standardization ensures that when the students get to the upper-level courses, their professors know precisely what they have been taught. By the time they get to be juniors and seniors, much of the support structure is stripped away. Xavier treats the progression up the academic ladder as a kind of weaning process.

Along the way, students are bombarded with information on careers, particularly in the fields of science and health. They receive brochures, for instance, explaining the requirements for getting into programs for allopathic medicine, veterinary medicine, osteopathic medicine, and dentistry, along with descriptions of each of the fields. The not-so-subtle message is that success is attainable, that becoming a physician is not an impossible dream. That message is reinforced by the university's practice of posting a photograph and a short biography of every student who gets accepted for training in the professions.

The approach seems to work. In 1993, forty-nine graduates of Xavier were accepted to medical schools, moving Xavier ahead of the significantly larger Howard University in the number of black graduates placed on the road to physicianhood. The following year, the number rose to fifty-five, and the year after that, to seventy-seven—putting Xavier far out front of any other university in America in the number of blacks placed in medical schools. "When we started doing these things," Carmichael said, "I never did think, to be honest, that we would be number one, but I knew we could do better."

Xavier's most impressive accomplishment, however, is not in the number of medical school slots it has won, but in its success in fostering an atmosphere of achievement. Most of the students don't begin as academic stars; although they are motivated, their grades and test scores are not the sort one would find at an elite institution. They are solidly in the middle—students whom, as Francis readily acknowledged, many schools would cast away without a second glance. But once the students are under Xavier's influence, their potential seems to blossom. Whimbey, who has continued to track progress at Xavier, noted in 1995 that in one summer in the program, the typical SOAR student gained about three grade levels on the Nelson-Denny Reading Test and the equivalent of 120 points on the Scholastic Aptitude Test (SAT). "This shows that the problem is in the educational system, not in the student's genes," Whimbey stated.

In a September 1993 article in *BioScience*, Carmichael and other Xavier faculty members tried to put their accomplishments into perspective by comparing students at Xavier to those at other institutions. They reported on a study by the Educational Testing Service that found that only 24 percent of African Americans with high ability (roughly those in the top 3 percent of blacks taking standardized tests) obtain a college degree and go on for graduate training. At Xavier, they looked at a much wider range of students (biology and chemistry majors scoring among the top 20 percent of blacks nationally). Nonetheless, with that more diverse group, Xavier's record was more than three times better than the national average. "Because we are comparing the top 3% nationally with the much broader group of those in the top 20% nationally who enrolled at Xavier, our comparison is, if anything, conservative," they crowed, in the diplomatic language of scholarly discourse. Biology professor Jacqueline Hunter made essentially the same point when we spoke in 1996. Of the 80-plus students who had gotten into graduate programs in medicine or the health sciences in 1995, she said, "probably ten may have gotten in no matter where they went to school, but the rest of those probably needed a Xavier."

Detriss Byrd, a freshman at Xavier, attributed much of the university's success to the dedication of the faculty: "The instructors don't hold your hand, but they're there whenever you need them. I mean, if you just need to talk more on a subject after class they're there." If not for such help, she added, "I would probably be on academic probation."

"You know right from the start that somebody here wants you to succeed," added Tamischer Baldwin, who entered Xavier along with Byrd. "They make you feel wanted, and they also make you feel like they're going to support you."

Baldwin looks upon the summer program as an important rite of passage: "It scared me when I was in SOAR. I was intimidated." But the situation changed quickly, she said: "Once you've seen so much difficult material, you don't let it intimidate you. And once it really counts, when it's part of your grade, then it's easy. . . . You get scared early, so you don't have to get scared once you get here." Nor does Baldwin fear what lies ahead: "We all know when we get to medical school that chances are it's not going to be all black. We know we are going to have to deal with racism, with people telling us that we can't [do the work], or that we took a spot from another white kid who would have been better qualified. We all are aware of that, and they are preparing us for [it]."

Through the years, Xavier University has launched a host of activities to supplement SOAR. Other short-term summer programs—MathStar, BioStar, and ChemStar—prepare younger high school students for work in specific subject areas. Meanwhile SOAR, which is geared toward students who are interested in the health sciences, has been renamed SOAR 1, to distinguish it from SOAR 2, which was initiated to assist students who are intrigued by computers and mathematics.

Many people talk about extending the school year, says Francis, "but we have [done it]. In the summertime we've got twelve hundred high school kids coming [to Xavier to study]." Most of these students may not be candidates for the Ivy League, but if they show some potential (especially if they are male, since a substantial majority of participants are female), Xavier tends to take them. "Is it fair to eliminate someone or not give a kid a chance just because they went to a lousy high school? Or just because they were poor? Or because [they had] a lousy adviser?" Carmichael asked.

Labat made essentially the same point: "Our kids are taught from the first grade up, either openly or subtly, 'You're not a good problem solver. You really shouldn't pursue this course. You really shouldn't go into science. You don't have the aptitude.' We teach them it is doable."

The faculty at Xavier also teach the students not to be apologetic for trying to learn. When we spoke in spring 1996, Francis had recently returned from a ceremony commending Xavier undergraduates who were inducted into Phi Beta Kappa, the national honor society. The students put on a skit, noted Francis, the essence of which was, "Don't ever apologize for being smart, for studying and for achieving." There is no shame, one student later told me in jest, in being a nerd at Xavier because "we have a school full of nerds."

As for why more educational institutions don't adopt a similar approach, Francis shrugged and replied, "It's hard work. You've got to have people who are committed." Xavier University is not alone, however, in demonstrating that academic achievement can be raised even among those who don't have the best start in life. Marva Collins made a big name for herself in Chicago, turning inner-city youths into motivated, successful, and committed students. As was noted earlier, at both the University of California at Berkeley and the University of Texas, mathematician Philip Uri Treisman reported stunning turnarounds in the achievement of mathematics students, and his success has inspired others to launch similar efforts elsewhere. A number of schools are also applying techniques that are based on or similar to the ones that Xavier has used so well.

A small program has operated in Washington, D.C., since summer 1989, with the express purpose of improving students' ability to take tests. It began in response to an academic embarrassment. In the 1988–89 school year, for the first time in thirty-four years, the city produced no semifinalists in the National Merit Scholars competition. School Superintendent Andrew Jenkins was mortified. He sought out Eugene Williams, then an assistant principal at a local high school, and told him to find a way to generate National Merit Scholars. "I didn't know how we were going to do it," Williams admitted.

Nevertheless, Williams threw together a smorgasbord of activities and established a program that is divided into two phases, one that lasts five weeks and one that lasts six weeks. In the first year of operation, a select group of students who were identified as having high potential spent four hours a day in class during the first phase, getting intensive work in honors English and mathematics, as well as in exercises specifically designed to help them do well on tests. The second phase ran for six weeks, during the evenings and on Saturdays. With guidance from the Princeton Review SAT Preparation Program, Williams's team drilled students in the types of activities measured by the SAT. The program was an immediate success. The thirty-two students who completed both phases increased their scores, on average, the equivalent of nearly 130 points on the combined verbal and mathematics sections of the SAT.

Williams expanded the program and continued to tinker with it. To him, the basic problem was clear: "While many of our youngsters had the knowledge base, many of them did not have good reasoning skills." He had heard, however, that Xavier University was doing wonders correcting such problems, that it had significantly raised students' performance on tests that were highly correlated with IQ, and his inquiries eventually led him to Whimbey, who was then living in Albuquerque. Williams brought Whimbey to Washington, where Whimbey shared much of the work he had done with SOAR.

When I visited the program in summer 1995, Whimbey's influence was obvious. Signs reading INTELLIGENCE CAN BE TAUGHT were posted everywhere, and the classrooms were a buzz of activity. Some students were working in pairs on mathematical problems, and others were doing vocabulary exercises. At one point, everyone came together to play a boisterous game of Pictionary—something of a cross between a spelling bee and Charades.

In one class, the subject of the day was Emily Brontë's *Wuthering Heights*. Meta Jones, a thin, quick-witted, recent graduate of Princeton University, was leading a spirited discussion analyzing the relationship between Catherine and Heathcliff. Her enthusiasm was contagious, fueled presumably, in part, by the fact that she had been a member of Williams's first summer enrichment class of 1989. That summer, her test scores had gone up the equivalent of 290 points on the SAT, lifting her performance from the high-average range into the exceptional category. Jones had gone on to become a National Merit Scholar. She has had plenty of company. For the past several years, Williams said, Washington has produced four or five National Merit Scholars annually; three-fourths, he estimated, have been through his Potential National Merit Scholars program.

Other institutions have reported results just as dazzling. Georgia Tech, for instance, noticed in the late 1980s that the performance of its black and Latino engineering students was lagging behind that of white students. The school's remedial activities clearly weren't working. So in 1989, the university jettisoned those activities and put together a tough five-week summer immersion program for minorities. The Challenge Program, as it was called, inundated participants with calculus and chemistry lessons taught by the regular Georgia Tech faculty and encouraged students to study in groups.

The result was a spectacular rise in grades and in retention. Shortly after the program started, minorities were outperforming whites, and the university was making plans to help other engineering schools in the region adopt Georgia Tech's techniques. "The change was in us and what we told them we expected of them," President John Patrick Crecine explained to a *New York Times* reporter. "In the past we told them they were dumb, that they needed fixing, and we had them in remedial programs."

"All we've done is assume that intelligence was never the problem but information was; so we just try to provide that," said Gavin Simms of Georgia Tech's Office of Minority Education and Development. During an interview, he acknowledged that Georgia Tech was not exactly working miracles, that after the first year of the Challenge Program, the minority students' performance lagged somewhat behind that of their white peers. Nonetheless, he pointed out, participants in the program graduate at a higher rate than do students who don't go through the program.

Certainly, no short–term program is going to wipe out the effects of years of educational malpractice, but the success of such efforts as Xavier's and Georgia Tech's strongly indicates that something more than good luck is at work. Maxine Bleich, a former executive of the Josiah Macy, Jr., Foundation, said that Xavier's work convinced her that college is not too late to overcome an early poor education. "From my life at the Macy Foundation, what was obvious was that they [Xavier] were making up, in an efficient manner, what was not accomplished in high school. So our view at the Macy Foundation was, 'Could we take those ideas and move them down to high schools?'" Bleich recalled.

In 1990, the Josiah Macy, Jr., Foundation created the New York–based Ventures in Education and named Bleich president. One of her principal tasks was to try to export Xavier's techniques ("cooperative learning," "collaborative competition," "vocabulary building," and lots of enthusiastic support) to high schools in low-performing areas across the United States.

In a 1990 study for the Macy Foundation, outside auditors looked at thirty-nine schools that were participating in foundation programs. These schools (in such places as Arkansas, New York City, and the Navajo Nation in Arizona) were serving more than three thousand students, the majority of whom came from racial or ethnic minority groups and most of whom were poor. The report of the McKenzie Group stated that the targeted students were leaping ahead of their peers. They were taking more mathematics and science courses and were performing better on standardized tests. Nearly all were headed for college.

More recent reviews have shown the same trends. A 1995 evaluation of Ventures in Education programs by the Wimeyer Group found that nine out of ten of the participants went on to college and that 40 percent were in mathematics- or science-related fields. It also found that the participants were fourteen times more likely to go to medical school than were other minority students. "Untold potential is being wasted because children are being miseducated," Bleich concluded.

Bleich is not alone in her frustration. Labat, of Xavier University, complained, in a moment of exasperation, that it is much easier to get the news media interested in black athletics or in black criminality than in blacks trying to learn. "Come here on a Monday morning in the heat of the summer at seven thirty and [and there will be] a tremendous number of African American kids walking into this building to come in and do academic work," she huffed, but the media, it seems, has little time for that: "No, they don't want to come tape that. They will tape a bunch of them standing on the corner and talk about how trifling they are. We have a quiz bowl every Friday where these kids are hyped up because somebody knew the answer to the number of electrons in a certain element. You know America; they're not interested in that."

Much of the nation "is never going to accept, to the degree that it should, that we have capacities," surmised Francis, president of Xavier. Certainly, many Americans—including many blacks—are not yet at the point where they believe that blacks are as capable as anyone else. A raft of public opinion surveys, most notably those done by the University of Chicago's National Opinion Research Center and the American Jewish Committee, have found that blacks tend to be considered less intelligent and lazier than are whites.

John Ogbu, the University of California anthropologist, is not certain that such perceptions can change unless black Americans force them to. He recalled:

> When I was in high school in Nigeria, when someone said "Japan," what came to mind was inadequate-made goods, shoddy things.

> When Japan proved they could make goods superior to Americans [that perception changed]. I think that recognition is not something bestowed on you, you earn it. Okay, we have to earn it by demonstrating that we are as smart [as anyone else]. . . . At the moment, we're handicapped, no doubt. Eighty-two percent of the kids that I studied in Oakland, thirteen-hundred-and-something black kids, from fifth grade to twelfth grade, reported that people in their families and communities believe that white people don't think blacks are as smart as whites. So *The Bell Curve* is nothing new to blacks.

Although the ideas presented in *The Bell Curve* are not new, they retain their power to harm, and the damage may be cumulative. Generations of black Americans have labored under—to use the phrase of Stanford University psychologist Claude Steele—a "suspicion of intellectual inferiority." And though other groups have shouldered a similar burden, none has shouldered it for such a protracted period or with so few places to turn for relief.

In the past, Asians were considered inferior to whites in virtually every sense (so much so that Asian immigration to America was essentially banned for much of the late nineteenth and early twentieth centuries), but they were never enslaved as a group in the United States (though "Chinese coolies" were exported to, and brutally exploited in, countries south of the U.S. border). Hence, Americans were never called on to rationalize or justify the subjugation of Asians. The United States, in other words, never invested quite as heavily in its stereotypes of Asians or Asian Americans as it did in stereotypes of blacks. But even if it had, the impact of such an investment would not have been the same for the simple reason that the Asian population in the United States was so small. As was noted earlier, large-scale Asian migration to the United States did not begin until the 1960s, when the American civil rights movement was at its peak. Indeed, the atmosphere created by that movement was largely responsible for the end of U.S. policies favoring immigrants from Europe at the expense of those from nonwhite countries. Consequently, the arrival of an unprecedented number of Asians in America coincided with a momentous shift in American racial attitudes and with the passage of laws making discrimination illegal. Moreover, as Ogbu and others have pointed out, immigrants' psychological frames of reference are anchored less in any lingering and unflattering American images than in an independent sense of identity derived from their respective homelands.

On the other hand, black Americans' generations-long passage through a sea of noxious stereotypes ensured that some of those stereotypes would be absorbed, that many blacks would come to believe, as the society insisted, that black brains were somehow deficient. The result is something of a psychological Catch–22. The belief that one is not intellectually inclined can itself be enough to prevent one from becoming academically proficient, which can make it impossible (assuming that one is so disposed) to offer proof that one is not mentally inferior.

Carmichael's eyes filled with tears when he talked of the SOAR participants who thank him for giving them the opportunity, finally, to see a large number of blacks achieving—to see, in effect, that failure by blacks does not have to be the norm. "Children shouldn't have to go through that," he said. The lesson of Xavier University and Georgia Tech, of course, is that they don't have to—not if they can find a way to filter out the drumbeat of voices telling them to turn away from the classroom and telling them that if they have ambitions, they should look to the stage, the ring, or even the streets, but not to the arena of intellectual achievement, where so many of their kind have already washed out.

Neither the faculty of Xavier University and Georgia Tech nor Treisman discovered anything magical, and there is nothing about their methods that is difficult to understand. Their approach can be reduced to six simple steps: (1) find a group of young people motivated to learn or find a way to motivate them; (2) convince them you believe in them; (3) teach them good study skills, including the art of studying in groups; (4) challenge them with difficult and practical material; (5) give them adequate support; and (6) demand that they perform. And, lo and behold, they do.

The second step may be the hardest, for convincing young people you believe in them is not an easy task—*unless you really do*. Given America's complex views on race, faith in young minority-group students is not always easy to come by. And it is not clear whether acting as if you do is sufficient and whether, as the South

African barrister George Bizos put it, "you become the person whose role you are playing."

Yet there is evidence, from the earliest days of industrial psychology, that people respond to positive reinforcement in the most unexpected ways. In a classic experiment carried out at the Hawthorne Works of Western Electric, a team of researchers attempted, between 1924 and 1932, to determine how to increase productivity of a small group of workers in a relay assembly test room. The investigators made an array of adjustments to improve working conditions in the room and, as they expected, the workers' productivity went up. But later, after they intentionally made conditions in the room less pleasant, they were astounded to find that productivity continued to increase. Any number of explanations were offered to explain the results, but the one that has endured has the virtue of simplicity: The employees did better work *because they were chosen* for the project and became the object of constant concern. They excelled, in short, because they were made to feel worthy.

This is not to say that inculcating a sense of self-esteem ought to be the main focus of educating anyone. The search for educational panaceas has led many down a dead-end road in search of feel-good but scholastically empty enhancers of self-esteem. Successful drug dealers, after all, can feel good about themselves and what they do. Poorly performing students can have plenty of self-esteem if they are convinced that doing well in school is not important; they find their self–respect, instead, in clothes, in games, or in bullying other children. Nonetheless, feeling good about one's prospects of learning, feeling capable of mastering difficult material, and feeling motivated to do so can be an extremely useful defense for a child who is surrounded by nay-saying and doubt.

Ideally, education should serve as bridge across the fetid swamp of low expectations, conveying young people to a universe in which any healthy dream is possible. It should be, to use Whimbey's phrase, "an equalizer." For some students, the lucky ones, it is; but for too many, the school system does little more than confirm that the murmurs of inferiority, rife in society, apparently have a basis in fact.

On March 16, 1996, the London *Daily Telegraph* ran an article by Alasdair Palmer entitled "Poor Whites Trashed." The essence of the article was summed up in the first paragraph: "On Wednesday Mr. Christopher Woodhead, the Chief Inspector of Schools, announced that white boys from poor and working-class families perform worse at school than any other racial group. More of them leave school earlier, with fewer qualifications, than blacks, Asians—or girls of any description."

The more "white" an inner-city school was, reported Palmer, the worse off its students were likely to be: "In those areas, blacks whose parents emigrated from the West Indies are staying in education longer and doing better. Blacks whose parents emigrated from Africa and Asians are doing better still. Lumbering behind them are the great white dopes.

"Disruptive and lazy immigrant children are thought to be responsible for the poor performance of inner-city schools. Yet it seems [that] the opposite is true: the most frequently disruptive element is not immigrant, but native."

Palmer saw the findings as a strong rebuttal to *The Bell Curve,* but his real interest was in what they said about the underclass—specifically the *white* underclass—and the collapse of pride and self-confidence among white working-class males. That collapse, in Palmer's mind, was connected to the fall of socialism and the rise of contempt for the indigent.

I found Palmer's political analysis significantly less compelling than the phenomenon around which he built his case— the problem of poor academic performance among a particular group of urban white males—and it struck me how easy it would be, had the failing children been other than white, for people to throw up their hands and say with a shrug, "What a shame that these kids just can't learn." The typical first impulse with white children is to assume that they can catch on and that any problems they may have in doing so are fixable. If we are serious about trying to achieve educational parity (or, for that matter, a race-neutral state), we must grant young children of color the same presumptions.

CHAPTER 4

The limits of desegregation

For a brief time in the early post–Jim Crow era, America finally seemed prepared to put black schoolchildren and white schoolchildren on an equal footing. In 1954, *Brown v. Board of Education of Topeka* ended the time-honored pretext that state-ordered separatism was equivalent to equality, but it did much more than that. It gave credence to the notion that a color-blind state was possible, that young black children and young white children would re-create the South and, in an almost biblical sense, lead their elders along the route of racial reconciliation. America's schools would be not only the great equalizer but the salvation of America's soul.

Such dreams, as it turned out, were premature. The order to desegregate schools became an occasion not for reparation and reconciliation but for resistance. The enduring images from that era are not of school yard harmony, but of terrified black children marching, under armed guard, into schools as vicious white mobs assailed them from all sides and as southern governors, winking from the sidelines, spouted sermons on the sanctity of states' rights.

I found myself reflecting on that history in 1996 as an educational drama that was reminiscent of those in the old American South unfolded in Potgietersrus, South Africa. Three black children were trying to enroll in a school in that Northern Province town, and an army of white parents were arrayed against them. "It is a matter of principle," the chairman of the parents group declared at one point, indicating that no price was too high to keep the Afrikaner-dominated school pure.

The parents maintained that they were not being racist. Like former governors George Wallace and Ross Barnett, who, at the height of America's desegregation battles, professed to be standing up for states' rights, the South Africans claimed to be motivated by a noble cause. They were trying, they said, to protect their language and their "Christian-Afrikaner-Boer culture and traditions" as they were entitled to under the law. Blacks in the region were not comforted by such assurances. Thousands marched on a local police station in protest against the school. As tempers flared and patience waned, the case quickly made it to the courts, and the three black children, along with eighteen others who had subsequently joined the case, were authorized to enroll.

When asked about the turmoil in the Northern Province, Tom Lodge, a political scientist at the University of Witwatersrand, gave a response with an upbeat spin: "The interesting thing is not that it's happening, but that it's happening as little as it's happening." He certainly had a point. Though Cape Town had witnessed a similar racial episode the previous year and minor disturbances had broken out at schools across the country, when contrasted with America's decades-long struggle for desegregation that spilled blood in cities across the nation, South Africa's experiment with equality in the schools was proceeding swimmingly.

Perhaps because South Africa's transition is going so much better than many dared to expect, a visitor to the country finds hope sprouting all around. It blares from billboards celebrating the "rainbow nation." It lurks beneath the often-asked query, "What do you think of our country?" And it reverberates in the voices of parents, who see the future in their children and believe that the schools will foster not only learning but goodwill among races.

"Ten years ago it was impossible to think of black kids in white schools, but today you see hordes of station wagons driving into town with black kids going to white schools," observed Joseph Thloloe of the South African Broadcasting Corporation. "Perhaps in a generation's time we will be able to create a nonracial society," he conjectured, when the children now "mixing at school" and unburdened by the past of apartheid have grown up disregarding race.

Bonganjalo Goba, national director of the Institute for Multi-Party Democracy, was similarly optimistic. Goba confided that he had not quite adjusted to South Africa's new ways and occasionally lapsed into the old rhetoric. "I will say something like 'white trash.'" But his sixteen-year-old son will not tolerate such language. He "will immediately object," Goba noted. "I look at him and say, 'Maybe that's a hopeful sign. Many of us still have hang-ups, but the young people, that is the hope of the new South Africa."

Oupa Molete, a Sowetan who works as a credit clerk in Johannesburg, remembered that not too long ago his eldest son, now a teenager, had to attend school in a building without a roof. When it rained, there was no class; he wondered aloud how much further ahead in his academic training his son would be if he had been allowed to attend a better school. Then he brightened and pointed out that things would be better for the black children coming along, that they would be educated with whites, without rancor and on equal terms.

Blacks were not the only ones placing their bets on the next generation. Valerie Moller, a social scientist at the University of Natal, observed that much of the older generation would never see life through a nonracial light. Although they may be "politically correct in their public utterances," their real racial views often come out "among their own kind." But young South Africans seem to be different. Even though many of her white and Indian students believe that greater opportunities for blacks will mean fewer jobs for them, they seem to accept that prospect with grace. They know that South Africa's future depends on the various racial groups working together.

What struck me, as I heard one person after another, black, white, and other, offer similar observations about those who are yet to reach adulthood, was how much their expressions of faith resembled the attitude of certain Americans a few decades ago—when it seemed that the passage of a few years, the mingling of races in the schools, and the coming to age of the young would purge society of its racial transgressions.

In May 1954, after the Supreme Court shattered the legal justification for school segregation, Thurgood Marshall, lead attorney for the black students and for the NAACP, made a bold and joyous prediction. Heartened by his hard-fought victory, Marshall told reporters (as recounted in the *New York Times*) that he thought it might take "up to five years" to eliminate segregation in education throughout America. By the hundredth anniversary of the Emancipation Proclamation—January 1963—segregation in all its forms would be eliminated, he prophesied.

Marshall obviously was overly optimistic, but, as I noted earlier, so were many other Americans. In the early years of the civil rights age people tended to be relatively optimistic about the ability of the state, aided by sociologists and other social and behavioral scientists, to accomplish whatever social objectives it deemed appropriate. In fact, *Brown v. Board of Education* focused only partially on questions of constitutional law. It was also, to the dismay of some contemporary critics, about some nettlesome questions in the sphere of social science that still reverberate through educational policy circles today: *How does a policy of racial segregation affect self-esteem? To what extent does self-esteem affect learning? Will black children be better or worse off in an educational setting that includes whites?*

In considering these questions, the justices drew heavily from the testimony of two social scientists—sociologist Louisa Holt and psychologist Kenneth Clark—brought in by the NAACP. Holt thought that legal segregation was profoundly damaging to the psyche of blacks and suggested that integration, perhaps as late as the junior high school level, could be something of an antidote. Clark reported on experiments he had conducted with three- to seven-year-old black and white children, asking them to choose either black or white dolls. Most black children seemed to prefer the white dolls, which Clark took to be an indication of self-hatred fostered by segregation.

The Supreme Court ruling, read by Chief Justice Earl Warren, echoed those concerns. To separate black elementary and high school children "from others of similar age and qualifications solely because of their race generates a feeling of inferiority as to their status in the community that may affect their hearts and minds in a way unlikely ever to be undone," he declared. And he quoted from a Kansas ruling that claimed that the sense of inferiority caused by legal segregation retarded "the educational and mental development of Negro children" and deprived them of other benefits. Not everyone was impressed with the Court's foray into the field of social psychology. The day after the decision was handed down, *New York Times* columnist James Reston harrumphed, "The Court's opinion read more like an expert paper on sociology than a Supreme Court decision."

Nonetheless, for years following that decision, integration—particularly of schools—was the elusive grail of the civil rights movement. Many blacks and a significant number of whites believed that if only black children and white children went to school together and got to know each other as human beings, cooperation and brotherhood would follow.

People have a tendency, regardless of nationality, to assume that children are gifted with a blank slate, that their openness and purity will make them less vulnerable to prejudice than their elders. Although that assumption may be true in some respects, it is also true that children live in the world that adults have created and pick up adults' practices and biases with amazing ease.

Ultimately, even the most integration-minded American intellectuals recognized that racial progress was not the inevitable result of getting black and white schoolchildren together, partly because desegregation was resisted at every turn, but also because as desegregation more or less proceeded, three facts became increasingly clear: First, desegregation is not the same as integration; children in the same school can be on different academic tracks or in different social circles, organized largely along racial lines. Second, black students don't necessarily achieve more in integrated environments than in largely black environments; factors that are largely independent of the racial makeup of the student body—as Xavier University's experience suggests—determine, in large measure, how well students do in school. And third, the mixing of black children and white children, in and of itself, does not automatically reduce prejudice or black students' sense of academic and social inferiority; rather, it can provide justification for bigotry.

In *Black and White in School*, the report of a three-year study of a model desegregated middle school pseudonymously dubbed

"Wexler," psychologist Janet Ward Schofield spelled out just how difficult it can be to make desegregation work. The Wexler school board strove to make the building as attractive as possible, supplying it with a university-quality swimming pool and tennis courts and intentionally siting it in a commercial area that was neither black nor white. High-quality equipment was brought in. The teachers, for the most part, were conscientiously "color-blind," meaning that they rarely explicitly acknowledged that the students were of different races and that some even claimed ignorance of the children's races.

Nevertheless, a racial hierarchy was quickly established. Nearly 90 percent of those who received academic honors were white, even though the school was roughly half black, and many blacks effectively ended up on the low-ability track. "The achievement gap," Schofield reported, "not only impeded both legitimate and illegitimate academic cooperation between blacks and whites but, on occasion, also led to misunderstandings between children. Furthermore, it helped to foster the belief that whites are brighter and more interested in learning than blacks."

When researchers asked one white girl whether attending the desegregated school had changed her ideas about blacks, she responded: "It made me prejudiced really. . . . You know, it is just so obvious that the whites are smarter than the blacks. My mother keeps telling me it's socioeconomic background, that the blacks . . . are nice people. But, I keep thinking every time I see a black person. 'Stay away from me.'" Black students at Wexler likewise tended to see academic achievement as "white." They were also much more likely than whites to be suspended for misbehavior.

Schofield noted that other studies of students in desegregated schools documented similar stereotypes about students' race and academic performance. By and large, white students did not believe they were biased; instead, they thought that their beliefs about the inferiority of blacks were based on the evidence of their own eyes. Even among close friends, according to at least one study, racial stereotypes seemed to be a factor. Though black students rated their white and black friends similarly in terms of desirable personality traits, white students rated their white friends more positively than they did those who were black.

In April 1996, a nonprofit group called ACORN (for Association of Community Organizations for Reform Now) released a report blasting New York City public schools for shortchanging minority youngsters. The group had sent black, white, and Latino "testers" on ninety-nine visits to various schools to ask about options for their children's education. The project was inspired by the experience of two ACORN-affiliated parents when they had investigated kindergartens. Both parents, one black and one white, had arrived at the same school simultaneously, but while the white parent was seen at once, the black parent was kept waiting for forty-five minutes. And though the white parent was shown classrooms for gifted children, the black mother was not. ACORN decided to try to determine whether racially colored treatment was the norm.

Time after time the investigators discovered that black and minority parents were treated differently. The whites were given tours of schools and offered (often without prompting) information on programs for the gifted. They were steered away from special education classes or from schools that employees deemed were not good enough for white children. Blacks and Latinos sometimes found that even getting into the buildings was difficult. And if they did get in, they were generally told only about the "regular" classes. Virtually no one seemed to care whether their children received a good education.

Administrators, secretaries, and even school guards, said ACORN, were deciding, with no knowledge other than the race of the parents, that white students belonged on the college-preparatory track and minorities belonged "on the track to academic mediocrity, if not outright failure."

In a 1995 review of research on school desegregation ("Review of Research on School Desegregation's Impact on Elementary and Secondary School Students," published in the *Handbook of Research on Multicultural Education*), Schofield concluded that desegregation has had much less of an impact than most advocates assumed it would, but that it nonetheless has been worthwhile. Desegregation seems to have helped, albeit slightly, to boost the reading scores of some black youngsters (though it apparently has had no effect on their mathematics scores) and has provided children with some useful, if limited, experience in navigating a multiracial environment. The modest results, she theorized, may not be a true reflection of the potential of desegregation, since desegregation has often occurred in the face of spirited resistance from whites and "under circumstances in which little if any serious attention was paid to creating a situation likely to improve either academic achievement or intergroup relations."

Schofield's point is well taken. In the more than four decades following the *Brown* decision, America has never managed to create a truly supportive environment for school desegregation. Instead, as author and children's advocate Jonathan Kozol claims, many American children are schooled under conditions of "apartheid." At a 1996 conference at Harvard commemorating the centennial of the *Plessy v. Ferguson* decision, Kozol spoke of a school he had visited in the South Bronx where there was only one white child among eight hundred blacks. That child, he observed, was a recent immigrant: "He was there by mistake." The *Brown* decision notwithstanding, America's schools remain largely segregated. Gary Orfield, a professor of education and social policy at Harvard, estimated that roughly two-thirds of black and Latino students attend schools in which most of their classmates are also members of racial minority groups.

Despite such disheartening developments, Clark, the psychologist consulted for *Brown v. Board of Education*, has maintained his faith in desegregation. In a 1992 speech before the Detroit Association of Black Organizations, he warned that black all-male academies would cause the students to feel inferior; they would conclude that something was wrong with them since "they can't be taught the way other teenagers are being taught." "Any board of education proposing this damaging psychological procedure would be shameless, or should be shameless," declared Clark, in a pointed reference to the Detroit school board that, prior to a court challenge (from the American Civil Liberties Union and the National Organization for Women Legal Defense Fund), planned to open three all-male academies with a special black-oriented curriculum.

Clark's strong words notwithstanding, many black parents and educators are so frustrated that they side with the Detroit school board. A national survey of black Americans conducted in 1992 and 1993 found that 62 percent were in favor of separate schools for black boys. The findings reflected the pessimism of a huge number of blacks about "the prospect of achieving racial and economic equality," concluded the study's authors, Michael Dawson and Ronald Brown, political scientists at the University of Chicago and Wayne State University, respectively.

Even many black parents who believe in the idea of integration wonder why they should try to force their children on whites who apparently don't care to associate with them. Others are so preoccupied with more pressing concerns, from violence in their communities to the lack of work, that desegregation seems not only like an unattainable dream but an irrelevant luxury.

Even to foreigners, the failure of desegregation is obvious. Lodge, of the University of Witwatersrand, though accustomed to the apartheid of South Africa, was astonished to be greeted by an American version when he took a temporary teaching position at Columbia University in 1990. His community in Montclair, New Jersey, seemed to be a "white island." The local school was predominantly black, and though it seemed decent, the majority of his white neighbors opted to send their children elsewhere—presumably to private schools where they would get a superior education. Lodge was convinced that race had something to do with the parents' decisions, just as he was convinced that the residential segregation he observed throughout New Jersey was not the result of happenstance.

Dumisani S. Kumalo, with the American Committee on Africa, thinks South Africa can learn from America's racial failures. "This nation is a great teacher because of how bad it is," he observed with a mischievous smile when we chatted in his New York offices.

This is not to say that the American experience with desegregation has been uniformly dismal. Philip Uri Treisman has reported impressive academic results with groups that are racially mixed and (in contrast to Xavier University's experience) has come to consider such a mixture critical to the success of his minority mathematics students. In interviews with black students at the University of California at Berkeley, he discovered that many black students "believed the lies that were out there" about their inability to do well in mathematics. Getting students to work together in mixed-race groups, he concluded, is critical to breaking down such stereotypes, for multiracial cooperation allowed black and Latino students to see white and Asian students "visibly struggling with the same problems" as they were trying to master. Black and Latino students quickly realized that their difficulties with the subject had nothing to do with race, that whites and Asians had identical difficulties.

By the same token, desegregation has enabled millions of people of different races to come together in some semblance of equality and call each other friend—a simple achievement that would have been immeasurably more difficult a couple of generations ago.

In a 1992 column in the *Washington Post*, Nat Hentoff recalled a comment made by Kenneth Clark shortly after the *Brown* decision. As a result of the Court's action and the collapse of segregation, Clark predicted, white youngsters in the future would be spared the burden of having to spend "so much valuable energy apologizing for injustices which they did not invent but for which they must share the responsibility."

Clark's prediction was only half right. Today's young people may not spend much time apologizing for the past, but they have not exactly conquered it. Instead, the children and grandchildren of that first desegregation generation are now finding their way into high schools and colleges where they are dealing with so-called self-segregation and other racial issues that Clark (and many of his peers) once believed would have been resolved long ago.

In recent years, colleges have become almost synonymous with racial tension as hundreds of campuses have weathered ugly controversies. Crosses were burned at Fredonia State College in upstate New York—an apparent response to a campus rally for racial harmony. Swastikas appeared on the doors of the rooms of black and Jewish students in a dormitory at Penn State University, and hate mail materialized in the mailboxes of minority students at Berkeley's Boalt Hall Law School. A series of incidents at Brown University—including "Nigger go home" scrawled on a bathroom dormitory mirror and the appearance of an anonymous note suggesting that an Asian student filled the "gook quota"—led the university to post a $1,000 reward for information regarding the perpetrators.

Meanwhile, groups of white students at an assortment of universities—including the University of Wisconsin, George Mason, and Duke—have flaunted Confederate flags, caroused in blackface, held slave auctions, and sponsored other events guaranteed to irritate black students. Black undergraduate groups have been no less belligerent—inviting to campuses such people as Khalid Abdul Muhammad, a formerly obscure Black Muslim functionary and self-declared "knowledge gangster" who rose to national notoriety by spreading the message that many of the problems of blacks are attributable to "that old no-good Jew, that old impostor Jew, that old hooked-nose, bagel-eating, lox-eating, Johnny-come-lately perpetrating a fraud, just crawled out of the caves and hills of Europe." A black student columnist for the *Columbia Daily Spectator*, Columbia University's campus newspaper, was so touched by Muhammad's insights that in 1995 he wrote a jeremiad of his own denouncing Jews as "leeches sucking the blood from the black community," which the newspaper published. Frequent as such controversies have become, they still are not the rule on college campuses, but they are indicative of an atmosphere that is rife with the potential for racial misunderstandings. It is an atmosphere that many students find draining.

When Carrie SiuButt, a native of Trinidad, came to the University of North Carolina (UNC) at Chapel Hill, she was eager to explore the cosmopolitan college scene. Though she had spent ten years in the multicultural stew of Miami, she thought that UNC would show her another side of America. Unfortunately, part of what it showed her was racism.

A pretty, dark-haired women whose ethnicity is not readily apparent, SiuButt remembers her first racial incident with absolute clarity. When she was a freshman, she was riding in a car with a friend when they spotted an interracial couple. Her friend stared in the couple's direction and spat out, "Nigger lover." SiuButt, who is of mixed black and Chinese parentage, was stunned. "That absolutely shocked me. She was supposed to be my friend, but after that incident, she was not. . . . I had never heard that said in my life." Here they were, at a great university, and "a clearly intelligent girl [was] shouting out, 'Nigger lover.'" SiuButt is still not certain what the woman assumed *she* was. Perhaps, she conjectures, the former friend thought she was Hawaiian. Nevertheless, more than three years later, SiuButt has not forgotten the episode. "It still bothers me that people talk like that."

What some students find nearly as disturbing as such incidents is the scarcity of meaningful interracial contact. Jae Lee, a Korean American who attends Duke University, sees little evidence of people picking friends without regard to race. Occasionally, he said, people of different races become buddies, but "I think it's very rare. . . . I'm not saying it doesn't happen at all. I'm saying that for the majority of the people here at this campus [it doesn't]. If you look on the campus you will not see two black people, three white people, and an Asian walking down the Bryant Center walkway together."

When asked why such patterns persist, many nonwhites (particularly blacks) profess weariness of reaching out to unresponsive whites. Edrienne Mason, a junior at Duke who is from Anchorage, Alaska, confided, "I came from a place where interracial interaction is very common and very accepted and I expected that to be [the case] here. When I got here I made an effort to diversify my circle of friends and meet a lot of people." She quickly found that race stood in the way. Mason was one of three black students among two hundred in her dormitory, and whenever the conversation turned to race, "everyone would turn to me as the spokesperson for the black race. 'So what's the black perspective?' or 'How do you feel about this?'"

At one point, during a conversation with a white student, they got on the subject of the schools to which they had been admitted, "and most of the places we got into were the same, except that I got into some Ivy League schools he did not; and he proceeded to tell me, 'Well, that's simply because you're black and I'm not.' So I became aware of the fact that racism here does exist, even though it might be subtle." Over time, she says, "I have lessened my efforts to reach out to others . . . and I began to be aware of the burden that minorities here have—that is, we have to bear the brunt for establishing positive race relations. . . . It seems as though the white students feel we have to be responsible for reaching out to them."

Many whites, on the other hand, express fear of rejection from hostile blacks. As Andrew Rosenblum, a white senior at Columbia University, put it, "Separating is easier to do than integrating. You don't have to take risks." Students find college a difficult-enough experience without taking on the mission of "diversity" outreach. "When students come to college they are leaving everything that's familiar and comfortable," commented Stacy Brandenburg, a white senior at UNC. Many naturally gravitate toward faces that look welcoming and familiar. "As soon as you arrive on campus," added Jonathan Gyurko, also a senior at UNC, "you need to look for a group to identify with—either through sports, or through the arts, or through your classes; but I think an easy one is to identify with your racial group."

That identification can extend even to student activities that, on their face, appear to be color neutral. "I've been involved with most of the theater organizations on campus. And I've started one of them," Gyurko noted. "And one of the problems is basically white students audition for all the shows. There are very few black students auditioning . . . [and] a handful of other minorities."

Gyurko sees an irony in that situation, since he believes the arts to be essentially color-blind and merit-based. Yet he knows that unless he makes special efforts to integrate his productions, they will remain virtually all white. "I'm going to be directing a play next semester," he confided, "and one of the things I would like to have in it . . . is some traditional African dancing. And to get the people to audition who I want to audition, I'm going to have to recruit within the BSM [Black Student Movement] and the black fraternities and sororities. . . . And, in the back of my head, I have concerns about [that]. Is it insulting to have to go and to make my pitch to specific groups to get them to audition?" He wondered whether he would be crossing some invisible line by essentially making a race-based appeal. In the end, Gyurko resolved to do it for the good of the production.

Brandenburg believes she understands why some minority students may be uncomfortable around predominantly white groups. When she took her first class in African American history at UNC, she was one of the few white students enrolled. She felt isolated and vulnerable. "I commented to a friend of mine later about this experience," Brandenburg recalled, "and she said, 'Well, that's what it's like for a black person every day they walk into a classroom.' And it was such a reversal of situations that it really opened my eyes." For black students on predominantly white campuses, the experience obviously doesn't end with being uncomfortable in a class or two.

Thomas Martin, a Duke University junior from Vienna, Virginia, and a member of the predominantly black Alpha Phi Alpha fraternity, maintained that black students like himself on a campus such as Duke are inevitably thrust into a white world. "You're almost forced into that." Yet, he said, "you don't get the sense of anyone accepting you, or of you fitting in." Martin joined Alpha Phi Alpha to have somewhere to belong. Why didn't he try a white fraternity, such as Kappa Alpha? "If I walk into that dorm," he said, indicating the nearby Kappa Alpha house, "they have a big Confederate flag on the wall. Why am I going to . . . throw myself at them when I can join another fraternity where I feel more at home?" The white fraternity's "old South night" gala, he said, was utterly off-putting. "I had problems with the idea of it. I certainly won't go to it. What could they possibly offer me as a black student?"

White and black fraternities—at Duke and elsewhere—have jointly sponsored campus activities. Alpha Phi Alpha and Kappa Alpha, for instance, put on a program that addressed affirmative action. Cosponsoring activities, however, is not the same as forming a common community. The latter requires confidence in the dream of integration that many students find all but impossible to maintain.

"I think back to when I was in high school, how this beautiful picture of Berkeley was painted as, like, the rainbow university, extremely liberal," recalled James Walker, a senior at the University of California at Berkeley. Reality was depressing by comparison. As for race relations on campus, he sighed, "There are none, very little. Blacks stay with blacks, for the most part. Whites stay with whites, Asians stay with Asians. Chicanos and Hispanics, they stay with their own."

The blame, minority students agree, cannot totally be laid at the feet of whites. With "a small black population on campus, some people feel pressured, you know, [that] we should stick together," said Kameron Green, a black freshman at Berkeley. Rachel LeForest, of Hunter College in New York, made a similar observation: "Being in the Black Student Union, I run into many people who have an animosity towards white organizers, and even though [they] will come together in a coalition to work on specific things, they feel white people are not welcome in the black sphere." Such sentiments, said Martin of Duke University, come into play when people consider which fraternity to join. "There are some black students in some white fraternities," he indicated, "but I think one of the unfortunate things is that . . . once a black student joins one of those fraternities . . . in many cases, that can alienate them from the rest [of the black students]."

Even though minority students admit their clannishness, they see it less as a function of self-segregation than as a means of emotional survival. Mason cited an incident from her freshman year at Duke as an example of the annoyances that blacks endure. After a classmate read aloud her paper on crime, she said, during discussion, that she thought all blacks were criminals, "including the one in this class." The only one in the class was Mason.

Anji Malhotra, a senior at Duke who is of East Indian extraction, also found dealing with white students stressful. "It wasn't so much like a specific sort of treatment, like a specific set of actions," said the twenty-year-old from upstate New York. "It was the way people looked at me and, I came to realize, the ways in which I was treated." She was at a fraternity party one night when the realization hit home. A white male friend turned to her and made what she took to be an insulting comment about her olive complexion.

Malhotra rejects the notion that minority students are rebuffing whites. Rather, she believes, it works the opposite way: "The white culture forms and then proceeds to alienate other students, to make students of color feel uncomfortable." Originally, she thought things would be different: "I didn't come to Duke . . . choosing to have minority friends, or wanting *just* that." But when white students are giving South of the Border parties and coming dressed up as gang members from Los Angeles or brandishing Confederate flags or printing ethnically insulting cartoons in campus newspapers, it's hard to feel like a part of their world. That doesn't mean that interracial relationships don't form, "but people have to make a considerable effort," Malhotra said.

Grace Chen, a sophomore at Duke, complained that Asian students have tried desperately to attract whites to their events, but white students rarely show. At one discussion of Asians in pop culture, the only whites in the room were with the student newspaper. "And one of the reporters said we [Asian students] need to make more of an effort to make the flyers more interesting so that white people will want to come. And it just really bothered me, because there were flyers all over the place, and she just made it seem like . . . it was our responsibility to draw the white people in to learn more about minority issues. I understand why you have to reach out to people, but after a while it gets tiring."

Geneva Weaver, of Duke, was weary of constantly being singled out, by teachers and others, as some sort of expert on urban ghettos. In a sociology class, she recalled, a teacher looked at her and said, "You went to an inner-city school. Can you tell us what it was like?" In reality, Weaver noted, the institution she had attended was anything but an inner-city ghetto school. Numerous other black students also commented on their resentment at being singled out as experts on race.

That resentment can sometimes come across as anger and can make whites—already wary of discussing race with blacks—shut down entirely. "I think one of the greatest fears that I have and that I think I share with a number of people is being labeled or called a racist . . . because that's such an ugly word," observed Susan Wasiolek, assistant vice president for student affairs at Duke. "It's almost like . . . a man being accused of molesting his child or battering his wife. It's one of those accusations or allegations that is so very, very difficult to overcome." Rather than take that risk, many whites—on campuses as well as in the society at large—prefer not to engage.

James Johnson, professor of business administration and geography at UNC, confided that it was difficult to get white students to discuss race. After the O. J. Simpson verdict, Johnson brought a raft of polling data to class to stimulate a discussion of racial polarization. "You could hear a pin drop," Johnson said. Generally, when issues such as affirmative action or racism come up in class, "people go quiet, real quiet." That does not mean students have no opinions. "Where I see the animosity is on course evaluations. They won't say it to your face, but they will say, '[There's] too much of this [racial] content in here.'"

Slayton Evans, a black professor of chemistry at UNC, believes that white students "back off of this issue not so much not to offend, but because they just don't know. The level of ignorance is too high. . . . These issues have never come up and the forum for dialogue hasn't been nurtured in high school. They come here, and there is no history; they don't think about these things critically; they don't read about them critically; and I think the result is that if we ask people about these issues, and try to stimulate critical discussion, people beg off."

By the time students get into college, "there are pressures and there's a kind of silence. There's a silence about difference, so that you don't have the kinds of discussions that could foster understanding," conjectured Peter Kuriloff, a professor of education at the University of Pennsylvania. "And that's only one piece of it. I think people pull into their own camps, hunker down, and try to be safe."

The racial conversations that do take place on campus are commonly spurred by crises, and when the crises die down people go their separate ways. In 1992 black UNC students led a series of demonstrations demanding the construction of a freestanding black cultural center. The demonstrations set off an intense campus debate, which ultimately resulted in the university's commitment to build the center. White students (and some trustees) fretted that such a center would sanction segregation. Proponents of the center assured them that the center would be open to and welcome everyone on campus. When I visited the campus in late 1995, the university was attempting to raise more than $6 million in additional funds for the center but, in the interim, allowed a suite of rooms in the student union to be used as a temporary facility for the center. The space was used almost exclusively by blacks. "I don't see a lot of other white students in there," observed Amy Piniak, a senior at UNC who writes for the campus newspaper. "And I don't know if that's because they don't think they'll be welcome. . . . But I think a lot of students have the impression that it's the *black* cultural center; it's not for them."

White students at Columbia University feel much the same about the Malcolm X Lounge on their campus. There's a "tacit understanding among students that this is specifically a lounge for black students. And the irony of it all is that it's right next to the

Hartley Kosher Deli," noted Lea Gold, a white, Jewish sophomore from Lakewood, New Jersey. For Gold, the situation is depressing: "You don't come to a school like Columbia to sit with your own."

Piniak, of UNC, got her first taste of campus clannishness during her freshman year, when a black high school friend came to visit. "I was giving him the grand tour, and every black student that walked by would say 'hey' to him and completely ignore me. . . . At the beginning, it made me really mad. . . . I was thinking more in terms of 'I'm a Tar Heel, he's a Dukie, and you're saying hey to *him* and not to me.' It frustrated me." Things got better, she found, "once I actually got to know people."

Recognizing how hard it can be for people of different races to find common ground, some students have taken action to combat the problem. At Duke a group of students formed Spectrum, an organization that encourages interracial dialogue and sponsors an experiment in interracial living. The Spectrum House, located in the same quad complex as several fraternities, opened during the 1993–94 school year. It is home to thirty-five to forty students a semester, who are specifically seeking to avoid the racial-exclusion trap. The large, first-floor sitting room, with several comfortable chairs and sofas, is a common meeting place where residents can study, debate, or merely lounge around. It is a setting designed not only for comfort but for conversation. Malhotra, who served as president of Spectrum, described it as "a safe haven . . . where minorities could feel comfortable being part of the mainstream culture."

Christian Grose, a senior from a small rural area in North Carolina, recalled that, originally, practically all his friends were white. After a black professor challenged him and his white dorm mates to embrace diversity, Grose applied to Spectrum House. Geneva Weaver, a black sophomore, came for similar reasons. "There were not really that many options to get to know a lot of people after freshman year," she said. She thought Spectrum would allow her to expand her circle of friends and to enrich her intellectual life.

The United Cultures organization at the University of Maryland has much the same mission as Spectrum: to battle "self-imposed student polarization" and "foster cultural sharing, understanding, and student togetherness," according to a university press release.

Minority students who join such organizations sometimes still suffer from what SiuButt, a founding member of UNC's Human Relations Coalition, called "racial fatigue," the weariness that comes from the almost constant strain of dealing with whites who are in the dark about minorities. As Carmen Alexander, a black sophomore who lives at Spectrum, remarked, "We're not here to educate people about what it's like to be black." She wondered, "How many minorities are tired of talking about [race and] how many white people are tired of listening?"

Edgar Beckham, formerly a dean at Wesleyan University and now a program officer at the Ford Foundation, finds nothing distressing in the current state of race relations on campus; by any measure, he pointed out, things are better now than before the desegregation era. "One has to remember that until the 1960s, Duke didn't have a racial problem . . . because they didn't admit any blacks to Duke. So Duke has racial tension. Hallelujah! Our society is making progress and that racial tension proves it. . . . Imagine thirty years ago a debate, an acrimonious debate on the Chapel Hill campus, about where to locate a black cultural center. I mean, my goodness, how far we've come. I mean in those areas, how long has it been since they were lynching blacks?"

Beckham believes that students have always gravitated toward homogeneous clusters—even when race was not at issue. "I was on a campus in the early fifties that was virtually entirely white," he recalled, "and one of the things faculty members deplored most was that all of those white men formed little enclaves called fraternities and got into them and avoided really significant intellectual encounters." Black students who hang together are, in Beckham's opinion, merely doing what whites have done all along.

Beckham finds the term *self-segregation* offensive. "It's like misappropriating the term Holocaust and using it for some minor evil. . . . Imagine walking into a restaurant in New York City and seeing a black family at a table and several white groupings at other tables and asking, 'Why is this restaurant segregated?' Well, it's not segregated. I mean, segregated restaurants didn't let black people in. So when you take the notion of segregation, that evil system, that worked in such a corrosive way to prevent people from having opportunity and then you use that term to describe people walking into the same eating halls, going through the same lines, and then choosing where they are going to sit and having as much free choice as everybody else, to call that segregation is downright silly."

Certainly, race relations on campus today are decidedly more relaxed than they were during the dawn of desegregation. Evans remembers those days well. He came to UNC in the early 1970s and agreed, his second year at the school, to teach a huge class in sophomore chemistry. Because the class was so large, the university controlled registration by giving out tickets admitting only a specific number to sign up for the course. The first day of class he was astonished to find the lecture hall filled to overflowing, with people sitting in the aisles and standing in the back. After class was over, Evans said, "I asked two of the students, 'Are you registered for this course?' They said, 'No.' I said, 'Well, why are you here?' And they said, 'We heard there is a black professor in chemistry. We came to see.' I was shocked. . . . They had never seen an African American [professor], much less in science."

Troy Duster, head of the Institute for the Study of Social Change at Berkeley, argued that campuses may not be as segregated as they seem. "The closer you get to any group, the more you see internal differential, heterogeneity, extraordinary complexity. So the all-Asian table is upon closer inspection, Korean Americans, Japanese Americans, Hmong, Laotians, Cambodians. You think you're seeing Asians, but what you may be seeing closer up is extraordinary heterogeneity inside these groups. The all-Chinese table [consists of people from] Taiwan, Hong Kong, mainland China, and American-born Chinese. . . . If you're white or black, what you see is the Asians in the corner."

By the same token, Duster contended, people look at the so-called black table and don't recognize that it is not monolithic. "You find kids coming from first- and second-generation [college] families" but also students from families who have never had anyone in college. There are black kids from the Oakland streets socializing with black Valley girls: "All this at the 'black' table."

A lot of colleges, nonetheless, have expressed growing concern over students' tendency to hang out together along ethnic lines, and many have commissioned studies or convened committees to get to the bottom of things. A 1991 report of the diversity committee convened by UNC found a "chilly" climate for minority students on campus. Black students said they felt unwanted and reported hearing "racial epithets at mixers and other social events." Black students were also concerned about "a lack of awareness of these problems on campus, a lack of openness to discuss racial issues, and a sense of threat evident among white students."

The Institute for the Study of Social Change also released a report in 1991 (updated in 1995) that found a complex web of interactions among students. The report noted: "While there is evidence that both undergraduate and graduate students increasingly cross ethnic boundaries for friendship and cooperative academic endeavors, there is also a blossoming of segmented voluntary associations targeted at and appealing to different segments or specific ethnic or racial populations on campus."

Columbia University issued a study in 1992 that concluded:

> Students tend to see the campus as quite fragmented in general, and they perceive different groups as more and less isolated: Orthodox Jews are seen as the most isolated group, followed by blacks, Asians, Lesbians, gays, Latinos, and whites, the least isolated group.
>
> Of all respondents, 65 percent think spending a lot of time on campus with people of one's own racial or religious group is a "natural thing to do," but 61 percent feel that it reduces the quality of the Columbia experience and 50 percent think it encourages antagonism among groups. At least half of the undergraduates are ambivalent about separatism.

According to Roger Lehecka, Columbia's dean of students, part of the problem with race relations on campus is that students are only at a university for a brief time. "No matter how much racial awareness you instill in a student body in a given year, a new class arrives the next year lacking awareness." A deeper problem, however, is that universities do not exist in splendid isolation. Though they may strive for ivory-tower values, they ultimately reflect the values of the society that spawned them.

In the wake of the article published in the *Columbia Daily Spectator* in 1995, Columbia's president, George Rupp, issued a strong statement rejecting "unequivocally the anti-Semitic sentiments expressed in this article" and urging mutual respect and civility. "We would be foolish to pretend that Columbia is completely free of the poisons of bigotry that surround us today," he added. "But the greater truth is that our whole history and our experience at Columbia and America contradict the impulse to divisiveness."

In fact, America's history is not nearly as simple as Rupp pretends. His is the hopeful rhetoric a college president is duty bound to deliver. But American history, as Rupp well knows, has not been characterized by a resounding and continuing rejection of divisiveness. The truth is less flattering and significantly more ambiguous. Americans have always believed, for the most part, in cooperation and harmony even as we have embraced chauvinism, clannishness, and prejudice. Students at America's major universities fully reflect the nation's ambivalence and complexity. Consequently, even on the most polarized campuses, many students manage to reject tribalism and insularity.

Mario Anderson, a twenty-nine-year-old black undergraduate at Berkeley, is originally from New York State. When I ran into him just outside Sather Gate in December 1995, he was waiting for a white friend with whom he planned to have lunch. He appeared momentarily perplexed when I asked whether students were racially divided.

Upon reflection, he pointed at the student-activity tables set up along Sproul Plaza and observed, "If there is any sort of separation, it's usually based on culture, like for example . . . Asians students out here have many, many groups on Sproul Plaza as you can see from their tables; so, to that extent it's based on culture."

He was clearly uncomfortable, however, describing the phenomenon as separatism, saying instead, "There are certain cultural nodes that, of course, would fall along ethnic or so-called racial lines, but then, from these nodes, you have sort of all of these tendrils that intermix with each other. . . . I'm very much in the sort of intermixing tendrils, where people freely mix with each other."

Gladys Brown, director of the University of Maryland's Human Relations Program, pointed out that most minority students had a choice. No one forced them to go to largely white schools, and they did not come merely to practice self-segregation. "Racial minorities come here because they want to learn how to navigate the system," she said. Sadly, part of the process for this generation of nonwhite students consists (just as if did for their parents) of learning how to function in a society in which they feel less than welcome. Many come with high expectations of racial harmony and leave with shattered dreams. Others find reasons to hold on to their faith, even if it is tempered with skepticism.

When I asked a group of Spectrum residents how they felt about the prospects for racial harmony, the responses ran the gamut. "As far as minority-white relations go, I have no hope whatsoever. But as far as maybe a relationship among minorities, I'm a little more hopeful; but even then I'm still kinda doubtful about that," replied Lee.

Chen was disappointed with the attitudes she had found in college but was far from despair. "In a way, I'm hopeful that maybe it will be different outside of the college." Grose's view was more upbeat, precisely because of his experience at the university. "I could have easily gone through Duke with only really knowing white people," he said, but instead he had discovered friends of myriad colors.

Paul Choi was hopeful that interracial relations would improve, primarily "because of what I've been able to accomplish in my own personal relationships with people." If meaningful interracial connections are to be made outside the campus, they will come about not through formal diversity activities or through some real-world clone of Spectrum, but through "individual relationships among millions of people." Society will change for the better, Choi stated, when people begin "treating each others as individuals, and not simply as races." Choi is no doubt right. Yet, if students have such a difficult time seeing beyond race on college campuses, it seems unlikely they will suddenly become color-blind when they leave—when there is generally less incentive and there are fewer opportunities to forge relationships (or even just to communicate) across racial lines.

The problem, from Duster's perspective, is not merely that students from different racial groups sometimes don't know how to talk to each other, but that they have fundamentally different approaches to racial issues. Even when a white student and a black student both favor interracial progress, they tend to define it differently, Duster noted:

> The black student says, "Are you in favor of more affirmative action admissions?" and the white student says, "No, I'm in favor of individual meritocracy." The black student says, "Are you interested in getting more black faculty in here?" and the white student says, "Only if they're qualified, 'cause I ain't playing no affirmative action." And so on. And finally the black student says, "Well, then you're a racist." And the white student says, "What! I wanted to have a beer. I wanted to hang with you. You call me a racist? . . . You're being politically correct, because you think if I don't agree with you on the political stuff then you can't be my friend." And so off they go into their corners.

Universities are trying an array of measures to get minority and white students more in tune with each other. Berkeley has an "American cultures" requirement, meaning that all undergraduates must take at least one course on the contributions of different ethnic groups. UNC's "cultural diversity" requirement has essentially the same purpose. The University of Maryland at College Park requires each department to promote diversity in its recruitment and through cultural activities. At the same time, campus administrators are sanctioning a host of themed dorms—such as the Massachusetts Institute of Technology's Chocolate City (a black section of a dorm for more than twenty undergraduates)—and minority-oriented fraternities and sororities. In fall 1995, UNC proudly announced the formation of Alpha Pi Omega, the first American Indian sorority in the nation.

It remains unclear, however, whether all these activities are promoting division or harmony. A March 1995 survey of attitudes at the University of Maryland showed that even opinions about the values of such activities are racially polarized. As the report stated: "Some of the survey results indicate a type of backlash occurring against UMCP's efforts to promote diversity, where white students view the efforts as 'too much' and other students view the same efforts as 'too little.'" These attitudes are not unlike the reactions to analogous efforts in the workplace.

In recent years, students who have already splintered along racial and ethnic lines have had to confront one of the most divisive issues of the current era: affirmative action. No other single issue has sparked as much debate on college campuses, and nowhere more so than at Berkeley.

In July 1995, the University of California's board of regents voted to abolish affirmative action throughout the state university system. The school has since shown intermittent signs of its old radical self. In October 1995, an estimated five thousand boisterous young people crowded into Sproul Plaza in a mass show of support for affirmative action. The sight of a raucous sea of students so touched speaker Jesse Jackson that he beamed and screamed, "Berkeley's back!"

No one had to ask what he meant. Since 1964, when the Free Speech movement erupted on campus and climaxed with the students' takeover of Sproul Hall, Berkeley and radicalism have been practically synonymous. In recent years, however, Berkeley seemed to be taking a conservative turn. Jackson was trying to take the students back to that earlier era, to a time when Berkeley's passion for social justice burned so brightly that the regents' vote on affirmative action would have been tantamount to a declaration of war.

Yet, as Matt Belloni, the twenty-year-old opinion-page editor of the *Daily Californian* pointed out during our conversation, the scene has changed quite a bit in the past thirty years. The *Daily Cal*, which has long treasured its independence from the university, had recently moved into a sixth-floor office of Eshleman Hall on campus. The building, a stone's throw from Sproul Plaza, houses a myriad of student organizations. Though the publication is still independent, the move seems to be a metaphor for the paper's moving closer to the system.

The paper's shift to the center was confirmed for many in September 1995, when the *Cal*'s multiracial staff voted to condemn the practice of race-based affirmative action. Belloni, a political science major from Laguna Beach, seated comfortably behind his desk in the corner, explained to me why they did.

Although the regents' decision was made in July, the young journalists mulled over their decision for several weeks, and when the staff finally took a vote, Belloni said, opinions did not split along racial lines. The editor-in-chief, Belloni pointedly noted, is Iranian, and blacks and Asians, as well as whites, sit on the editorial board. Belloni refused to say who took which side, but insisted that it was not a case of the whites and Asians voting against affirmative action and everyone else voting for it. "The main division was whether the student saw a need for diversity for diversity's sake."

The *Cal* editors concluded that race-based programs were not only unfair, but created a stigma against minority students. The editorial argued, instead, for what it called "socio-economic affirmative action," whereby race could neither help nor hurt a prospective applicant. Socioeconomic status, Belloni argued, is "a much more accurate level of representation of who needs what than a racial stereotype or a racial generalization. . . . Poor is poor, but Latino is not poor and Latino is not necessarily disadvantaged."

Before the regents' decision, Berkeley admitted half its students only on the basis of so-called academic index scores (essentially, grades and test scores). Of students in that group admitted in 1994, 0.1 percent were American Indian, 0.8 percent were African American, 3.3 percent were Chicano-Latino, 46.9 percent were Asian, and 40.7 percent were white. Another 45 percent of students were admitted after a range of criteria, including essays, honors, nonacademic accomplishments, and "diversity," were considered. The second group was substantially more integrated than the first: 2.3 were American Indian, 11.6 percent were African American, 30.6 percent were Chicano-Latino, 26.1 percent were Asian, and 25.9 percent were white. The remaining 5 percent of the students who were admitted were clearly at risk but nonetheless demonstrated potential; of those, 36.7 percent were black, 35.1 percent were Chicano-Latino, 17.1 percent were white, and nearly 10 percent were Asian or American Indian. Eliminating all "diversity" considerations presumably would make the racial composition of the second group, and perhaps the third group, much more similar to the first. An analysis in 1996 by U.C. Berkeley officials, for instance, projected a possible drop of more than 50 percent in black and Chicano admissions if racial factors were eliminated from the admissions process.

Clearly, a policy that simply substituted socioeconomic status for race would not necessarily ensure a diverse racial mix. There are, after all, huge numbers of poor whites and Asians in California who would take slots that currently go to so-called disadvantaged minorities. Nonetheless, Belloni does not find discriminating on the basis of race to be an acceptable remedy: "It's, like, do you kill a negative with a negative?"

He acknowledged that the paper's position mirrors a change on the campus itself. "The student body here is not the same as it was back in the activist sixties. . . . The pressures are so high on most students to succeed. It's, 'Well, do I want to go attend a rally on Sproul or do I want to study for my chem midterm?' It's the choice you have to make, and most students choose to study for the chem midterm."

Duster rejected Belloni's views on affirmative action, but agreed that Berkeley students have changed—and not merely in their passion for activism:

> In the sixties, when you only had 2.8 percent black students, 1.7 percent Chicano, you could literally afford a kind of gracious largesse about affirmative action. You could say as a white liberal on a liberal campus, let a few hundred more in. But [in those years] every student who applied could get in—if they had a 3.25 GPA and had SAT scores that were reasonable. Twenty years later, you got 23,000 applications for 3,500 slots in the freshman class. . . . The times are tougher, and the white students who in 1968 were about 80 percent of the student body are now down to 30 percent. See, context is everything. You can't say the students have gotten conservative. The demography of the state, the economy of the state, politics [have been] remarkably transformed.

Duster, a bearded, thoughtful, amiable black man, who in more than a quarter of a century teaching at Berkeley has mastered the art of placing facts in context, observed: "On the issues of race and access to institutions, no question about it, white students and Asian students are far less likely to be supportive of affirmative action than they were thirty years ago. However, in this society, on a continuum, they are still more liberal than their parents."

That fact comes as cold comfort to minority students and faculty at Berkeley and elsewhere who are dealing with the backlash against affirmative action—and with white students and faculty who seem to regard anyone who is black or Hispanic as incompetent. Columbia University's study of students' attitudes, for instance, found that 56 percent of black students and 44 percent of Latinos believed that, as a result of affirmative action admissions policies, faculty members doubted the academic ability of minority students. Furthermore, 80 percent of black students and 72 percent of Latinos thought affirmative action had created doubts about minority students among their white classmates.

Mason, of Duke, said she was ill prepared for the reception she got from many whites at the university who would imply, sometimes bluntly, that she was at the university largely because of her race—despite her stellar academic record. If they had asked, Mason observed, "I would be quick to say, 'You know, I consider myself to be a very competitive student and I work very hard and I feel like I deserve to be here. . . . Granted maybe there are stipulations made for minorities, athletes, alumni children, what have you, but all of us, almost, are in that category.'" Such exchanges, however, rarely take place.

Peter Kuriloff, of the University of Pennsylvania, recalled talking to a black student who questioned a grade and was told by the instructor, "Oh . . . this is [a] good [grade] for black students." The student was deeply offended, he said, at "the subtle assumption that she was here because of affirmative action." Minority faculty members often make the same complaint. As Robert L. Hampton, dean for undergraduate studies and associate provost for academic affairs at the University of Maryland, acknowledged, "Clearly, some people look at me and say I'm here because of affirmative action or [refer to me as] a black dean. And I say, 'No, I'm a dean.' And to that extent, we all suffer from that affirmative action mentality."

William "Sandy" Garrity, an economist at UNC, believes that the affirmative action presumption puts a great deal of psychological pressure on black faculty and students to prove themselves that's "very different from what other groups have to confront." That pressure is likely to get much heavier before it lets up, as universities and American society in general sort through the maze of issues swirling around affirmative action. That such an examination is focused, in large measure, on the area of university admissions is perhaps inevitable. For one thing, college admissions procedures, unlike most hiring decisions, are relatively open to public examination. If one racial group is treated differently from another (admitted with significantly lower test scores, for example), the double standard is readily apparent. Moreover, the fact that test scores and grades are so central to the admissions process means that applicants can be easily ranked on the basis of what many consider to be objective criteria. And to have those criteria set aside in the service of social engineering is something that many people find deeply troubling, for it seems to violate the idea of fairness—of rewarding people for hard work and ability—that universities, at their best, are thought to exemplify. A university education, say critics of affirmative action, should go to those who most deserve it, and given the centrality of a skilled workforce to the nation's future, to those who will be best able to compete in an increasingly and unmercifully competitive world. Political correctness, argue the critics, has no place in decisions that will determine, in substantial measure, the future leaders, and indeed the very fate, of the United States. Not that applicants generally see college admissions in such sweeping terms. Yet even the most apolitical student recognizes that young people embody and symbolize, as nothing else can, a nation's political, intellectual, and ethical potential—that they are vessels of hope for human progress. Yet the young are also society's soldiers, the ranks from which frontline troops are traditionally drawn—not only for foreign wars, but for those right at home, including, inescapably, the war over "preferences" and affirmative action that has become, for the current generation, every bit as maddening, perplexing, and rife with moral ambiguity as the war in Vietnam was a generation or two ago.

CHAPTER 5

Should affirmative action be kicked out of college?

Sometimes when I am asked whether I am for or against affirmative action, I find myself being evasive. It isn't because I don't have an opinion or am reluctant to voice one, but because the question is impossible for me to answer honestly (never mind fully) with a simple yes or no. It's somewhat like being asked whether you are for taxes or, better yet, abortion. No one in his or her right mind is unequivocally "for" either. Yet many people accept both, if unhappily, because they seem better than the available alternatives—because they are, in short, a lesser evil.

To make matters even more complicated, affirmative action is not simply one thing. Sure, governmental bureaucrats have their definitions, and courts and law professors have theirs. And anti–affirmative action ideologues have yet another. The truth is that the definition changes, often radically, depending on who is using the phrase. It can mean everything from quota programs for supposed incompetents to extending a hand to eminently qualified people previously held back by bias. Often, when the phrase is used in what passes for public dialogue, it has no real meaning. It's hurled as part of a broad indictment summing up the case against minorities (usually blacks) and, sometimes, women for taking jobs (or promotions or places in schools or universities) that they simply don't deserve.

In *Affirmative Action Reconsidered,* published over two decades ago, economist Thomas Sowell made a point that remains relevant: "Many different policies have gone under the general label of affirmative action, and many different institutions—courts, executive agencies, and even private organizations—have been involved in formulating or interpreting the meaning of the label. The conflicting tendencies and pressures of these various institutions have shifted the meaning of affirmative action and produced inconsistent concepts as well. There is no way to determine *the* meaning of 'affirmative action.'" That is not to say that the words have no meaning—merely that they do not have a common meaning.

Frederick R. Lynch, in *Invisible Victims: White Males and the Crisis of Affirmative Action,* came up with the following: "I use the term 'affirmative action' to refer to a system of racial-and-ethnic preferences or 'quotas' that have been the real-world results of 'goals and timetables.'" In *In Defense of Affirmative Action,* author Barbara Bergmann used a different definition: "Affirmative action is planning and acting to end the absence of certain kinds of people—those who belong to groups that have been subordinated or left out—from certain jobs and schools."

Allow me to put forth a working description that is less partisan. This is not a technical definition, since affirmative action (and the justification for it) must meet some fairly specific legal tests in many circumstances, especially when it is court-ordered or engaged in by governmental agencies. It also has taken on particular meanings to the people who speak the patois of corporate "diversity" and "equal opportunity." For the moment, however, I think it's useful to present a definition that encompasses an array of things that many intelligent people mean when they discuss affirmative action. Let's assume that affirmative action means programs or policies that, in the interest of equity and/or heterogeneity, consciously take race, ethnicity, or gender into account (to whatever extent) in making decisions about employment, admissions, or the allocation or awarding of other valuable benefits or resources.

Is that something enlightened people should be for? I think not (and this is an important caveat) if they exist solely in the abstract and idealized world—in the world in which so many economists seem to live: a place of perfect knowledge, perfect competition, and perfect access to information and opportunity, all of which ensure that society will function in a perfectly bias-free way. I have not yet seen that place and have strong suspicions it does not exist. In the world in which I live, I think affirmative action is an often-justifiable, limited, and seriously flawed method of dealing with a set of problems that really require a much better solution. I also believe it is an issue that, in terms of public debate, primarily involves ethnic and racial "minorities," since affirmative action for women doesn't seem to get people nearly as riled up.

Supreme Court Justice Harry Blackmun, as I noted previously, nicely laid out the basic paradox. Race-conscious strategies were necessary, he maintained "in order to get beyond racism." Certain people must be treated differently, he reasoned, so that eventually they could be treated equally. It is a powerful and provocative pronouncement. It is also arguably wrong. And it has been under attack since the day it was made. In an article published in the *University of Chicago Law Review* in 1979, the year after Blackmun delivered his dictum in the *Regents of California v. Bakke* decision, Duke University law professor William Van Alstyne delivered a bitingly contemptuous reply. Race-based policies, he insisted, are nothing more than a Lorelei—a mythical, seductive nymph whose sweetly beckoning voice lures sailors to be shipwrecked on a rock.

> [G]etting beyond racism in this fashion ... is as little likely to succeed as the now discredited idea that in order to 'get beyond' organized government, it is first indispensable to organize a virtual dictatorship that, once it extirpates the evils that made organized government necessary, will itself just naturally wither away. We have not seen governments wither by the paradox of assigning them even greater powers. We shall not now see racism disappear by employing its own ways of classifying people and of measuring their rights.
>
> Rather, one gets beyond racism by getting beyond it now; by a complete, resolute and credible commitment *never* to tolerate in one's

own life—or in the life or practice of one's government—the differential treatment of other human beings by race.

Other than to warn the government against getting into the "racial spoils" business, Van Alstyne had no concrete and feasible suggestion about how exactly to foster or create a society-wide "complete, resolute and credible commitment" to eschew bias in all its forms. And in the years since he penned that article, no one else seems to have come up with such a suggestion either. So the battle about affirmative action rages on.

Nonetheless, I accept the point. You don't get rid of racism—not anytime soon and possibly ever—by putting the government or businesses or universities into the racial bean-counting business. In fact, there are a host of reasons why some people (including some of goodwill) may come to see affirmative action—however defined—as not merely a lesser evil, but an outright evil. They may do so because however it is explained, affirmative action, in its most energetic incarnation, is about trying to fight bad discrimination with remedial, benign, or good discrimination. Such a strategy, as Mamphela Ramphele, vice chancellor of the University of Cape Town, observed, "has no inherent moral-ethical basis." Justifiable as discrimination against a manifestly privileged class may be, it is not an approach that automatically leaves one on the moral high ground.

To make matters worse, affirmative action does not distribute its benefits equally—even among the targeted groups. Clearly, those who are best positioned to take advantage of it reap the largest rewards, and that situation raises the inevitable question of intragroup equity. "Personal enrichment should not be confused with black empowerment—one cannot be fabulously rich on behalf of others," Ramphele pointed out. Virtually the same point was made in a 1996 analysis of an Ohio state program for minority businesses. The study found that half the money paid to minority contractors went to 2 percent of Ohio's certified minority businesses. Governor George Voinovich pronounced himself "shocked."

The dirty secret of life, as Jimmy Carter indelicately pointed out some years ago, is that it simply isn't fair. That would be true even if affirmative action had never been invented. By the same token, the hiring and promotion process has never been fair. If anything, affirmative action has made it fairer, but because affirmative action is not fair itself, it gives unfairness a focus. It is vulnerable and always has been—as any lesser evil is—to moral (even if insincere) opposition. Consequently, opponents of affirmative action have been able to make a compelling, if not particularly credible, case that they are the true architects of equality, defenders of righteousness, and heirs to the philosophical legacy of Martin Luther King, Jr.

One of the authors of the so-called Civil Rights Initiative, a ballot measure devised to eliminate state-supported affirmative action programs in California, told me with manifest sincerity in 1995 that his proposal was just reaffirming the language of the Civil Rights Act of 1964. "I mean that's in all our literature," said Tom Wood. "We are living in a regime now, in a country now, where there are laws on the books that put somebody like me in a different legal position from a woman or a racial minority." Courts had declared that it was all right to "discriminate against whites or males or both, and increasingly Asian Americans . . . and, you know, I think that that needs to be changed. I don't think it's right. I don't think it's good educational policy. I don't think it's good social policy. I don't think it's good constitutional philosophy."

Glynn Custred, coauthor of the initiative, agreed: "Some people have said that we're abusing the term 'civil rights,' but we don't think this at all, simply because what the 1964 Civil Rights Act did, and what that whole movement is about, was to focus on individual rights. . . . What we're trying is to get back to that original intent." Colorado Attorney General Gale Norton made a similar point in 1996 when she urged state colleges and universities to drop race-based scholarships. She believed, said Norton, *like Martin Luther King*, that people should be judged "not by the color of their skin but by the content of their character."

The "color-blind" argument was made most notably by Supreme Court Justice Clarence Thomas in *Adarand Constructors v. Peña*—the case of a white Colorado Springs–based contractor who sued the federal government because a Hispanic-owned company, despite a higher bid, was awarded a federal subcontract. The Supreme Court reversed a lower court's ruling that the set-aside policy (favoring blacks, Hispanics, Native Americans, and Asian Pacific Americans) was constitutional. In a separate opinion agreeing with the Court's 5–4 decision, Thomas wrote: "I believe that there is a moral and constitutional equivalence between laws designed to subjugate a race and those that distribute benefits on the basis of race in order to foster some current notion of equality. . . . In my mind, government-sponsored racial discrimination based on benign prejudice is just as noxious as discrimination inspired by malicious prejudice. In each instance, it is racial discrimination, plain and simple."

Justice John Paul Stevens bluntly rejected the comparison. "There is no moral or constitutional equivalence between a policy that is designed to perpetuate a caste system and one that seeks to eradicate racial subordination," he wrote. Nevertheless, Thomas's reasoning resonated not only in the Supreme Court but among millions of Americans who have concluded that affirmative action does more harm than good.

In *Ending Affirmative Action*, Terry Eastland revisited the early days of the modern civil rights era. In the 1950s and early 1960s, he maintained, civil rights leaders fought for race-blind laws, so people could be judged "not by the color of their skin but by the content of their character." Martin Luther King and company, Eastland claimed, "were gratified whenever the law inched toward colorblindness, which it did on many occasions." But then something went dreadfully wrong: "In the latter half of the 1960s, when the architects of affirmative action began their work, they had to loosen the constraints of colorblind law and morality, for otherwise it would not have been possible to establish public policies that treat blacks differently. Once this crucial first step had been taken, preferential affirmative action could evolve into an enterprise aimed at securing more equal outcomes for certain other minority groups and women."

The early engineers of affirmative action were liars, in Eastland's opinion, for they claimed that their departure from the standard of color blindness was temporary. "It would have been shocking had they said that affirmative action was going to be permanent, for colorblindness lay then, as it still does today, at the core of American ideals," Eastland concluded.

Eastland's notion of what lay at the "core of American ideals" during the 1960s is undoubtedly quite different from that of most blacks who lived through those years—when black churches were burned and bombed to intimidate black clergy, when blacks attended previously segregated colleges only because of court orders and under federal protection, when civil rights workers were beaten and shot and left for dead. At the least, in those years, America was torn between opposing ideals—segregation and integration, color blindness and brutal racism. But Eastland touched on an important point: Today, whatever Americans may actually feel and however they act, the vast majority do not think of themselves as racists. If it is not exactly color blindness that we believe in, we do tend to believe that there is something wrong with policies that, in an obvious way, discriminate against whatever racial group claims us as members. Affirmative action, to those who believe they are harmed by it, feels a lot like plain old discrimination, however someone else may justify it. Society's opposition to discrimination may not be quite as sweeping as some people like to think; still, the foes of affirmative action are not necessarily being insincere when they claim, on the basis of one sentence from King's 1963 speech, to be his latter-day disciples. They are, however, likely to be ignorant of what King actually believed.

The January 1965 "holiday anniversary issue" of *Playboy* featured—along with literary offerings by Vladimir Nabokov and Jack Kerouac and a fantasy pictorial history of harems—what was billed as the longest interview King had ever granted any publication. During that conversation, King was asked about his support for a $50 billion program of aid for America's blacks. Did he think it was it fair, *Playboy* inquired, "to request a multi-billion dollar program of preferential treatment for the Negroes or for any other minority group?"

"I do indeed," responded King. "Can any fair-minded citizen deny that the Negro has been deprived? Few people reflect that for two centuries the Negro was enslaved and robbed of *any* wages—potential accrued wealth which would have been the legacy of his descendants. *All* of America's wealth today could not adequately compensate its Negroes for his centuries of exploitation and humiliation. It is an economic fact that a program such as I propose would certainly cost far less than any computation of two centuries of unpaid wages plus accumulated interest. In any case, I do not intend that this program of economic aid should apply only to the Negro; it should benefit the disadvantaged of *all* races."

King went on to argue that the law was full of precedents for "special compensatory programs" and specifically cited American Indian projects, unemployment compensation, and manpower retraining initiatives. "The closest analogy is the GI Bill of Rights," he said. "Negro rehabilitation in America would require approximately the same breadth of program—which would not place an undue burden on our economy." A program of "preferential employment of the disadvantaged," said King, could be sold to the country much as special treatment for veterans was sold.

"If a nationwide program of preferential employment for Negroes were to be adopted, how would you proposed to assuage the resentment of whites who already feel that their jobs are being jeopardized by the influx of Negroes resulting from desegregation?" asked *Playboy*.

"We must develop a federal program of public works, retraining and jobs for all—so that none, white or black, will have cause to feel threatened," King replied. In the same interview, he also addressed the question of "preferential treatment in housing" and whites' fears of integration, making the point that if housing for blacks was improved, "many white people would be surprised at how many Negroes would choose to live among themselves." King also called for more preventive medical service, training for jobs, high-quality education (immediately), and eventually the eradication of America's slums.

"Young boys and girls now in the ghettos must be enabled to feel that they count, that somebody cares about them; they must be able to feel *hope*. And on a longer-range basis, the physical ghetto itself must be eliminated, because these are the environmental conditions that germinate riots. It is both socially and morally suicidal to continue a pattern of deploring effects while failing to come to grips with the *causes*. Ultimately, law and order will be maintained only when justice and dignity are accorded impartially to all."

The reality of King's views, in short, is much more complicated than the "content of their character" sound bite. Though King did see color blindness as an ideal, he did not believe America was on the verge of attaining it. Instead, he saw a need for special efforts to make black Americans whole. In the same "I have a dream" speech that has so inspired the anti–affirmative action lobby, King also insisted that America had presented blacks with a "bad check" and that the country had an obligation to make that check good. If King's call for "special compensatory programs" was not exactly a demand for affirmative action as it is now known, he was clearly demanding some form of governmental activism aimed largely at blacks. Wiping out slums, eradicating poverty, ensuring access to a decent education—all these things and more, he saw as partial payment of an incalculably colossal debt.

There is no way of knowing where King would stand on affirmative action if he were alive today. It's clear, however, that his views cannot be summed up with "ignore color, ignore history, ignore present circumstance, and just treat everyone equally." When people claim that King was philosophically opposed to affirmative action, they are simply wrong. It is true, however, that King recognized that to target blacks for benefits to the exclusion of whites would be to invite resentment and resistance.

That resentment, which has the virtue of being morally defensible, has inevitably grown as affirmative action has expanded. Indeed, the number of aggrieved persons doesn't necessarily bear any relationship to the number who are actually harmed. In 1994, for instance, some five thousand white would-be firefighters in Los Angeles were told that they could not take the required exam because a consent decree with the Justice Department left little room for whites who were not already in the hiring queue. The exclusionary policy set off howls of protests from aggrieved white job seekers and from critics of affirmative action. "Now, if you stop and think about this for a minute, how many of those 5,000 guys would have passed the qualifying exam?" asked Custred. He answered his own question: "A fairly small number." His point, of course, is that it was not merely the handful of whites who might actually have been hired who felt wronged by affirmative action, but virtually all who thought they were qualified for the test.

Even without the toxin of white (especially male) resentment—which, whether rooted in actual injury or simply in its perception, is undeniably heartfelt—affirmative action would not be an easy sell.

Group-based burdens and privileges, by their very nature, challenge the ethic of individualism that Americans like to believe lies at the core of our collective success. They also, in the eyes of many critics, run counter to the spirit—and perhaps the letter—of the U.S. Constitution.

In recent years, federal courts (including, most notably, the Supreme Court) have increasingly accepted the argument that when the government makes racial distinctions, for any reason, it perpetuates a racial tribalism that has no place in an egalitarian democracy and risks violating the equal-protection guarantees of the Fourteenth Amendment. So declared the U.S. Fifth Circuit Court of Appeals in 1996 in ruling against an affirmative action program at the University of Texas School of Law.

The case was brought by four white students who sought admission to the school in 1992. Three were rejected, and one was admitted too late, he said, to enroll. The plaintiffs were all decent but less than brilliant students. Lead plaintiff Cheryl Hopwood, for instance, had a 3.8 undergraduate grade-point average at California State University-Northridge and ranked in the 83rd percentile of those who had taken the Law School Admissions Test (LSAT). That was not quite good enough for the University of Texas School of Law—at least not if one was white. Yet, as Hopwood was surprised and angered to discover, she probably would have been a shoo-in if she had been black or Hispanic. When Hopwood's lawyers reviewed the records of the candidates who were actually admitted, they found that only one of forty-one black students and three of fifty-five Mexican American students outstripped her academically. They also found that the law school had set up an admission program that made it particularly vulnerable to a legal challenge.

In winnowing the pool of applicants, the school began by computing a "Texas Index" for the four thousand or so persons who applied annually. The index, a composite of undergraduate grades and LSAT scores, enabled the admissions office to rank all candidates. Those with high scores almost certainly got in, and those with relatively low scores were almost certainly excluded. The action focused on those in the middle.

To select from the roughly nine hundred people they would have to admit to get a class of five hundred, the university officials sifted through the ranks of good but not exceptional students, looking for qualities that might set them apart. The problem, in Hopwood's eyes, was that they looked a lot harder at (and more kindly on) blacks and Mexican Americans than at whites. Not only were the minorities' applications reviewed by a special subcommittee, the cutoff scores were set lower. As a result, blacks and Hispanics were admitted with worse academic records, on average, than most of their white classmates.

Among Texas residents, the typical successful applicant, irrespective of race, had a B-plus average. (For whites it was 3.56, for blacks 3.30, and for Mexican Americans 3.24). The average LSAT score was 164 for whites, 158 for blacks, and 157 for Mexican Americans—placing those groups in the 91st, 78th, and 75th percentiles, respectively. The racial-ethnic gap among non-Texas residents was slightly higher.

Mark Yudof, dean of the law school, frankly acknowledged, in an interview with the *Los Angeles Times*, that the standards for minorities and whites were different, but added, "I don't think you can have a public institution that is lily white." In fact, like many institutions in the South, the school had been completely white until the dawn of the civil rights age. When Heman Sweatt, a black veteran and Houston postal carrier, applied to the law school in the 1940s, Texas initially responded by opening up a second-rate school for blacks, just as the state of Oklahoma had done earlier for Ada Lois Sipuel. This time around, however, the Supreme Court went further than it had with the Sipuel case. Refusing to accept the state's assurances that the new school was in any way "equal" to the University of Texas School of Law, the Court ordered Sweatt admitted in 1950—effectively laying the groundwork for its 1954 decision on *Brown v. Board of Education of Topeka*.

Though Sweatt got into the school, he encountered such hostility that he fled without a degree. The law school cited that unfriendly reception, and lingering mistrust of the school among blacks, as justification for the program. "As late as 1971—twenty years after Sweatt left the law school humiliated by the taunts and threats of students and faculty—the entering class had no blacks," the school told the appeals court. The program the University of Texas developed, however, bore an unfortunate resemblance to a plan used in the

1970s by the medical school of the University of California at Davis.

Allan Bakke, after being rejected by that medical school, had sued—and was ordered admitted after essentially making the same arguments as did Hopwood. The California program, much like the one in Texas, considered minority applicants separately from those who were white. The special admissions program was open only to blacks, Mexican Americans, Asians, and American Indians, whose applications were reviewed by a special committee. Bakke claimed that the process violated the state constitution, the 1964 Civil Rights Act, and the Fourteenth Amendment. The Supreme Court justices, in a 5–4 decision, agreed that the program violated the 1964 law. But they also agreed, by the same 5–4 majority, that the Fourteenth Amendment does not necessarily prohibit states from making racial distinctions. They could not agree on much of anything else.

Writing for the majority, Justice Lewis Powell wrestled with the concept of color blindness, noting that when members of Congress had urged passage of the civil rights laws, they were not talking about some hypothetical world in which whites might be discriminated against but about the real world in which government-supported segregation denied blacks any semblance of equal treatment. Nonetheless, he observed, unless the equal-protection clause truly covers all races, it would be an oxymoron. "Preferring members of any one group for no reason other than race or ethnic origin is discrimination for its own sake. This the Constitution forbids," he concluded. Yet, Powell made a crucial distinction between discriminating solely on the basis of race and making race one factor in a complicated selection process. He cited Harvard University's admission program, which allowed race to be a "plus" but not the decisive factor, as a model worth emulating.

In a separate opinion, Justices William Brennan, Byron White, Thurgood Marshall, and Harry Blackmun declared that the fact that different justices came to different conclusions "should not and must not mask the central meaning of today's opinions: Government may take race into account when it acts not to demean or insult any racial group, but to remedy disadvantages cast on minorities by past racial prejudice, at least when appropriate findings have been made by judicial, legislative, or administrative bodies with competence to act in this area."

The fifth circuit appeals court in New Orleans effectively rejected the Bakke precedent and declared that the school could not use race, even as a "plus" factor, in admissions. To Judge Jerry Smith, who wrote the opinion, the University of Texas program was a clear instance of a school lowering standards and favoring certain minority students "to the detriment of whites and non-preferred minorities." And for no good purpose. Under the so-called strict-scrutiny justification, the government's use of a racial classification had to satisfy two tests. It had to (1) serve a compelling governmental interest and (2) be narrowly tailored to achieve the goal. Since the law school failed, in the court's opinion, to meet the first test, there was no point in determining whether it met the second; failing either one was enough to place the program in violation of the equal-protection clause of the Fourteenth Amendment. The equal-protection clause, Smith wrote, "seeks ultimately to render the issue of race irrelevant in governmental decisionmaking." He reasoned that programs that discriminate against whites and "non-preferred minorities" could not accomplish that end.

Smith disposed of Powell's argument for racial diversity by noting that in the Bakke case, it "garnered only his own vote and never represented the view of a majority." Moreover, he asserted, the promotion of diversity "fosters, rather than minimizes, the use of race" and, as such, promotes racial stereotypes and could fuel hostility. As for Blackmun's dictum that race-conscious remedies might be necessary to achieve a race-neutral society, he pointed out that other justices disagreed.

Smith also rejected the remediation argument. Sure, the school had discriminated in the past, but that was years ago, and most of those who were guilty of discrimination were no longer around. At any rate, he wrote, "A broad program that sweeps in all minorities with a remedy that is in no way related to past harms cannot survive constitutional scrutiny."

Smith made it clear that he had no problem with discrimination, as long as it was not racial: "A university may properly favor one applicant over another because of his ability to play the cello, make a downfield tackle, or understand chaos theory." A school could properly discriminate, he argued, for a host of other reasons as well, including a student's participation in extracurricular activities or simply because an aspirant was the child of an alumnus. A school might also attempt to foster diversity among its recruits—but, again, not by favoring people because of their race. Plaintiff Hopwood, argued Smith, might even be a good candidate for admission on diversity grounds: "She is the now-thirty-two-year-old wife of a member of the Armed Forces stationed in San Antonio and, more significantly, is raising a severely handicapped child. Her circumstance would bring a different perspective to the law school."

Smith's argumentative tone suggests, among other things, that he had no interest in presenting himself as a dispassionate jurist—and certainly not as someone who is neutral on the subject of affirmative action. Instead, he captured, in legalistic language, the outrage that many nonlawyers have felt for a long time. "Preferences" for minorities, he said in effect, have no place in American society—certainly not in American law—and it is time to begin stamping them out. But even if that perception is true, it's worth asking whether the educational system is the place to wage the battle over affirmative action.

In 1984, a decade before *The Bell Curve* was published, Charles Murray argued (in a *New Republic* article entitled "Affirmative Racism") that "preferential admissions by race" were harmful to blacks. Blacks typically enter elite universities significantly less well prepared than whites, Murray wrote, and hence are unable to keep up. Their disappointing performance fueled stereotypes: "What students and instructors see in their day-to-day experience in the classroom is a disproportionate number of blacks who are below the white average, relatively few blacks who are at the white average, and virtually none who are in the first rank. The image that the white student carries away is that blacks are less able than whites." Instead of fighting racism, Murray concluded, affirmative action actively encourages it—stigmatizing all blacks, irrespective of their abilities, and making it less likely that even capable blacks would be able to enjoy either academic or professional success.

In a response published a few weeks later, Derek Bok, then president of Harvard University, chastised Murray for cataloging "only the disappointments and failures of preferential admissions without recognizing its many success." He also cited a survey of Harvard undergraduates in which the majority of blacks and whites who were polled professed confidence in the ability of black students. Less than 5 percent of black Harvard undergraduates "felt they had moderate or severe doubts about their own academic ability, and over 75 percent reported no doubts whatsoever," wrote Bok. "Almost 60 percent of white undergraduates believed that they had no such doubts about blacks, and barely 10 percent indicated moderate or severe doubts." Bok acknowledged that many white students suspected that "others" might question the abilities of blacks, but read no significance into that finding. He also pointed out that racial prejudice and resentments had existed long before affirmative action was born and reminded Murray that as recently as 1965, blacks were all but absent from predominantly white universities. "Only slightly more than one percent of the nation's law students were black, and a mere handful of blacks attended the predominantly white graduate schools of medicine and business. Little or no progress had been made in raising these proportions over the preceding generation," Bok noted. He then went on to challenge Murray to "explain in detail just how his policies would work and why they would fare any better now than they did prior to 1965."

That challenge, in effect, has gone unanswered, even as the assault on affirmative action has grown more virulent. Still, despite the considerable ideological baggage Murray brings to the issue, the question he raises is not trivial. Can lowering admissions standards in the name of inclusion ultimately do more harm than good? Custred, the California State University anthropologist who coauthored the California anti–affirmative action initiative, has no doubt that it can. An approach that essentially says, "we have so many spots for blacks, so many for Hispanics, et cetera," Custred said, encourages beneficiaries to see themselves not as individuals but as members of distinct racial and ethnic groups. "This encourages resegregation; it encourages the feeling that, 'If in fact we come from a lower socioeconomic status and our grades are not as good as these race horses that they have at MIT and Harvard, there is something wrong with us as a group.'"

In fact, the reaction of students—minority and white—is a good deal more complex than Custred seems to realize. It is true that suspicion of the intellectual inferiority of certain minority groups is rife on college campuses. The problem is almost certainly more pervasive than was suggested by the numbers cited by Bok at Harvard. It may even be worse than was indicated by the Columbia University study noted in Chapter 4, since when asked about racially charged subjects, people tend to downplay any suggestion that they may harbor racist thoughts. Yet as the various studies and the testimony of students themselves make clear, it is not so much fear of competition that drives minority students to frustration as it is the constant, sometimes subtle, questioning of their ability by others—specifically, by faculty and white students.

That questioning of minority students' aptitude, Murray and Custred have argued, is a direct result of affirmative action. The solution, they have proposed, is to let students go only where their abilities would naturally take them—instead of encouraging them to compete in arenas where they are hopelessly outclassed. In other words, many minority students who now go to Harvard, Yale, and the University of California at Berkeley should instead go to lesser places like California State University or George Mason University. By the same token, many of those now admitted to state universities should set their sights on junior colleges or perhaps trade schools.

Still, one has to wonder whether the presumption of intellectual inadequacy is rooted primarily in—as opposed to rationalized by—affirmative action. As psychologist Jeff Howard, an expert on education, was quoted as saying in Chapter 2, a "rumor of inferiority ... follows minority children to school." And that rumor seems to exist independently of any affirmative action program. Also, as the minority students I interviewed made plain, the problem of acceptance on college campuses has to do with a myriad of factors, of which academic performance is only one. The classmate who told Duke student Edrienne Mason that she considered all blacks to be criminals, for instance, was presumably motivated by something other than intellectual questioning of affirmative action programs. Although eliminating affirmative action may make students like that classmate more comfortable—if only because it would reduce the number of black students around her—it would not necessarily make things better for those minority students whom Custred said he is concerned about. Those who remained on campus would still have to put up with offensive racial attitudes, and those who left the campus or were not admitted would be deprived of all the benefits a good university can provide.

Charles Young, chancellor of the University of California at Los Angeles, sees the elimination of affirmative action as a prescription for social disaster. He acknowledges that in many universities, including UCLA, there is something of a two-tier system—that many students of color would not have been accepted purely on the basis of their grades and test scores. However, he rejects the notion that these students are floundering. "We've seen the graduation rates for all groups rise rapidly. The completion rate for minorities is higher than it was for nonminorities a few years ago." And society is better for their having been educated at UCLA, he insists. "We have now brought a lot of people who were outside the mainstream into the mainstream of America; and as difficult as the situation still is with regard to stresses and strains and potential confrontations and disruptions, it would have been far worse without it."

When I asked Young about the Murray-Custred solution, a look of exasperation swept across his face. "Here we are in Los Angeles, the most ethnically diverse city in the history of the world. We have an obligation to try to help the community in which we live—not to say, 'Oh, well, all the good white folk get into the University of California and the good black and brown folk get into [lesser schools]."

As for the stigma of affirmative action, Young observed: "There is no one admitted to UCLA who doesn't meet the standards, and they are very high standards; no one who is not basically able to do the work, do it effectively, and to graduate with pride." Given that fact, he said, there is "no reason for people to be stigmatized. . . . They're not going to be given a gift degree." The stigma, Young concluded, is rooted not so much in reality as in the attitudes of those who "feel African Americans are inferior to whites."

At any rate, Young suggested, the alternative to affirmative action is not pleasant to contemplate: "We're going to have more black janitors, more black sales clerks, but you're not going to have more African American leaders, or Chicano-Latino leaders, and real contributors to our society unless they have a real opportunity for education."

Journalist and author Nicholas Lemann has unearthed an intriguing bit of support for Young's thesis. He tracked down one of the black students who took the medical school slot that might have gone to Bakke and discovered that Bakke's potential loss might have been society's gain. In a June 1995 article in the *New York Times Magazine,* Lemann reported that Patrick Chavis had established a booming practice in the poor, predominantly black and Latino city of Compton, California.

In accepting Chavis, who grew up on welfare and is the oldest of five children, the University of California at Davis gambled and won. Though smart enough to do the work medical school required, he did not test as well as some whites who were turned down. Yet today he is a successful physician, delivering health care in an area that sorely needs it. While still in medical school, Chavis and some black classmates set up a clinic to serve poor residents and volunteered their services; they could not get their white classmates to help. Most of his fellow black classmates, Chavis told Lemann, continue to work for poor people. Many, including Chavis, would probably not have become doctors following the Bakke decision. "If Chavis hadn't gotten into medical school," Lemann pointedly observed, "patients wouldn't be treated by some better-qualified white obstetrician; they'd have no doctor at all and their babies would be delivered the way Chavis was—by whoever happened to be on duty at the emergency room of the county hospital." Chavis's career choice, Lemann noted, was not necessarily totally altruistic; he did not, after all, have precisely the same options as his white peers: "The idea that, as an obstetrician-gynecologist, he could build a practice on the west side of Los Angeles based on middle-class white women is a joke."

As for Bakke, his legal victory may have been his crowning achievement. "He does not appear to have set the world on fire as a doctor. He has no private practice and works on an interim basis, rather than as a staff physician, at Olmsted Community Hospital," reported Lemann. But that Bakke has not become a star is irrelevant to those who, like Van Alstyne, see affirmative action as simply a bad idea. Indeed, Van Alstyne argued that it was Bakke's less-than-stellar credentials that explained the medical school's willingness to sacrifice him. Bakke's interests were given short shrift by the school's faculty, he observed, because he was too poor a student to be anything like them. "If we should assume anything about that faculty . . . we might more safely assume that the faculty 'represented' not persons in Bakke's position at all but only outstanding students, persons who do especially well in academic life, who do equally well through medical school, and who are thus sufficiently outstanding to have been granted academic appointments in a great university," Van Alstyne wrote.

His point was that Bakke's political interests were not protected by the school, since he never was given consideration by people remotely like himself. But Van Alstyne also underscored an important reality: that the frontline battles of academic affirmative action do not pit highly accomplished whites against incompetent or unaccomplished minorities. They more typically pit groups of people against each other who, though apparently competent enough, are something less than sure bets. The whites who are the most affected are those who, *even were it not for affirmative action*, would be borderline choices by the educational institutions they are trying to enter, and the minorities, though generally somewhat less well academically prepared than the whites, are not all that far behind.

That issue came to the fore with a vengeance during the Hopwood trial, when Samuel Issacharoff, a University of Texas lawyer arguing the case for the university, suggested that three of the four plaintiffs were less than exceptional students. (The fourth, as was noted, had won admission, but apparently too late to attend.) Issacharoff attributed Hopwood's high undergraduate grades to the fact that she had matriculated at easy institutions. He characterized the second plaintiff as the only one among 4,500 applicants to the law school who had flunked out of college. "He was in the beer-drinking major," scoffed Issacharoff. The third plaintiff, he said, had been unable to come up with strong letters of recommendation.

Issacharoff's point—though made from the opposite side of the debate—is essentially identical to Van Alstyne's: that white applicants who are bumped by academic affirmative action are not at the front of the achievement line. They are not the "race horses" who seem destined for greatness, who seem destined, in other words, to make a significant mark on society. Are they nonetheless more entitled than a somewhat less accomplished minority candidate to a cherished slot in the entering class of a prestigious university? It's impossible to answer that question with an unequivocal yes unless one assumes that the small differences in test scores reveal something extremely important, that whatever the tests measure (be it intelligence, aptitude, or ability) is pretty much fixed, and that a university's sole criterion for choosing among candidates should be past academic performance as opposed to, say, the candidates' hypothetical potential for making a noise in the world.

None of those assumptions can be accepted as gospel. An analysis by the NAACP Legal Defense and Educational Fund, for instance, found LSAT test scores to be a very poor predictor of how well black students performed at the University of Texas School of Law. Sophisticated educators have long understood that grades and test scores can tell them only so much. In his response to Murray's *New Republic* article, Bok made that clear. Admissions officers, he wrote, "do not feel that high scores on SATs and other standardized tests confer a moral entitlement to admission, since such tests are only modestly correlated with subsequent academic success and give no reliable indication of achievement in later life."

Also, as Lemann observed: "An education-based meritocracy makes its judgments about people before they've done anything, based on a measure, school performance, that depends heavily on who their parents are and what kind of environment they create. People tend to shy away from meritocracy in pure form, or at least to want to sand off its rough edges, because it doesn't seem genuinely to offer equal opportunity to everyone. No American institution of higher learning is willing to select solely on the basis of (as opposed to mainly on the basis of) merit as defined by grades and test scores."

Nor, for that matter, should major universities be interested only in candidates they know are certain to shine. Being accepted to a university, it's important to note, is fundamentally different from being hired by a firm. Most employers aren't in the business of taking big risks. They try to hire people they think can do the job. Universities also want (or should want) people who can do the work, but their institutional function is almost the opposite of that of profit-seeking businesses; it is not simply to add value to their enterprises, but to add value to the students. Their express purpose, in other words, is to help people improve themselves—not just to reward those who have already been well schooled.

The university is different from a private business in one other important respect. Its mission is not to make money, but to make a difference in the larger society. Universities are not just turning out interchangeable automatons, but individuals who will take different paths in the world. And unpleasant as it may be to acknowledge, race still plays a substantial role in what one does with one's life.

A 1996 study by researchers at the University of California, San Francisco (UCSF), found that Chavis and Bakke were, in a sense, characteristic of black and white physicians. Minority physicians were much more likely than whites to serve other minorities. They were also more likely to serve poor communities and uninsured patients, whereas white physicians seemed reluctant to work even in relatively affluent nonwhite areas. Thus, 52 percent of the patients of black physicians in California were black, 54 percent of the patients of Latino physicians were Latino, but only 9 percent of the patients of nonblack physicians were black, and only 20 percent of the patients of non-Latino physicians were Latino. In short, the physician's race was, by far, the single most significant predictor of the racial mix of his or her patients.

"What was most striking is that we found there were fewer physicians available in affluent minority communities than in poor, nonminority communities. So what determines the number of available physicians in a community is race and ethnicity, not income levels," said Kevin Grumbach, an assistant professor of family and community medicine at UCSF, who was one of the authors of the report, published in the May 16, 1996, issue of the *New England Journal of Medicine*. The article concluded:

> Black and Hispanic physicians locate their practices in areas with higher proportions of residents from underserved minority groups. In addition, they care for higher proportions of patients of their own race or ethnic group and patients who are uninsured or are covered by Medicaid. . . . The fact that the physician's race or ethnic group predicted whether he or she would care for greater-than-average

> numbers of black or Hispanic patients, while the ranking of the medical school was not predictive, suggests that differences in practice locations . . . are at least in part reflective of the . . . physicians' decisions to practice in areas with higher proportions of members of their own race or ethnic group.

Miriam Komaromy, assistant professor of medicine at UCSF and the study's principal author, saw the statistics as a strong argument for affirmative action. "Minority physicians, particularly black and Hispanic, serve minority populations to a greater degree than white physicians in the same communities," she said. "So training members of minority groups for medical careers is going to be extremely important to get care to underserved populations." Komaromy conjectured that changes that "result in a decrease in the number of physicians from minority groups are also likely to result in poorer access to health care and may ultimately result in reduced health and well-being for a substantial portion of the population." She concluded, in effect, that refusing to take race into account when selecting those to be trained as physicians could quite literally result in the loss of lives.

Shortly after he attended the thirty-year reunion of his Amherst class, Hugh Price, president of the National Urban League, reflected on the fact that many of his classmates, despite their stellar education, were "not raising any Cain professionally. They're not the top professionals." He wondered aloud about the function of a great university. Is the mission "to pick the students who are going to do the best in the freshman class?" he asked. "Or is the mission to try to make a variety of judgments about who's likely to be at the top positions thirty years out?" If the University of California at Berkeley, for instance, accepted only those with the top grades and test scores, "you're not going to get the people you would be proudest of thirty years later. You'll get some of them doing it that way," he acknowledged, but such a process would ignore the qualities of grit and determination that make people into world-class successes.

Neil Rudenstine, Harvard's current president, made the same argument in his president's report, reprinted as a cover feature of the April 1996 edition of *Harvard Magazine*. Standardized tests, he conceded, are somewhat useful in predicting students' performance for the first year or two, but they are far from perfect measures. For one thing, the ability to do well on such tests is correlated with a variety of factors other than merit, including the ability to pay for test-preparation courses or attending a superior high school. And there is so much the test cannot measure—judgment, decisiveness, creativity—that are essential in the world.

Grades are even a less perfect measure. In addition to the problems of grade inflation and disparate standards, there are huge differences in the courses offered. As Patrick Hayashi, associate vice chancellor for admissions and enrollment at Berkeley pointed out, students get extra points on their averages for taking advance placement courses and honors courses, "but those courses aren't randomly distributed in high schools. There are far fewer . . . in the poorer high schools. So it's just logistically impossible, in some instances, for a student who's gone to a poorer high school to have the same grade point average as someone who's gone to a richer high school."

Several years ago, UCLA's law school had a system that relied almost exclusively on grades and test scores. "They turned away an awful lot of people here who ended up going to Harvard . . . because Harvard looked at the whole individual," said Chancellor Young. The law school scuttled the system because administrators were unhappy with the results. Those looking for a model of meritocracy, Young asserted, are seeking something that does not and cannot exist. "The University of California is a modified meritocracy. It comes about as close to being a meritocracy as you can come." In his mind, a so-called meritocracy that focused only on academic numbers would not only be "thoughtless" but "dullsville."

Carol Christ, vice chancellor and provost at Berkeley, reached the same conclusion. Even if the regents' resolution had not shaken things up, she thinks it was time for the university to rethink the way it was admitting students—and for reasons that had nothing to do with affirmative action. The heavy emphasis on grades and test scores that undergirded the Berkeley admission process, she said, was, in part, merely an efficiency measure. During the 1980s, when applications mushroomed, a professor came up with the numbers-based system as a way of "handling all these applications with minimal individual effort." Under that system, half the school's students were admitted purely on the basis of academic index scores—computed from high schools grades and SAT scores. The remainder were evaluated on the basis of several criteria, including essays, volunteer experience, academic awards, and "social diversity" characteristics—all mapped out along an "admission matrix." That process "has really stopped serving us very well," said Christ, who believes that it is time for the university to develop a system that would do a better job of sizing up the entire human being. Such a system could also counteract the drop in minority admissions that eliminating affirmative action measures would otherwise produce.

Even some of affirmative action's most vocal foes, however, aren't crazy about the idea of basing admission just on the numbers. "To do it strictly on test scores, I would object to that myself," says Custred. Instead, he suggested looking more closely at "promising students in the socioeconomic disadvantaged areas, taking into account that their grade point average is somewhat below the highest, and their SATs weren't that good."

The notion that socioeconomic status should replace race as a qualifier for special preferences has, in fact, become something of a staple among those who, for a variety of reasons, don't like the idea of focusing so much on race. Many believe that racism is simply no longer the barrier that it once was and that educational policymakers should recognize that fact. As Matt Belloni, the opinion editor of Berkeley's *Daily Cal,* put it: "The stereotypes that were true in the sixties, that if you were black you couldn't succeed in white society, those aren't necessarily as true anymore. It's whether you have enough money to compete."

In this age of expanding opportunities for minorities, the children of rich black physicians have become nearly as notorious as Cadillac-driving welfare queens were a few years back. As Patrick Baikauskas, an Illinois politician who proposed that race-based affirmative action in federal hiring should be replaced with a system that favors the poor, asked, "Why should the son of a wealthy black doctor get preference over a white coal miner's daughter?"

David Jayne, a legislator from Michigan who was sponsoring a measure to outlaw affirmative action programs in his state, asked a variant of the same question: "Why should a rich black kid whose parents are doctors from Birmingham get preferential treatment over a poor white kid born to a welfare mom from Mt. Clemens?"

Bernard Anderson, an assistant secretary of labor and a former professor of economics, argued that the push to eliminate race-based admissions criteria is predicated largely on a misperception—on the belief that "as a result of the widening opportunities available to black people in the 1960s, 1970s, and 1980s, we now have a large middle class that is no longer in need of any special consideration . . . and if you work harder to level the playing field in education, training, and other fields before someone applies to college, or before they apply for a job in a major corporation, that's the way to just sop up the remaining inequality." To Anderson, however, that assumption ignores the painful reality that the size of the group that "is still not on a level playing field" is huge.

Anderson is right. In truth, the sons and daughters of rich black physicians are a distinct minority of those benefiting from affirmative action, and they are at least as likely to be competing with the children of rich white physicians as with the children of poor coal miners from Appalachia or of white welfare recipients from Mt. Clemens. Yet, the basic point—that wealthy black children don't need affirmative action—is probably correct, and that problem theoretically could be solved by refusing to take race into account for families whose income is, say, more than $100,000 a year. Such a remedy, however, would exclude less than 2 percent of black households. The number excluded would shrink nearly to zero if wealth was determined on the basis of net worth, rather than income. Conventional wisdom notwithstanding, the reality is that whatever problems people have with affirmative action will not be solved simply by eliminating well-to-do blacks from consideration for academic preferences.

In fact, most currently popular proposals for economic-based affirmative action would remove racial points not just for rich minority students, but for all minority students. In an article published in *Current* in 1995, author Richard Kahlenberg noted that one consequence of race-based affirmative action had been a growing anger among poor and working-class whites. "On a political level, with a few notable exceptions, the history of the past twenty-five years is a history of white, working-class Robert Kennedy Democrats turning first into Wallace Democrats, then into Nixon and Reagan Democrats and ultimately into today's Angry White Males. Time and again, the white working class votes its race rather than its class, and Republicans win," he wrote.

A class-based approach, Kahlenberg argued, would reverse that trend. It would also be more morally defensible—not to mention more effective—in reaching those persons who truly need help. Determining who qualified, he maintains, would be relatively easy and could be done by looking at such things as parental income and net worth, the quality of the high school attended, family structure, and neighborhood influences. Kahlenberg acknowledged that few blacks and Latinos are likely to benefit under such a system partly because, as was noted earlier, even within the same economic class, whites and minorities perform differently on tests, but that is not so bad: "If the goal is to provide genuine equal opportunity, not equality of group result, and if we are satisfied that a meritocratic system which corrects for class inequality is the best possible approximation of that equality, then we have achieved our goal." Moreover, he suggested, a class-based approach would not leave beneficiaries with that awful stigma attached to race-based affirmative action. The stigma, he maintained, "is bound up with the question of whether an admissions criterion is accepted as legitimate. Students with good grades aren't seen as getting in 'just because they're smart.' And there appears to be a societal consensus . . . that kids from poor backgrounds deserve a leg up. Such a consensus has never existed for class-blind racial preferences." Kahlenberg suggested that to make things more equitable, universities should also eliminate "unjustified preferences," including those for the children of alumni.

In fact, as Kahlenberg acknowledged, a number of universities, including Berkeley, have long given special points to applicants who demonstrate some form of socioeconomic disadvantage. Still, Kahlenberg and others who focus on economic disadvantage are on to a critically important issue. It is obvious, for instance, that the massive financial shift over the past two decades from grants to loans in college financial aid has had a devastating impact on the poor—especially on the poor who are black. In an era of rapidly rising college costs, programs that provide poorer students access to a college education are essential. But to see such programs as the solution to the affirmative action controversy is naive at best.

If disproportionate numbers of black and Latino students end up being beneficiaries of economic affirmative action as opposed to race-based affirmative action, there is no reason to believe they will suffer any less stigma than they do at present because such programs would still be seen (much as welfare is now) as some sort of "minority" program. Moreover, it is doubtful that the kind of consensus that Kahlenberg theorized actually exists.

Sure, there is a general sense in society that poor people deserve a bit of help, but that does not mean, as Kahlenberg suggested, that rich alumni would be willing to give up the admissions preferences their own children enjoy to make way for poor students. To the contrary, the well-to-do are eagerly taking every advantage that money can buy. Not only are they sending their children to expensive prep schools and laying out cash for test-preparation courses, but many are engaging the services of pricey consultants to assist in the college applications process. As *The New York Times* reported on April 17, 1996, "For a fee of $1,000 to $2,500, a consultant will go to work on a ninth- or tenth-grader and suggest courses, tutors, summer programs and after-school activities to make the student a more attractive college applicant." Wealth generally brings with it a certain sense of entitlement and presumed privileges, including the prerogative to pull strings to get one's children into fancy schools. And I strongly doubt that the rich will give up such perquisites merely to mollify Kahlenberg.

If the movement for assistance to the poor was really as strong as Kahlenberg believes, the replacement of financial grants to the economically disadvantaged with (often unaffordable) loans would never have taken place. Moreover, the assumption that class should trump race in admissions decisions ignores an important reality: The poor, as a class, were never enslaved and never barred from receiving an education. The poor *were* discriminated against by fancy country clubs and realtors in fancy neighborhoods, and they still are. If the appetite for remedying that problem actually exists, I see no sign of it. Instead, America seems to be moving in the opposite direction: The gap between the rich and the poor is growing apace. As the *Wall Street Journal* reported in 1996, the heads of major American companies now receive more than two hundred times the pay and benefits of ordinary workers, which means that an already wide divide has become a colossal chasm—with the disparity having nearly quintupled since 1965. Moreover, speculated *Wall Street Journal* reporter Joann Lublin, the gap is almost certain to widen even further—thanks largely to "overly generous" corporate directors and to the practice of rewarding America's corporate chieftains (whose huge pay packages tower over those awarded CEOs in Europe and Japan) with huge chunks of stock. But if Kahlenberg is right, so much the better. Still, affirmative action was never meant to redistribute America's wealth and privileges among the poor (laudable though that goal may be). Rather, it was explicitly intended to deal with the problem—and the lingering effects—of discrimination.

Bob Laird, Berkeley's director of admissions, believes that the suggestion that race-based affirmative action should be replaced with socioeconomic preferences ignores "the way disadvantage actually operates in this country, that there is a compound disadvantage with race and socioeconomic status." And he points to the "growing body of literature which says even middle-income African-Americans . . . face a significant amount of disadvantage that is not equated simply by adjusting gross income figures."

In a review of Kahlenberg's book (*The Remedy*, which is an expanded version of his argument for class-based affirmative action), William Julius Wilson made a similar point: Race is a component of "disadvantage." And he raised the possibility that Kahlenberg's scheme might end up devastating the black middle class, that it would result

> in the systematic exclusion [from educational institutions] of many of those blacks from middle-class families who are still suffering the cumulative effects of race. This could create a situation in which, for example, African-Americans who are admitted to Harvard represent the bottom half of the socioeconomic continuum in the black commu-

nity, while those who are above the median are excluded, because they no longer fall within the affirmative-action pool. They are therefore left to compete with middle- and upper-income whites who are not burdened by the handicaps of race.

As the work of Claude Steele and others suggests, affluent blacks (excluding those in the multimillionaire category, who presumably have enough resources to overcome any barriers put in their way) do indeed face hurdles not generally encountered by middle-class whites. That so many Americans apparently wish to deny that fact does not make it any less of a reality. It does, however, explain why some people are so insistent on the use of nonracial strategies to deal with problems that are fundamentally racial in nature. If we Americans can sell ourselves on the idea that class trumps race—that the white coal miner's daughter is, in fact, more deserving (or, at least, more disadvantaged) than the son of a black postal worker, then we can also sell ourselves on the idea that the burdens of race are not really that heavy, that America has effectively evened the playing field and therefore has no special obligation to the minority groups—particularly the blacks—that it once mistreated (a long, long time ago). Although it is probably true that Americans, as a group, are no longer a racist people, it is not true that race no longer matters in America or that pretending that it does not will return us to a state of racial innocence—or even erase the stigma of race.

"My sense is that, given this society, there will always be a stigma attached to students of color whether there are preferences or not," observed Laird, Berkeley's director of admissions. "Something like eleven percent of the freshman class at Harvard comes in through some degree of preference extended to sons and daughters of alumni," he added, "but I never have the sense of the legacy student feeling, 'Oh, I don't really belong here,' or 'I haven't earned it.' The whole thing is, 'Hell I'm here, that's what counts.' And we see that also among other groups of students who have had preferences extended to them. There doesn't seem to be the burden. That's why I think it's so clearly tied to race."

Martín Sanchez-Jankowsi, outreach and faculty assistant for affirmative action at Berkeley, wondered whether a far-reaching and effective class-based program could even get off the ground. "The Constitution says nothing about discrimination on the basis of classes," he pointed out. "We pride ourselves on discrimination [based on] class. We think we're superior to people that didn't discriminate . . . on class. . . . Capitalism has won the day based on discrimination. The only thing the Constitution prohibits is essentially discrimination on the basis of race, creed or religion."

There is a big difference, obviously, in the way most people regard so-called racial preferences and the way they look at preferences extended to the children of alumni or to athletes or talented musicians. The rich kid and the athlete are considered to be valuable additions to the university. American society has never placed a great value on either poverty or minority racial status. It is unlikely that it is about to start; the welcome society extends to the children of poverty will never be quite as unconditional as that extended to the children of wealth—whatever their ethnicity.

Genaro Padilla, vice chancellor for undergraduate affairs at Berkeley, acknowledged that as a Latino originally brought in (among other reasons) to help diversify the English department faculty, he is a beneficiary of affirmative action. "I'm proud of that," he said. "I also understand that it carries with it a certain . . . assumption about whether or not I should have been at Berkeley." He is therefore particularly mindful of the potentially harmful effects of the affirmative action stigma, of the whispers that some of his Latino students hear in which their ability is questioned. Those students, he says, "carry the weight of that anxiety, that stigma, and it can be very damaging." He tries to talk to them and to tell them that he understands because he, for the past quarter of a century, has had to deal with those questions himself. And he makes sure his young charges understand that however they got into the university, affirmative action is not going to enable them to pass chemistry tests or, eventually, to receive tenure; they will do the work or will fail. He also believes, however, that it may be necessary for an entire generation to "carry that burden of doubt."

Over breakfast one morning, Eva Paterson, executive director of the Lawyers' Committee for Civil Rights in San Francisco, related an anecdote she had heard from California politician Willie Brown. Brown, a strong advocate of affirmative action, compared American history to a four hundred-year-old poker game in which one side always cheated. At some point, the cheating stopped, and one player had one chip and another had one million. Suddenly the player who had been cheating died, and his grandson took over and promised never to cheat again. "If you just keep playing poker, this person with one little chip is never going to catch up," reasoned Paterson, "unless some of those chips, which are ill-gotten gains, are given to the person who was cheated."

Paterson acknowledged that turning over those "chips" could create questions about the ability of the disadvantaged player, but she argued that there is no perfect way to deal with that dilemma: "Those who feel that they would be stigmatized," she says, can always say no. "But I assure you there will be plenty of people who will say, 'Thank-you, I will take the contract, that choice of law school, or that job or that promotion.'"

Certainly, the critics are right when they say that under certain circumstances, affirmative action advances minorities with less-than-sterling academic accomplishments at the expense of whites and, increasingly, Asians with weightier credentials. But as I pointed out in *The Rage of a Privileged Class*, that does not necessarily mean these minority students are unqualified, for

> determining what it means to be "qualified" is not as easy as it is often made to seem. Ted Miller, who was associate dean of admissions at Georgetown Law . . . , points out that many older white professors there—"if they were being honest"—would admit that they could not have met the standards exceeded by the school's typical black student of today. As the number of applicants to law schools escalated during the 1940s, notes Miller, schools turned to the LSAT as "an artificial means" to help them sift through applications. And as the numbers continued to increase, the minimum score needed to get into the more exclusive schools (the "qualified threshold") rose. Yet many of those who met the lower standards of the past nonetheless turned out to be distinguished lawyers. Obviously, they were not "unqualified," even if their test results would not win them admission to a prestigious law school today. By the same token, reasoned Miller, as long as the black students admitted were capable of doing the work, who was to say they were "unqualified"?

James Doherty, a white lawyer in Washington, D.C., made that point in a letter to the editor of the *Washington Post*. "When I was at Georgetown Law during the '50s there was a saying: 'Harvard is particular about whom it lets in, and Georgetown is particular about whom it lets out.' In my case, I surely would not have been admitted under today's standards," wrote Doherty, in joining a spirited debate over racially disparate admission standards at the Georgetown University Law Center.

Does the fact that white students years ago were not as well prepared as today's typical minority applicant make it all right to give minority students the edge over today's white students—who are much better prepared than were their predecessors in Doherty's day? Wood, the anti–affirmative action leader, said no. He argued that to do so would still be to make an unacceptable sacrifice "in terms of academic preparedness of the students."

People who are for affirmative action essentially argue that the choice is not between good and bad students but among various groups of good students, some of whom, admittedly, are better students than others, but all of whom are capable of doing respectable college work. Both sides agree that if Wood's proposals were followed, the ethnic makeup of certain universities would change drastically.

Chancellor Young estimated that at UCLA, the number of black and Mexican American students would drop—not to where it was in the pre–affirmative action days perhaps but dramatically nonetheless. The number of white students, he conjectured, might go up somewhat. And the number of Asian students would skyrocket—"especially if you do it on an economic basis." Already, Young noted, the school admits virtually every well-qualified economically disadvantaged black and Chicano student who applies. But that is not true of Asian Americans. "A lot of them . . . are being turned away."

That fact has not been lost on Asian Americans and, indeed, has fueled one of the more explosive controversies over affirmative action in selective schools. Some Asian Americans wonder whether they have become the Jews of the 1990s, whether they are being sacrificed, despite their academic accomplishments, for a political agenda that does not serve their best interests.

In San Francisco, a group of Chinese American parents filed a suit because a 1983 desegregation consent decree limited their number at a prestigious and selective public high school. As a result of the consent decree (which restricted the enrollment of students from any one race to 40 percent at so-called alternative schools), Lowell High School was rejecting Chinese applicants to admit whites, non-Chinese Asians, Latinos, and blacks who scored lower on a standardized test. Lee Cheng, a student at the Berkeley law school who is a Lowell graduate, found the situation at Lowell absurd. Cheng, whose parents immigrated to San Francisco from Taiwan in the 1960s, considers it a "great historical irony that Asians are being labeled as non-disadvantaged." It seems to him that "in most circumstances, Asians have been and still are one of the most despised and hated groups" in the country. Cheng was particularly offended by the situation at Lowell, where, he claimed, lawyers were getting rich monitoring a consent decree that discriminated against Chinese Americans.

Cheng's experience under the consent decree was one of the factors that led him to law school. "I'd always been told that under the law in America everybody is equal. . . . That concept made me feel better whenever I was beaten up because I was Chinese or called a 'Chink.'" Lowell undermined some of his faith and led him to oppose the affirmative action program at Berkeley. Before the regents demanded that the University of California schools eliminate all racial and ethnic considerations, he was working with a group of Berkeley students to file a suit against the law school. He and his associates had already lined up potential plaintiffs—Asian Americans who were denied admission to the law school—but dropped the plan for a suit after the regents' vote.

Cheng recalled a painful incident that occurred at a party following exams. A white classmate, emboldened by drink, approached him and said: "I'm kind of surprised you're so opposed to affirmative action. Isn't that how you got here?" Cheng was stunned, but tried to explain, patiently, that he got in on his merits. Still, the comment rankled, fueling his belief that affirmative action actually encourages negative stereotypes that harm competent people like him. Reflecting on that incident, Cheng observed: "Apparently, he [the white classmate] thought that all minorities benefited from affirmative action, that all minorities needed a boost up." In effect, the implicit understanding that *some* minorities need special help leads certain people to believe that *all* (or at least *most*) minorities are intellectually inadequate.

Not all Asian Americans, of course, feel as violated as does Cheng. Henry Der, former head of Chinese for Affirmative Action (a San Francisco-based nonprofit organization), believes that Cheng is seriously mistaken. He pointed out that 70 percent of all Lowell students are Asians—counting Japanese, Filipinos, Koreans, Vietnamese, and others. In an essay exploring the impact of affirmative action on Asians and Asian Americans, Der wrote: "The nine distinct racial classifications, provided for in the Consent Decree, have actually worked to the advantage of Asian students seeking access to Lowell, including ethnic Chinese from Southeast Asia who classify themselves as 'other non-whites.'" Der also disagreed with Cheng's assessment of the situation at the University of California. Even before the regents decided to end affirmative action, Asian Americans, he pointed out, made up more than one-third of all University of California undergraduates—more than double the proportion of Asian American students who graduated from California high schools.

Tse Ming Tam, acting director of Chinese for Affirmative Action, noted that well over 80 percent of Asian Americans who applied to the University of California in 1994 were admitted to a university in the system (though not necessarily to the school of their choice). That figure, he said, is comparable to the percentages for whites and Latinos and higher than the percentage for blacks. If affirmative action is harming Asians, he wondered why all of a sudden so many Asians are appearing on campuses and in the professions: "You're telling me these Asian Americans were nonexistent prior to the implementation of affirmative-action programs?"

The answer, in many cases, would be yes; as I discussed previously, the elimination of racial bias in immigration laws in 1965, coupled with a huge upswing in the number of Asian refugees, has resulted in a massive increase in the Asian American population over the past three decades. The children of many first-generation residents are just now appearing in America's universities and graduate schools. Tam's larger point, however, that Asians have a history of discrimination in America, is irrefutable. The very fact that the immigration of Asians was effectively prohibited for much of this century is evidence of that discrimination. But how relevant is that past to today's reality?

Chang-Lin Tien, chancellor of the University of California at Berkeley, believes that some of it is quite relevant, in part, because it shows how far the country has come. "People forget how much progress [America has made]," he reminded me.

Tien's own introduction to America is unforgettable. Born in China and educated in Shanghai and Taiwan, he came to Louisville, Kentucky, in 1956 to study at the University of Louisville, where lunch counters, drinking fountains, and other public accommodations were still strictly segregated. His views were shaped by that experience in substantial measure, Tien said. "Today, I can still recall my shock when I first boarded a city bus and found that whites rode in the front and 'coloreds' rode in the rear. Just where exactly did an Asian fit in? I too have a skin color but I am not black. And if I chose the front section, what kind of statement was I making about the black men, women and children relegated to the rear?" Tien wrote in an essay published in 1995.

Such experiences made Tien into a supporter of affirmative action. Still, he personally knows what it feels like to be touched by the affirmative action onus. When he was appointed chancellor in 1990 (the only Asian American to head a leading U.S. university), "some people said, 'Oh you became chancellor because you are Asian-American. They need a token representation.' That's very hurtful," recalled Tien. He vowed to hold minority faculty to high standards so they would not have to bear the stain of having gotten ahead only because of their race. In fact, one of his first acts as chancellor was to review the materials of an Asian woman who was up for tenure. In the process, he became convinced that she was not well qualified and refused to approve her promotion. He told Asian American students, "If I approve [the appointment], I'm hurting all of you because I'm setting a second standard for you."

Yet, Tien also believes that prejudice would be widespread regardless of how qualified minority candidates may be. He has seen companies with countless Asian engineers, but only a handful, he noted, "reach a high level. . . . Even me myself right now, I'm still experiencing [prejudice] as chancellor." Society, he added, has not yet reached a state at which people can see each other without taking "race, or origin or color" into account.

Tien is struggling with the question of how best to balance the competing claims for equity. On the one hand, he sees "a society with a lot of hidden, or glass ceilings, or even very blatant [discriminatory] practices." On the other hand, he is acutely sensitive to the charge of reverse discrimination. He is all for fairness, but wonders what fairness is: "It's not a simple issue. What is good for the society overall?" He hears people demanding that the university admit solely on the numbers but observed, "No university admits entirely based on academic scores." Also, because he presides over a public university funded by taxpayer dollars, Tien and other heads of state institutions must strive to serve the educational needs of their respective fiscal communities. Must they presume, as Judge Jerry Smith submitted that they should, that the world is totally color-blind—and therefore judge a Bakke and a Chavis by precisely the same nonracial criteria? Must they pretend, in other words, that a doctor is a doctor and a lawyer is a lawyer and that it is therefore a matter of indifference whether color-blind admissions policies result in a scarcity of black and brown professionals? Or must they acknowledge, as Chancellor Young suggested, that, for the most part, white physicians have no interest in poor black communities and that color blindness will be a fiction as long as blacks are trained to be laborers and whites are trained to be corporate chieftains? Can a university afford to be color blind when society is full of people who, as Tien pointed out, refuse to stop taking race into account?

That Tien has found no easy answers is not surprising. He is struggling with one of the most Byzantine—not to mention sensitive—issues of the current age, and one made all the more difficult by the fact that there is no conceivable solution that will not leave some group feeling resentful and betrayed.

In March 1996, the *Los Angeles Times* ran a front-page story razzing California regents and other state officials who claimed to be in favor of abolishing university admissions "preferences." Despite their opposition to affirmative action for women and minorities, several regents, reported the *Times*, "privately used their influence to try to get their relatives, friends and children of business partners into UCLA, in some cases ahead of better qualified applicants who were turned away." The *Times* noted that one regent, who claimed to favor a "merit-based admissions policy," arranged for the daughter of a local builder to be admitted even though she had previously been rejected because of her mediocre academic record. "Meanwhile, the school turned thumbs down on more than 500 other students who . . . had better grades, SAT scores and [had taken more] honor classes" than the builder's daughter. Over the past decade and a half, the *Times* revealed, hundreds of requests from powerful public officials seeking special treatment had poured in through the university's back channel. Following the revelations, the *Times* tartly editorialized: "It's astounding that any regent wailing about the so-called unfairness of 'preferences' based on race or gender could then turn around and unabashedly work behind the scenes to promote the preferences of power, position and who-you-know. The undeniable message from those regents: Preferences are fine—as long as they benefit people like me."

There are any number of reasons why California's regents may be more comfortable with a system that rewards friendship, wealth, and connections than with one that awards "preferences" for race, but none of those reasons adds up to an argument for merit or even fairness. Whatever else the regents' behavior may show, it plainly demonstrates that some people who claim to favor a purely by-the-numbers meritocracy are either lying or deluding themselves. In other words, even if a fail-safe system could be devised that would unerringly cull out "deserving" candidates from those who are not, a huge number of those self-righteous souls who theoretically abhor favoritism would reject it; otherwise far too many people—including those who are white, well connected, and affluent—would miss opportunities to which they believe themselves entitled. One could argue that the need to eliminate favoritism for the rich and powerful is all the more reason to admit students strictly by the numbers. And that would certainly be true if one was fully confident that the numbers captured all the qualities that are considered important.

However, as I noted earlier, people who are involved in the university admissions process are notably lacking in such confidence.

They have seen too many cases in which people who don't look terribly good on paper end up blossoming in the right environment. They also realize that the function of a university—especially of a great university—is not merely to educate those who do best on tests; it is also to nurture talent that has not yet been realized, to develop potential that doesn't come wrapped in the traditional package.

Clearly, it would be better for all concerned if educational inadequacies were corrected before anyone applied for admission to college; it would be better, as well, if the United States was not so racially fissured. It would be great, in other words, if a Bakke was just as likely as a Chavis to end up serving a poor black and Latino population in Compton or East Harlem or if, for that matter, there weren't so many poor minority neighborhoods in the first place. But such, unfortunately, is not the case.

There is a certain logic to the Murray-Custred argument that the majority of blacks who are now at Harvard and Yale should go to No Name U and that those in strong state universities should go to community colleges, for it would perhaps solve what they perceive as a mismatch problem. If where one went to school was a matter of complete indifference, that might be fine. But if that was the case, well-to-do parents would not fight so hard to get their children into first-rank institutions. Harvard's dean of admissions made the point when he told a reporter for the *New York Times*: "We are in the business of choosing leaders for the next century." Obviously, where one goes to school matters—perhaps not as much as whether one goes, but to a considerable degree—not only for what one learns, but for the contacts one makes and the networks one joins. They are networks that, as anyone who goes to an elite school knows, can give one a huge head start in life.

Even historically black colleges, which presumably could benefit the most from access to a larger pool of attractive candidates who can't get into prestigious predominantly white universities, are not necessarily happy to see affirmative action programs abolished. Norman Francis, president of Xavier, worries that if major institutions disinvest in black Americans, "we will never then create the pool of professionals, either Ph.D.s or others" that the black community sorely needs. Black colleges and universities, he fears, "are going to carry the burden, just as we did after the Civil War—and even before the Civil War—for freed slaves. We *will* carry that burden, but the impact of what we will do will never be brought to the level that we [black Americans] need." Other black college administrators fear that the new environment may, in the end, even make it difficult for them to shoulder the burden of educating blacks—especially if the courts insist that they adhere to color-blind principles that would make it impossible for them to keep their institutions predominantly black.

Balancing the needs of those who have been disadvantaged against those who feel entitled is never an easy proposition. Reflecting on the situation in South Africa, whose racial disparities make those of the United States look tiny, observed Ramphele, vice chancellor of the University of Cape Town: "There are limits to the extent to which one can correct past wrongs. For example, those excluded from educational opportunities in the last five decades cannot hope to be placed in the same position they would otherwise have been in, nor can much be done about those educationally disadvantaged over the last decade or two beyond remedial education. One may have to make peace with the past. Acceptance of the cruel reality of the legacy of disadvantage is a challenge which political leaders have to face up to instead of creating unrealistic expectations among ordinary people."

Ramphele's point is well made and well taken. Yet as Xavier, Georgia Tech, and other universities have demonstrated, educationally disadvantaged is not the same as educationally hopeless. Even when they start from behind, people can often live up to any reasonable expectations with which they are confronted if they are given the proper environment. The job of any university—particularly of a public university—is to help students discover what they are made of and to challenge them to fulfill their promise, even if that promise is not readily apparent. A great university, in other words, does not just take sure bets; it does not simply process people who are already on a gilded path; it also takes risks.

On March 5, 1995, the *New York Times* dropped the following nugget of information into an article exploring the issue of affirmative action in higher education: "[A] study of three classes of Harvard alumni over three decades found a high correlation between 'success'—defined by income, community involvement and professional satisfaction—and two criteria that might not ordinarily be associated with Harvard freshmen: low S.A.T. scores and a blue-collar background." (Unfortunately, Harvard's admissions office, after repeated calls, refused to release any more detailed information on the study to my researcher.)

It does not take a Harvard study, however, to recognize that the point made by Hugh Price, of the Urban League, is right: Picking people merely by test scores and grades is not going to identify all those who would make you proud. Carol Christ said that Berkeley understands that fact and, therefore, even as the university eliminates a system of race-based advantages, it is endeavoring to come up with a "holistic" approach.

Certainly, such an approach could easily end up being nothing more than an exercise in racially obsessed subjectivity—affirmative action under another name. As Cheng, the student at Berkeley law school, pointed out: "It's not hard to fudge around with subjective factors." Yet the reality is that until some perfect measuring instruments come along, it would be irresponsible for human beings not to try to exercise real-world judgment in making decisions about potential and merit.

The Fourteenth Amendment does not say, or even imply, that universities should admit students only on the basis of a mechanistic system that fails to acknowledge the existence of racial disadvantage. It doesn't say that college administrators must close their eyes to the fact that growing up in a black urban slum is different (and, in virtually every respect, more dangerous) than growing up in most white blue-collar suburbs. It doesn't mandate that medical schools should train physicians with no interest in poor minority communities or that schools of public affairs should educate civil servants who don't speak the language or care about the troubles of those they would presume to serve. It doesn't prohibit institutions, including those of the state, from trying to look at each applicant as a human being and from trying to judge how much that person has overcome and how far he or she is capable of going.

A system that intelligently tried to take the totality of one's experiences into account and to select and nurture those who are truly most deserving would not eliminate questions of race from the admissions process, for race is a fact of life and, for some people, a component of the barriers they have had to overcome. It would, however, mean that race is not inappropriately taken into consideration, that Latino or black is not, ipso facto, taken as a surrogate for deprived.

Would such a system differ in practice from affirmative action as it is now implemented in many colleges? Certainly, it should because it would require most institutions to look a lot harder than they do now at the people behind the application packets. Can universities do so effectively? Not without spending a lot more time investigating those who apply. Not without giving up some of the false security of numbers—SAT scores and grade-point averages—for the acknowledged uncertainty of human judgment. Not without devoting more resources and more thought to admissions than is currently the norm and not without doing (in the manner of Xavier University) everything possible to see to it that people, once admitted, realize their potential.

It's understandable, given all the philosophical, constitutional, and even moral problems with affirmative action, that any number of people would prefer simply to see it (and anything reminiscent of it) disappear. As is true of any lesser evil, affirmative action is not a beautiful thing to gaze upon, and, to make matters worse, it reminds us of some unpleasant and ugly things about ourselves. Nonetheless, as Americans contemplate throwing out much of what has gone under the name of affirmative action, we must also seriously contemplate whether we are prepared to pay the long-term price of replacing a bad system with one that—in insisting that we blind ourselves to American racial reality—is incalculably worse.

CHAPTER 6

Does affirmative action have a future?

Divisive as affirmative action is in universities, it can be positively galling in the workplace. Money, power, and status are at stake; insecurities and rumors abound. In such a volatile environment, the very suspicion that racial favoritism is being practiced (and thus standards are being compromised) is often enough to ignite sparks—all the more so when those suspicions are vented in the pages of a national magazine.

In autumn 1995, the *New Republic* made the *Washington Post* Exhibit A in a spirited inquiry into the problem of affirmative action gone awry. The famous *Washington Post* nameplate leaped out of the cover in letters nearly as large as the magazine's. The synopsis on the contents page was intriguing: "Twenty years ago, *The Washington Post* was lily-white and disconnected from the majority of the city it covers. Today, after an energetic diversity campaign, black staffers are bitter, coverage of race issues is regularly neutered and white staffers are lashing back with a vengeance. A case study in affirmative action." (In the interest of full disclosure, *Newsweek*, for which I am a contributing editor, is owned by the Washington Post Company.)

The piece was written by Ruth Shalit, a Princeton graduate in her mid-twenties with a quickly growing reputation for intelligence, pugnacity, and journalistic style—qualities that had helped her to thrive and stand out in Washington's mass media shark tank. Shalit also, unfortunately for her, had a habit of professional irresponsibility, having committed plagiarism at least twice in an extremely public fashion with nothing but carelessness as an excuse.

Shalit's piece was exhaustive and provocative: a thirteen-page lightly illustrated treatise that the *Post* staff generally found about as pleasant as a midnight mugging. The "growing backlash against affirmative action" was the focus of the sprawling article that aimed to diagnose the malady not only at the *Post,* but in the newspaper industry—and American society—writ large. During the past decade, Shalit noted, the newspaper business had been on a binge of "preferential minority hiring." So even though many newspapers across the country were cutting back on staff, the number of minorities the *Post* employed was growing explosively—and perhaps indiscriminately—for the *Post* was becoming darker quicker than just about any other newspaper. Over the past several years, the percentage of minority news professionals at the prestigious newspaper had increased to roughly 18 percent. And though the *Post* clearly was well meaning in hiring them, those good intentions seemed to have led the newspaper astray. In Shalit's opinion, the *Post* had become editorially spineless in its coverage of minorities, often leaning over backwards to avoid giving offense. It had also become institutionally polarized—riven with a "sort of post–affirmative action racism"—that resulted in white and minority reporters and editors seeing each other in the worst and most insulting light.

Shalit quoted columnist Richard Harwood bemoaning the fact that as a result of the fixation on racial preferences, the newspaper no longer sought journalists who were simply "the best." The *Post,* as seen through Shalit's eyes, had become a place where white journalists felt angry and threatened, suffocating under the dictates of corporate diversity. When they were not making nasty anonymous comments about their black colleagues ("She can't write a lick"; "he's dumb as a post"), they were grousing about a system of coverage that endlessly glorified black families in a "hacky sentimental" way. Black staffers fared no better. They felt underappreciated and perennially frustrated and were convinced that the newspaper was blocking their careers. Moreover, whatever their color, when the subtext was race, *Post* reporters felt called on to produce banal pabulum—"blandly upbeat to the point of sycophancy"—particularly when covering the city's mayor.

The management, blithely out of touch, was peopled with characters plucked from the annals of some fantastical, loony cartoon. All the managers were apparently brainwashed and hopelessly steeped in the dogmas of diversity and affirmative action. Instead of putting out a respectable newspaper, they passed their working hours in noisy adoration of the gods of proportional representation. Deputy managing editor and diversity czar Michael Getler, reported Shalit, "now spends his days patrolling the newsroom, blasting stereotypes and preaching inclusion." Meanwhile, Jeanne Fox-Alston, director of hiring and recruitment, a schoolmarmish type complete with a gray topknot, sat astride a burgeoning bureaucracy busily winnowing out white men.

The *Post,* in Shalit's eyes, was not only practicing poor management and poorer journalism, it was perhaps even breaking the law. By slavishly attempting "to reproduce in its building the precise ethnic makeup of its community" (a goal the *Post* management denied), the newspaper was engaging in a practice that was "arguably illegal." And even if the *Post* was doing nothing criminal, it was certainly betraying its journalistic mission. "A newspaper's mandate—to be an arbiter of truth, an enemy of euphemism, a check on social complacency—is directly at odds with the ideology of diversity management, with its ethos of sensitivity and conflict avoidance at all costs," wrote Shalit.

As she wound down, Shalit made a pointed observation and raised a good, and vital, question: "After encountering the racial strife at *The Washington Post,* it's tempting to despair that major American institutions will ever achieve both racial integration and racial harmony. If the *Post,* which tries so hard and means so well, is failing so dramatically to achieve its goals, what hope is there for the rest of us?" Maybe it would be better, she suggested, if instead of urging people to focus on their resentments, the *Post* simply encouraged them to do their jobs. It was a call for (if not exactly benign neglect) a kind of benign indifference—to worries about diversity and to the people the newspaper covers—as the road back to virtue and objectivity.

The article hit the *Post* newsroom with the impact of a torpedo, setting off cries of anguish, anger, and betrayal—much of it duly chronicled in the pages of the *Post*. Howard Kurtz, the *Post* media writer, reported that the essay provoked two black *Post* reporters to distribute a memo assailing "gutless colleagues" who chose anonymously "to disparage black staffers and the newspaper's effort to diversify." "Before the smoke cleared," Kurtz revealed, "Executive Editor Leonard Downie Jr. fired back with a blistering letter, accusing author Ruth Shalit of engaging in 'big lie propaganda' and 'racial McCarthyism.' He also called her piece 'amateurish,' 'false,' 'preposterous,' 'shameful' and 'maliciously hurtful.'"

Kurtz also reported that the *New Republic* employed no black staffers and that *Post* publisher Donald Graham had written to the magazine calling it "the last practitioner of de facto segregation since Mississippi changed." "Looking for a qualified black since 1914," was Graham's suggestion for a new *New Republic* motto. Kurtz duly noted Shalit's plagiarism problem as well: "Twice in the past year, the *New Republic* has acknowledged that she used material from other publications without attribution. Shalit blamed both instances on confusion involving computer processing and said she was 'very depressed and sick at heart' over the mistakes. This is, quite clearly, a sensitive subject," Kurtz dryly observed.

In a long letter to the *New Republic*, Graham and Downie reaffirmed their commitment to diversify the *Post* staff and denied they had a goal to mirror the area's ethnic makeup precisely: "Our stated goal for many years has been to try to have our new hires be 50 percent women and 25 percent minorities, consistent with filling every vacancy with the best-qualified person possible. This has never meant turning away any journalist because he was a white man nor lowering our standards to hire any woman or minority journalist."

Letters went out from a battalion of other *Post* people, many focusing on mistakes in the *New Republic* piece, both petty and large. Getler noted that Shalit had misreported the month of their interview. Fox-Alston pointed out, among other things, "I do not have gray hair and have never, ever, worn my hair in a topknot." James Ragland, a black former reporter for the *Post*, complained that Shalit had misrepresented his reasons for leaving and bitterly added, "She propped all of us up as cardboard figures without sufficient portfolio, and then dismissed us collectively as wayward offspring of affirmative action."

Warren Brown, the *Post's* automotive writer, lambasted Shalit for having a poor sense of history: "You've obviously never read a 'prediversity' newspaper. I did. I grew up in segregated New Orleans reading the now-defunct New Orleans *States-Item* and the still published *Times-Picayune*. Even as a kid, I knew what was going on in those newspapers: Black criminals were clearly identified by race. If there was no racial identification, that meant the perpetrator of the crime was white. Black people never got married, according to those newspapers. . . . Black people never did anything well, except maybe sing and dance. White people were pretty damned near perfect. But, I suppose you call that kind of journalism 'truth.'"

Not content to confine their responses to the mails, several *Post* writers addressed the controversy in the pages of the newspaper. Columnist Donna Britt accused Shalit ("who in her article took quotes out of context, who failed to use statements she got from whites that refuted her premise, whose multitude of inaccuracies extends even to physical descriptions, who reported false rumor as fact without checking with all involved and who twice in her short career 'accidentally' plagiarized other writers' work") of being "exactly the type of marginal reporter she accuses certain minority journalists of being."

Richard Cohen also responded in his column, not to attack the *New Republic* piece but to agree, in prose less polemical than Shalit's, with one of her key points. To a white man, wrote Cohen, "a message has been sent. He feels himself operating under a quota system, and no amount of assurance that goals are not quotas is going to ameliorate the emotional impact. Somehow, a goal feels like a quota, and a quota feels unfair. The *Post* insists its standards have not been lowered. Okay. But for white males, a barrier appears to have been raised."

Shalit herself seemed astonished at the viciousness of the *Post's* counterattack. In a lengthy interview in the December 1995 issue of the *America Journalism Review*, she came across as someone who was more than a little battle weary, but far from apologetic. Reporting the piece, she said, had been difficult because people feared retribution from the *Post*: "It was wild. It was like doing a piece on the CIA. I had reporters calling me from phone booths. I met reporters in cafes in Arlington [Virginia]. This was something that people wanted to talk about, but they were afraid."

She attributed many of the charges of inaccuracy to fear generated by the *Post's* executives: "After the piece was published he [Downie] called a meeting of 400 staffers in which he denounced me personally and said nothing in the piece was true and invited staffers to give testimonials to racial harmony. In that climate it's understandable, although unfortunate, that reporters would feel compelled to distance themselves from quotes that were accurately reported and offered in context."

Shalit acknowledged that she had made some factual errors in the article, but made it clear that she had learned her lesson (at least when it came to reporting on fellow journalists): "What this has taught me is that whenever you go after journalists, especially one of the biggest, most powerful media institutions in the country, you've got to make sure your piece is triple riveted and that you've gone over every line, and you don't give them any weapons to use against you because they will."

When I visited the *Post* in January 1996, emotions were still a bit raw. Some of the people to whom Shalit had talked felt terribly ill-used. "I mean she almost committed a felony in terms of the amount of mistakes in that article for someone who had such extraordinary access here," groused Getler. His frustration with Shalit was palpable. "It just pisses you off," he said at one point, "when somebody comes in and . . . takes five-year-old stuff, and doesn't see the new stuff, and doesn't understand that these are the toughest issues in America." Getler acknowledged that some racial resentments existed at the *Post*, but felt the problem was not nearly so bad as the *New Republic* piece alleged. "We have not had huge eruptions," he said, "except the ones caused by this article, which made many black reporters . . . think that their white colleagues were slurring them anonymously." He had tried, he said, to get people to talk frankly about the issue "especially in the aftermath of

The New Republic thing [but] it was very hard to get any whites to talk, because they felt if they talked . . . they would be liable to be tagged as racists."

Fox-Alston, director of recruiting and hiring, attributed some of the tension Shalit witnessed to simple misunderstandings. Whites are understandably upset when their white friends who apply for jobs at the *Post* "sometimes barely get the time of day" while minority candidates, often with less experience, get hired. "It doesn't matter that some of the minority reporters we're hiring tend to go into the [less prestigious] suburban jobs and many of the white reporters we're hiring may go directly to national staff, or into very high profile jobs on the metro staff." Another part of the problem, she said, was that the *Post* could only hire a fraction of those who applied: "We may hire fifteen, twenty reporters in a year in which we have a lot of turnover. . . . But we could hire fifteen or twenty reporters in a week's time based on the number of people who are interested in coming to work here. . . . So, we're turning down a lot of people. And I think even without the racial element involved, there would be a lot of disappointed people. . . . I think the racial element just turns up the heat."

Disappointment, of course, doesn't necessarily end when journalists actually make it to the *Post*. As Getler noted in a 1993 report on the newsroom, dissatisfaction inside the paper is easy to find. "To say many people are unhappy may be less accurate than [to say] many people simply are not very positive about their situations here," he tactfully observed. And yet, the *Post* is hardly unique; discontent is pervasive in big-city newspapers, as is grumbling about the trade-offs demanded by so-called diversity initiatives. How deep such resentments run is unclear, for the subject of race within newsrooms, as Getler noted, is more often mumbled about than openly engaged.

Foreign editor Eugene Robinson, who is black, confessed that had I asked him, before the Shalit affair, whether there was much resentment against blacks at the *Post* "I would have pretty unhesitatingly said, 'No,' because I didn't have that sense; and now I guess I say, 'I don't know.' Obviously there are some folks who have a problem, and for whom anybody black who has gotten a certain beat or gotten onto a certain staff, or risen to a certain level here is, in some sense . . . [the beneficiary] of some sort of favorable treatment. And I, to this day, like to believe that's not a widespread feeling among whites at the *Post*. But I don't know." He had been unsuccessful, Robinson acknowledged, in getting people to identify any minority staffer they thought had received special treatment. "So that makes me wonder if it isn't a more generalized feeling that in fact doesn't have a lot of body and substance when you talk about specific individuals."

Graham saw attitudes at the *Post* as a reflection of those in the larger society: "I would seriously doubt that there is any organization in the twentieth century in America . . . where you can walk around, talk to people, and not find people saying discrimination on the basis of race or sex are major factors."

Graham's perspective on race—and on much of life—is not necessarily what would be expected of a scion of one of America's preeminent newspaper families, but he opted, before he took his place at the head of the family business, to see the world from a less privileged vantage point. He was drafted in 1966 and shipped to Vietnam; subsequently, he spent over a year as a Washington, D.C., police officer. Those experiences gave him insight into workplace tensions—and the handling of racial issues—at institutions other than the Washington Post Company.

"I joined a D.C. police department that was eighteen percent black in a city that was seventy-two percent black in 1969," Graham recalled. "The riot [set off by the killing of Martin Luther King, Jr.] had taken place in 1968. The following year had seen a series of police-community incidents which had been triggered by police officers using weapons." The new police chief, Graham remembered, decided to be aggressive in recruiting minority officers: "I spent the following fourteen months riding around in scout cars with whites and blacks, and I heard a lot of bitching by whites about blacks and by blacks about whites." In those days, whenever some police officer was promoted or not promoted, race was likely to be blamed. "Were a lot of nasty words said in locker rooms?" Graham asked rhetorically. "Yes." But he believes that offensive comments would have been made even if no special recruitment effort had been undertaken. And he has no doubt that, on balance, the city was better off for having widened the pool of applicants.

"It is true . . . that this paper has looked, and looked hard, for talented minority journalists. We have searched harder for minority journalists than we have for whites. But had we not searched, our normal process of employment would not have turned up many minority journalists," concluded Graham. "I think this paper is hugely better for the presence of many talented minority journalists—many of whom are here because we went out of our way. It would be a better world if the processes by which we normally hire people turned up equal numbers of whites, blacks, Hispanics, Asians, and others, men and women, but up to now that has not been true."

Though the *New Republic* piece made Shalit a source of derision at the *Post*, the sense among many journalists outside the newspaper was that Shalit was on to something important, but that her extremely sloppy job of reporting made it hard to know just what to make of her observations. Reese Cleghorn, dean of the University of Maryland school of journalism and publisher of the *American Journalism Review,* summed up the feeling nicely in a column in the *Review*. Shalit's article, he wrote "included factual errors on a scale that normally would result in probation or dismissal of a writer at a good news organization." Nonetheless, he pointed out, the article performed—or at least set out to perform—an important service: "It explored, at length, a subject that is almost an official taboo in newsrooms that are seriously striving for diversity."

Did the *Post*'s striving cause it to go overboard, to sacrifice good journalism and become a cheerleader for black causes in the service of demographic engineering? Though it is true that the *Post* has made an obvious effort to increase its coverage of the lifestyles of black Washington, and has done some forgettable features on blacks, I see no evidence of a *Post* policy of sugarcoating sordidness in Washington's minority communities. Indeed, the *Post* ran Leon Dash's decidedly downbeat (though Pulitzer Prize–winning series) on the family and legacy of Rosa Lee: a black Washington grandmother and heroin addict, crippled by illiteracy, who taught her grandchildren to shoplift, turned her daughter into a prostitute, and worked off her daughter's drug debt by selling drugs herself. What the *Post* controversy does illustrate, however, is that journalists—the creed of objectivity notwithstanding—are no more comfortable dealing with racial conflict and certainly no more color blind than are other Americans. At the *Post,* as at other newspapers, the recruitment of blacks and other people of color has forced staffers to confront—or tiptoe around—their colleagues' racial anxieties. One black *Post* staff writer, for instance, told me she dreaded dealing with a certain white editor whenever she reported a racial controversy, for instead of simply editing the story, the editor would become defensive and generally ended up defending the whites who were portrayed in the story in an unflattering light. Not having spoken with the reporter's editor, I have no idea how that editor views their partnership, but it is clear that it is a relationship that is not relaxed when it comes to race.

Indeed, major metropolitan newspapers, as was noted earlier, are rife with racial tensions, and "diversity" efforts in newspapers—no less so than in other types of organizations—have set off resentments and resistance up and down the line. The big difference between journalistic institutions and others, however, is that journalists have the explicit task of exploring social tensions, even occasionally in their own places of employment. And in the past few years, as racial issues have exploded on the American scene yet again, they have also shaken and polarized newsrooms.

The 1992 Los Angeles riot touched off a spate of race-relations reporting, and in exploring the racial crisis in society, many of those newspapers discovered the magnitude of the problems within. The *Los Angeles Times,* for instance, was roiled by controversy when a black staffer charged, in the wake of the riot, that minority journalists had been bused in from outlying bureaus for use as "cannon fodder" during the chaos. A *Times* reporter, who was also president of the local chapter of the Asian-American Journalists Association, echoed the complaint: "[W]hen the riot spread and it became apparent that a number of white reporters could not gain access to the scene, minority reporters from the suburbs were shipped into the danger zone."

Ron LaBrecque, who wrote about the controversy for the journal *Spectrum,* thought that the minority journalists' complaints were not without foundation. Though many black reporters eventually got bylines in the paper, he observed, for the first few days of the disturbance "not a single black staffer, with one unplanned exception, wrote or edited any of the *Times'* dozens of stories, although blacks were dispatched to report from the scene." City Editor Leo Wolinsky heatedly rejected the charge that minority journalists were used as cannon fodder. "I hate to do this kind of racial countdown but this was necessary for a response," he told LaBrecque, detailing the deployment of forces on the scene: "On the first night there were ten whites, five blacks, one Asian-American and two Latinos. On the second night there were eight whites, four blacks, two Asian-Americans and three Latinos. On the third night there were nine whites, five blacks, two Asians and one Latino."

"I'm a little raw on this," Wolinsky added. "It's just an absolutely outrageous claim. Let me go a little further than that. It's a racist claim, that me, as a white person, that I decided that the lives of white people were more important than black people. I find that so disgusting, I find that so revolting, it almost makes me sick to my stomach."

The *Times* was not the only newspaper in which internal tremors were felt from the explosion on the streets in Los Angeles. The riot inspired the *Akron Beacon Journal* to produce a lengthy series on race—for which it won the Pulitzer Prize—and, in the process, to explore the tensions simmering in its newsroom. The final story in the series, drawing on comments made by staffers in focus groups, found a cauldron of frustration and resentment that the normally fearless journalists were reluctant to address. A white staff member explained, "If you say you don't think whites are being treated fairly, you run the risk of being branded a racist. I can't risk that." One black journalist characterized the internal inquiry as a painful process akin to "opening the door on . . . incest or what the priests in the Catholic Church have been doing for years." To the extent that the unusually guarded staffers were able to speak their minds, it was generally to voice complaints.

Many black journalists were convinced that news coverage was racially biased and that they were, by and large, excluded from power, for although the newspaper's publisher was black, most of the top positions in the newsroom were held by whites. Whites felt that blacks were preferred for jobs and promotions and that fearless, hard-hitting reporting was being weakened as the newspaper embraced "minority perspectives." One white staffer admitted he was "never more outraged in my life" than when reporters were told to ask people's race over the phone to ensure diversity in coverage. One black journalist, after listening to the gripes of whites, admitted, "I'm surprised to hear them saying they feel victimized, too."

In the process of putting together its series on race (prompted not by the Los Angeles riot but by former Ku Klux Klanner David Duke nearly winning the Louisiana gubernatorial contest), the New Orleans *Times-Picayune* discovered that its staff was no less divided. Tensions ran so high that an outside "diversity expert" was called in to help. Sig Gissler, an ex-newspaper editor and professor of journalism at Columbia University, who visited the newspaper, called the process "staff group therapy." In an article in the *Media Studies Journal,* Gissler described some of the anguish that process had produced: "Looking back, Keith Woods, a black journalist who pushed the project as city editor and now is a columnist and editorial writer, says he lost friends and suffered some of the deepest pain in his life in the process. While proud of the project, he says, 'As a human being, I don't want to do that again.'" Another editor confided to Gissler than the enterprise got off to a shaky start. When a black staff member suggested that the series touch on slavery, "White people in the room rolled their eyes and said, 'Jesus Christ, why do we have to talk about slavery? It happened 300 years ago.'"

Even newspapers that have not tackled huge race-relations projects have seen race become a source of internal discord. A white reporter and columnist for the *Burlington Free Press* in Vermont was fired in 1993 after complaints came in about his supposedly insensitive coverage of a race-relations forum. His supporters claimed that the journalist, Paul Teetor, was a victim of racially discriminatory policies, of a "quota-based system that the Gannett company relies on to measure the racial correctness of its editorial product." Teetor sued. Gannett settled in 1996.

Such controversies are unlikely to vanish any time soon. For affirmative action and so-called diversity initiatives, as Shalit suggested, have brought blacks and other minorities into journalism organizations in unprecedented numbers, and those organizations are still struggling to assimilate them. Few thoughtful people, however, believe that the old days—when newsrooms were as white as a Ku Klux Klan rally at midnight—were actually better. In those days, as the *Post*'s Warren Brown suggested, news about blacks wasn't sugarcoated; it just didn't exist. Nor was there much chance of racial conflict in the newsroom, since everyone was of the same race.

I got a clear insight into the attitudes that flourish in such environments some two decades ago—not in a newsroom, but in the New York offices of *Esquire* magazine. At the time, I was a young (maybe twenty-one or twenty-two years old) columnist-reporter for the *Chicago Sun-Times*. Though I had only been in the business a few years, I was acquiring something of a regional reputation. I had already won a few awards and had compiled what I thought was a reasonably good array of clippings. Many of the articles dealt with race, but many others focused on subjects ranging from politics to crime. I hoped to break into magazine writing by garnering a few freelance assignments from *Esquire*, so I had made an appointment with one of its editors.

At this point, I have no recollection of the name or title of the editor with whom I met. I do remember that he was a pleasant and rather gracious man and that he was sufficiently important to make me believe that he spoke for the publication. What he had to say was sobering. He wasn't sure, he confided, how many black readers *Esquire* had, but he was reasonably certain the number was not high. Since I had not inquired about his readership and, in fact, had not even given the matter much thought, the statement took me a bit by surprise. But it soon became clear where he was headed—and that was to the door to bid me adieu.

I had been a longtime reader of *Esquire*, and it had never previously occurred to me that I was not supposed to be, that it was not me whom *Esquire* had in mind as an audience—never mind as a contributor. I don't know whether the editor bothered to read my clippings, but then, the clips were somehow superfluous; the very fact that I had written them made them so. All the editor saw before him was a young black guy, and since *Esquire* was not in need of a young black guy, they were not in need of me. If they, perchance, did need a black perspective—and this certainly was not explicitly expressed, though I sensed it—why in the world would they take a chance on an unknown when big names like James Baldwin were around? I left that office in a state of controlled fury—not just because the editor had rejected me as a writer, but because he had been so busy focusing on my race that he was incapable of seeing *me* or my work.

For most of this century, white newspaper editors lived in the same world as that *Esquire* editor. It is a world in which blacks only occasionally surfaced—usually as harbingers of something awful—before blessedly vanishing from the scene. Some magazine editors live there still—as *New York* magazine periodically reminds me, generally when it publishes stories enumerating and honoring New Yorkers who are "the best."

One such edition—from March 20, 1995—has lain on my desk for months. "The Best Lawyers in New York," reads the cover line. Inside, a piece by Robin Pogrebin groups the New York bar into various categories—personal injury, corporate, criminal defense, civil rights, and so on—and provides a list and brief biographies of the lawyers who excel in each. Accompanying the piece are several individual photographs, along with a handsome group portrait of conservatively attired attorneys who, we are told, are simply "the best."

What struck me when I first read the article was that (as best as I could determine from the photos, bios, and names) all New York's leading lawyers are white. Women are sprinkled throughout the list, but blacks, Hispanics, and Asians apparently don't qualify. The writer's description of how the list was put together provides a good idea of why that is so.

"The lawyers in this article have been selected by a jury of their peers—a grand jury actually. Our method was to talk to more than 200 New York attorneys, asking them to recommend others in their practice areas. Inevitably, lawyers being lawyers, the process gets abused. Hidden agendas are pursued, and prejudices are indulged. Most obviously, white male lawyers—who clearly continue to dominate the field—tend to nominate other members of the club."

The paragraph annoyed me when I first read it—and it still does—partly because I see it as an excuse for the reporter not doing her homework, but also because it condones, even as it acknowledges, a system of selecting "the best" that excludes anyone who doesn't belong to a segregated club.

The writer, I'm sure, was more than competent according to the usual criteria. Yet I found the article, even as a light feature, woefully inadequate—even taking into account the fact that *New York* magazine targets a readership of New York elites (and would-be elites), who are therefore presumed to be predominantly white. Among other things, it is not credible. To imply that all the best lawyers in New York—including those in the civil rights and criminal fields—are white is simply inaccurate. If a black writer had been assigned to do a piece on, say, the "most beautiful" New Yorkers and returned with an article that featured only Hispanics and blacks, the editors would no doubt have noticed that something was askew. Pogrebin's editors apparently did not.

Are they bad people? I seriously doubt it. Are they often blind to people of achievement who are not white? I suspect so, just as the *Esquire* editor was blind to anything about me except the color of my skin. Does the fact that they—and their staff members—were apparently selected without regard to affirmative action make them more competent? Obviously not. A city magazine staff that ignores large parts of the city is not my idea of a staff brimming with competence or merit. Unfortunately, in a society as racially sick and segregated as ours, race and merit are sometimes intermingled entities. The *Los Angeles Times* first discovered that fact in 1965, when it attempted to cover the Watts riot without any black reporters and ended up deputizing a black advertising salesman who had never previously written a story. The salesman did an atrocious reporting job. Yet, as bad as his work was, it was infinitely better than that produced by experienced white journalists who did not dare to go into Watts and had no idea of why it was burning. Merit—not just in news reporting—is the ability to provide an organization with attributes, experiences, skills, even wisdom, that it would otherwise lack and that cannot always be found, to use Graham's words, through the "normal process of employment."

In the March 13, 1995, issue of *The Nation*, Katha Pollitt ruminated on what the normal process had produced at some of America's leading opinion journals as she made some broader observations about affirmative action. Many intellectuals had concluded, she observed, either that the civil rights movement had been so successful that affirmative action was unnecessary or that affirmative action is "a bureaucratic hindrance that fuels white resentment and condescends to deserving nonwhites."

Pollitt went on to say, "I'm not sure whether those who make these arguments are naive or devious. But in my little corner of the work world—liberal opinion magazines—nothing could be further from the truth. In the thirteen years I've been associated with *The Nation*, we've had exactly one nonwhite person (briefly) on our editorial staff of thirteen, despite considerable turnover. And we're not alone." *The Atlantic*, *Harper's*, the *New York Review of Books*, and the *Utne Reader*, she noted, had no nonwhites on staff. *The Progressive*, *Mother Jones*, and *In These Times* had one apiece. And the *New Republic* and the *New Yorker* were not doing much better, with two and three (or perhaps six "depending on how you define 'editorial' out of 100 plus"), respectively. Of the magazines she surveyed, only *Ms.* came off reasonably well, claiming three out of eleven minority staffers, including the editor-in-chief, Marcia Ann Gillespie, who is black.

Far from living "in the color-blind America of conservative fantasies," Pollitt concluded, most people—including liberal magazine journalists—live in segregated islands accessible, for the most part, only to people like themselves: "The workplace is white because the social world is white, and vice versa. Merit doesn't really come into it."

An executive from the business side of the magazine world made much the same point about the noneditorial departments of magazines in a 1993 article in *Folio*—a publication that targets managers of magazines. "In 1985," wrote Rodney English, "I asked an ad director at the company where I was a circulation director why there were no blacks or women on his staff. He told me that he didn't hire blacks or women because the decision-makers at ad agencies and corporations aren't comfortable dealing with blacks and/or women. Selling pages, he carefully explained to me, was not about numbers and demographics. Selling pages comes from that special relationship between the salesman and the client."

To the extent that executives see color more clearly than competence—and assume that minority staffers can only write for or sell to other members of minority groups—they are likely to defend their hiring decisions with what amounts to rationalizations for racial prejudice. Still, English saw signs that in the several years since he had the first conversation with the ad director, things might be changing—ever so slightly—for the better.

English noted that the ad director, since promoted to associate publisher, has apparently become more enlightened: "He has hired a number of women. He has yet, however, to hire any person of color." English went on to observe that through his work with a publishing program housed at Howard University, he "had the opportunity to talk to dozens of talented, angry and frustrated black and brown Americans who love magazines and their unique role in American society, yet who chafe and struggle in a work environment almost uniformly dominated by white Americans."

Even when it comes to selecting which models get portrayed on which magazine covers, prejudice is very much a player. When fashion model and writer Veronica Webb interviewed *Allure* editor-in-chief Linda Wells for *Essence* magazine, Wells explained that sales were lower when a non-white person was pictured. "Wells admits she feels 'irresponsible' for not being able to show a wider variety of images, but the objective of a cover is to appeal to the majority of the buying public," wrote Webb. "'I don't know how to change the magazine-buying habits of the consumer,' says Wells. 'We're in a situation right now where only four or five models sell. I could try to put out a greater number of covers with people of color, but sales are my report card, and I could lose my job if they failed to meet expectations.'"

A few years ago, during a visit to a big-city newspaper, I encountered an executive I had known for some time. He was interested in getting the publication to hire more journalists of color and solicited my advice on recruitment. I offered a few ideas, most of which seemed obvious to me, but he was clearly impressed, for they were things he apparently had not thought of on his own.

"Wouldn't it be great," he said, "if we could hire you to coordinate our minority hiring?"

I smiled and gently told him that the idea struck me as somewhat silly, that the editor-in-chief was responsible for hiring and that if he was talking about making me editor of the newspaper, that might be something worth talking about.

I'm not sure he got my point—which was that cordoning off someone and putting him in charge of minority hiring was likely to create as many problems as it solved. I was all for the newspaper hiring more minority journalists, but felt it needed to take place in a sensible way and that if the editor was unable to identify talented people of color, perhaps there was something wrong with the editor—something that would not be cured by simply bringing someone in to remind him that journalists came in more than one shade.

Some time after that, I had several long conversations with the publisher of another newspaper who was in the process of putting together his management team. He was interested, he said, in hiring some minority senior managers, so I gave him some names of people who might be likely candidates. Over the next several months, I watched as he put his team in place—a team, as it turned out, that was totally white. Only after he had largely assembled that group did he begin to have serious conversations with some of the nonwhites I had recommended.

To this day, I don't doubt the man's sincerity; he did want to hire some minority managers, and eventually he did so. But what was clear to me was that to him, minority recruitment apparently meant the recruitment of people who couldn't be trusted with the organization's most important jobs. His first priority was hiring people who could do the work—meaning whites—and only after that task was complete would he concern himself with the window dressing of diversity.

Over the years, I have learned that affirmative action in theory (however defined) and affirmative action in practice are two different things. In the real world it is much more than simply opening up an organization to people who traditionally have been excluded; it is attempting, usually through some contrived measures, to make organizations do what they don't do naturally—and it goes down about as easily as castor oil.

Shortly after I announced my resignation as editor of the editorial pages of the New York *Daily News*, I took one of my white staff members out to lunch. He told me he had enjoyed working with me and was sorry to see me go. Initially, he confided, he had cringed when he had heard that I was coming, for he had feared that I would be just another affirmative action executive, presumably incapable of doing the job competently. He admitted that he had been pleasantly surprised.

I was pleased but also saddened by his confession—pleased that he felt comfortable enough to tell me how he truly felt and saddened that the very fact that a person of color got a high-ranking job would lead him (as it had led so many before him) to question that person's credentials. Yet, having occasionally been the target of affirmative action recruiters, I am fully aware that (whatever they may say in public), they don't always pay as much attention to credentials as to color. Therefore, I understand clearly why even the ostensible beneficiaries of such recruitment tactics may find affirmative action, as practiced by major corporations, distasteful and even offensive.

A decade and a half ago, I received a call from an associate of an executive search firm who, after verbally tap dancing for several minutes, essentially asked whether I wished to be considered for a job as a corporate director of equal opportunity. At the time I was stunned, for it was clear to me that I had absolutely no credentials for (let alone interest in) the job. I was an expert neither on personnel or on equal-employment law; I was, however, black, which seemed to be the most important qualification. I laughed and told him I thought not—that I saw my career going in another direction. I nonetheless wondered just how serious the inquiry could be, since I seemed (to me, at least) so unsuited for the position.

Since then, I have received other calls from headhunters or representatives of search committees, sometimes pushing jobs that have seemed every bit as outlandish. At one point, a man called to discuss the presidency of a major foundation. I confessed I didn't understand why he was calling *me,* and he assured me that the client was extremely interested in having me apply for the job. The man's earnestness intrigued me enough that I sent him a résumé. I never heard from him again, which confirmed, in my mind at any rate, that his interest was anything but genuine. I imagined him sitting in his office with a long list of "minority candidates," from whom he would collect résumés and promptly bury them in a file, merely so that his clients would be able to say they had "considered" minorities. Indeed, when the foundation head was finally named (he was a white man with a long professional association with the foundation trustees), it was clear to me that the supposed search had been a sham. After one takes a few such calls, one realizes that the purpose is often defensibility ("Yes, we took a hard look at fifteen minority candidates, but none quite fit the bill") and that the supposed high-level position is merely bait to attract the interest of people who don't really have a shot—but in whom everyone must pretend they are interested because an affirmative-action program is in place.

Some time after publication of *The Rage of a Privileged Class*, the black employees of a large, international corporation invited me to talk about the findings in my book at one of their corporate-wide events. In talking with my hosts, I quickly discovered that they were not merely interested in my insights. They wanted me (in some delicate way) to send a message to the management.

They were frustrated because a corporate affirmative-action program, of which the management was extremely proud, was not doing them any good. Mid-level managers, it turned out, got diversity points for hiring or promoting minorities, but the corporation had defined minorities in such a way that everyone who was not a U.S.-born white man qualified. In other words, the managers got as much credit for transferring white men from Europe, Australia, and Canada as they did for promoting African Americans. And that is exactly what they were doing, according to the black employees, who wanted me to let the management know, in a nice and extremely subtle way, that such behavior was unacceptable.

I'm not sure what message the management ended up extracting from my speech, but I am sure that the frustrations those black employees felt are widespread in corporate America—and, indeed, in corporations outside America. In South Africa I often heard complaints from black professionals that were nearly identical to those of blacks in the United States.

Bonganjalo Goba, national director of the Institute for Multi-Party Democracy, noted that instead of being trusted with "really serious executive-level decisions," blacks in corporate South Africa were typically given "social responsibility portfolios," jobs in which their major responsibility was representing the company before various black and social service constituencies.

Sam Tsima, a human resources consultant to one of South Africa's largest banks and chairman of the Johannesburg branch of the Black Management Forum (a nonprofit association of professionals), had essentially the same grievance. Though blacks finally had won political power, he observed, "the corporate world belongs to the other side." Still, companies can no longer afford to have only white managers: "They've got to get blacks in and they have got to be seen to be doing it."

So corporations lured blacks with exorbitant perks and salaries and then parked them in "soft" jobs, so they could "parade the people on the outside and say, 'Yes we do have black people.'" Such practices, Tsima feared, could "automatically make affirmative action lose credibility." So the Black Management Forum continued to fight for "meaningful involvement" for blacks in the corporate world. But though often demeaning and not particularly satisfying, those dead-end yet well-paying jobs were difficult to resist, Tsima acknowledged: "At the end of the day, people need to survive."

Brigalia Bam, general secretary to the South African Council of Churches, was even more outspoken. The relatively small number of well-educated blacks were being used "for tokens in companies everywhere," she said. "And the anger and frustration, already it's growing, because some people accept these jobs, and they know that you're just a token. You have no power base. You are just there so that the company looks good." At the same time, she said, South African corporations were dealing with "serious hostility" from whites who felt threatened by the attention and positions that blacks were suddenly receiving.

Bam noted that she had been named to three huge corporate boards: "I know I am in those corporations because it's the right thing to do. . . . The in thing now is to get black women." But in many cases, she said, the corporations are unwilling to take their new board members seriously: "They suddenly bring you to a corporation and think you are going to be sitting there smiling and feeling good, because you are the chosen black."

In time South Africa presumably will learn how to incorporate blacks fully into its corporate sector; its demographics give it no choice. But after three decades of various kinds of affirmative-action activities, blacks and other minorities in the United States, where the demographics are somewhat less compelling, are still fighting for full integration into the mainstream business world.

The Federal Glass Ceiling Commission, a bipartisan body named by President George Bush and housed in the U.S. Department of Labor, concluded that the upper echelons of the business world are practically unreachable for persons of color. "Consider: 97% of the senior managers of Fortune 1000 industrial and Fortune 500 companies are white; 95 to 97% are male," said the 1995 study. It went on to report that few women and minorities are well positioned to move up: "The critical career path for senior management positions requires taking on responsibilities most directly related to the corporate bottom line. But the relatively few women and minorities found at the highest levels tend to be in staff positions, such as human resources, or research, or administration, rather than line positions such as marketing, sales, or production."

African Americans, concluded the commission (on the basis of focus groups it had convened), saw the glass ceiling as "virtually impenetrable." They felt that "their talent, education and experience are not valued in corporate America. At the same time, they feel they have no choice but to continue to fight against what they consider unfair and outright racist patterns in corporate advancement." Asian and Pacific Islanders felt "they are not being treated equally and they believe their superior educational achievements and high performance is not translated into access to senior decision making positions." Hispanics "believe that the glass ceiling is keeping them from moving beyond a certain level and they feel that they are always being watched and judged."

Of course, critics of affirmative action attribute many of those problems to affirmative action itself, to its tendency to make people think of themselves as separate groups, to its emphasis on numbers instead of qualifications, to its celebration of victimization instead of accomplishment—which they believe becomes a self-fulfilling prophecy. If you think of yourself as a victim, they say in effect, so will everyone else.

Anti–affirmative action advocate Erroll Smith, for instance, recalled meeting with the chairman of the Los Angeles branch of a Chinese-owned bank shortly after the 1992 riot in Los Angeles. The man told him he was interested in doing business with the black and Latino communities. "He said he saw the Hispanic community as a growing community, with a lot of potential, and they wanted to get a position there," said Smith. His main reason for wanting to do business with blacks, however, was to make sure he was in line with federal regulations and would not get into trouble with the law. Smith found that reason to be both shocking and telling: "He saw the Latino community as an opportunity, but he saw the black community as an obligation and a liability—the Los Angeles black community, the wealthiest, most affluent, perhaps most well-educated black community in the nation. Our best and brightest, he saw as a liability and an obligation." Smith blamed that attitude on blacks' demands for "preferences" and affirmative action, which he and other critics insist limit the respect given minorities who benefit from such policies.

In fact, Smith said, he objected in principle to any policy that depends on portraying blacks as helpless and disadvantaged, a policy that he saw as "marketing" folly: "In the marketplace people will generally accept you based on their perceptions of your competence, notwithstanding race." Despite that fact, Smith asserted, civil rights leaders had gone to extraordinary lengths to portray blacks as "poor, disadvantaged, helpless people." They had waged, perhaps unwittingly, what amounted to a massive public relations campaign against blacks. Consequently, "all around the world people look at us as poor and disadvantaged. . . . And people don't want to do business with losers. People want to do business with winners."

Some of Smith's logic escaped me. Latinos, after all, also benefit from affirmative action. (And the Los Angeles riot was as much a Latino riot as a black riot, though—and this may have been Smith's point—the picture presented to the public by much of the media led most Americans to believe otherwise.) Nonetheless, Smith was adamant in his insistence that affirmative action (at least in its most aggressive forms) contributes to the perception that blacks are damaged goods and that it was time that blacks outgrew it.

There are "too many affluent African Americans in this country to say that we're an oppressed people," he declared. "We have too little participation in entrepreneurship; too many of us standing [under] the glass ceilings of corporate America complaining about the fact that somebody won't let us be captains of their ship." The solution, Smith believes, is for more blacks to become captains of their own ships.

When Getler, of the *Washington Post,* called race in the workplace one of "the toughest issues in America," he was right. It seems mentally and emotionally to tie into knots just about anyone who seriously grapples with it. It makes one yearn for a simple solution. Still, when I talk to people like Smith, I find myself a bit perplexed by the notion that affirmative action is at the root of so many of America's ills: that it has almost single-handedly undermined blacks' entrepreneurial accomplishments. By the same token, I find myself unpersuaded by the arguments of such people as Glynn Custred that affirmative action is primarily responsible for the failure of many whites to take blacks' intellectual achievements seriously.

In my high school, the so-called affirmative action stigma was not an issue. Everyone in the school—which was overwhelmingly white—was reasonably intelligent; at least we had all passed a test certifying that we were able and literate. No one had been given an edge for reasons of race or ethnicity. Yet it was far from a color-blind place. Much of the socializing, particularly after hours, was along racial lines. And a white classmate openly extolled the virtues of Nazism.

One day, I was singled out by the English teacher to read a composition of mine in class. As I read, I heard one of my classmates whisper to another that I must have copied the essay from a book. I took the comment as something of a compliment, as an acknowledgment that the piece was far too good for a typical high school kid to have written. Yet, I wondered, as I made my way through the composition, whether his remark was, at root, racial, whether he was really saying that he couldn't conceive that a black kid could be so much smarter than he. I didn't bother to confront him, so I really don't know. I do know, however, that the problem of racial stigma did not begin with affirmative action.

In "The Ethics of Living Jim Crow," an autobiographical essay published in *Uncle Tom's Children* in 1940, Richard Wright told of his first job at an eyeglass lens-grinding company in Jackson, Mississippi. He landed the job, in part, because the boss was impressed with his education, particularly with his two years of algebra. Wright was promised an opportunity to learn, and, as he put it, "I had visions of 'working my way up.' Even Negroes have those visions." But even though he worked hard at the factory and did his best to please, he discovered, over time, that nobody was teaching him a skill. His inquiries into the reason only provoked outrage. Finally, a co-worker shook his fist in Wright's face and advised him to stop making trouble: "This is a *white* man's work around here, and you better watch yourself."

Such sentiments obviously would not be voiced in most companies today. The civil rights revolution has seen to that. Still, it's worth recalling that the days of blatant discrimination are not exactly ancient history. In *The Declining Significance of Race*, William Julius Wilson noted that visits to black colleges by corporate recruiters jumped from an average of 4 in 1960, to 50 in 1965, to 297 in 1970. The reason for the jump is obvious. It is not that employers suddenly stopped being prejudiced, it is that it suddenly became obligatory—as it now has in South Africa—for companies to show they were willing to give blacks a chance. The positions initially made available—again, as in South Africa—were largely for show.

The foes of affirmative action argue that the past is largely irrelevant, that even left totally to their own devices, few bosses these days would dare to discriminate. Indeed, Dinesh D'Souza went so far as to assert that even in the absence of affirmative action, corporations today are more inclined to discriminate in favor of blacks than against blacks. Constance Rice, western regional counsel for the NAACP Legal Defense and Educational Fund, emphatically disagreed. She also stated that the enemies of affirmative action are lying when they say "that people don't judge you by the comfort level, and the chemistry, and who makes someone feel better, and who's more comfortable, and who can tell their jokes in front of you." Hiring and promotion decisions, she believes, are based primarily on "nonperformance criteria."

Rice cited the case of a woman in a law firm where she once worked. The woman was the best strategic thinker around but was not physically attractive. As a result, Rice noted, the woman was "left out of the team meetings—the early-morning meetings with clients in Tokyo. . . . She was the smartest one on the litigation team.

And the women the men would have in the rooms were the women they wanted to sleep with. We were all qualified, because we all graduated from the top law schools. We clerked. We all got hired because we're all capable. But in terms of that group of highly capable people, the star wasn't included. . . . That's what happens. People do not make decisions rationally based on who's the best."

Those who would dismantle affirmative action, said Rice, "want to pretend that the market forces are going to produce . . . meritorious decisions and all the cream is going to rise to the top. Well, it never has worked that way. And it isn't about to start now." As for the stigma of affirmative action, she dismissed the notion as nonsense: "The biases were already there. . . . Our presence, just our presence, means that race is in the picture."

Bernard Anderson, whose responsibilities as assistant labor secretary include the Office of Federal Contract Compliance Programs, said he sees plenty of evidence of continuing discrimination in the cases handled by the office. People of color with training and experience are "treated like shit in too many places on the job."

Even in the labor department, said Anderson, he had seen signs of racial prejudice. The solicitor, who is black and a Rhodes scholar, appointed two other blacks with impeccable credentials to top positions. "And the black lawyers were very empowered and encouraged by all of this, but a number of the white lawyers, and these are all career people, were just shaking in their boots." By and by, Anderson recalled, a "poison pen memorandum" found its way around the department. The missive made insulting, scatological comments about the people who were appointed. It also charged that they were unqualified and declared that affirmative action had gone too far.

One could argue that the kind of backlash Anderson cited would not exist if it were not for affirmative action. It's harder, however, to dismiss his evidence of ongoing discrimination in industry—particularly in light of several highly publicized cases that seemed to stem not from affirmative action but from old-fashioned bigotry.

Denny's restaurant chain, for instance, agreed—in a settlement with the Justice Department—to put a government-appointed civil rights monitor on its payroll, after being hit with a slew of complaints alleging discrimination against customers and employees.

Shoney's, another large restaurant chain, settled a suit for over $130 million that alleged, among other things, that managers were told to keep the number of black employees down in certain neighborhoods. Even the U.S. Department of State, though it denied it engaged in discrimination, settled a discrimination suit by agreeing to pay black foreign service officers nearly $4 million in compensation and by granting several retroactive promotions.

But even if Anderson is wrong and such cases are exceptions to the norm, Rice's point about how hiring works in the real world is not easily disposed of. In his memoir, *A Good Life*, Ben Bradlee, the former executive editor of the *Washington Post*, told a charming and revealing story about hiring Sally Quinn—a striking blond with scant experience who went on to become a star *Post* writer and eventually Bradlee's wife. Originally, Quinn had applied for a job as secretary to Phil Geyelin, the editorial page editor. She did not get the job, partly because she could not take shorthand and partly because, Bradlee implied, "I suggested that anyone that attractive could make work difficult."

Shortly thereafter, however, a job opened up for someone to cover parties, and again, Quinn was suggested. "She was perfectly suited for the job, except for one small problem: she had never written a word in her life," recalled Bradlee. "She was a young Army brat who had worked as the social secretary for the Algerian ambassador, Cherif Guelal. She had worked in Bobby Kennedy's 1968 campaign, and she knew everyone in town." Bradlee told Geyelin he was considering hiring her, even though she had no experience. "Well, nobody's perfect," responded Geyelin, and Bradlee made the hire.

Putting aside whatever the anecdote says about sexism in the newspaper business a quarter of a century ago when Quinn was hired, it is thoroughly revealing of just how unimportant traditional credentials can be when the "right" person comes along. Though it's inconceivable that anyone with a similar lack of experience would be hired as a writer at today's *Post*, it remains the case in virtually every corporation in the world that merit is a flexible concept and often encompasses qualities no résumé would ever contain.

Indeed, two economists, Jeff Biddle of Michigan State University and Dan Hamermesh of the University of Texas, found that beauty (which outside the acting and modeling industries is not most people's idea of a job qualification) has a significant bearing on success. Relying largely on surveys done in the United States and Canada, in which interviewers not only collected information on income but rated people's attractiveness, they attempted to quantify the value of beauty using a variety of statistical tests.

"All of these tests reinforce the conclusion that whatever the causes, people who are better looking receive higher pay, while bad-looking people earn less than average, other things being equal," they reported in the December 1994 issue of the *American Economic Review*. And that statement was as true for men as it was for women. Among men, those viewed as "below average or homely" were penalized about 9 percent in hourly earnings. Those seen as above average got an extra 5 percent.

After conducting a follow-up study on lawyers—published as a National Bureau of Economic Research working paper—Biddle and Hamermesh found that after fifteen years in the business, good-looking lawyers made about 12 percent more than did those who were less attractive (despite similar academic profiles).

It's difficult to know just what to make of such findings or of research that has found that tall people generally are more successful than are short people or that thin people do better than fat people except that clearly something other than professional competence is being rewarded. Indeed, most people who have any experience in the world know that the real workplace bears little resemblance to the meritocratic model so often offered up to vilify affirmative action.

The meritocratic model embodies two crucial assumptions: (1) that merit (essentially meaning qualifications) is easily determinable and (2) that it is somewhat static; it is like money you put in a bank, which is to say that you bring it to the enterprise and watch it grow (slowly but surely) to the benefit of both you and the enterprise. In reality, however, the workplace operates much more like a casino. You bring your qualifications to the table and wager them. If you are among the fortunate few, you win early and often and ultimately end up with a huge fortune; otherwise, you perhaps walk away with little more than the shirt on your back. The workplace, in other words, sees a few big winners and a great many losers, and who becomes which often rests—at least in part—on little more than chance. Merit is anything but static. It responds dramatically to cultivation. Among those who are fortunate, merit—or, at least, what passes for merit (which may, in reality, be nothing more than a degree from an Ivy League school or a recommendation from a friend of the boss)—is spotted early and those who are presumed to possess it are developed at crucial junctures.

In other words, to argue that affirmative action is unfair because it results in unqualified people getting promoted above qualified people is to ignore the fact that part of becoming "qualified" is receiving certain opportunities and promotions. CEOs, in short, are not plucked out of hats (well, maybe some of them are); typically, they are plucked out of the ranks of people who have been division heads and senior vice presidents, and these people, by the same token, are selected from those who have headed departments. If one group of people gets on the track to head important departments and another group is systematically excluded for whatever reason, those who are excluded never end up developing the "merit" that would enable them to succeed on a large scale.

I have met numerous senior executives, some of whom I have gotten to know quite well. I have met relatively few, however, who struck me as being so brilliant, so loaded with talent, that everyone around them paled by comparison. What has struck me more often is how ordinary they are—though their experiences have usually been anything but ordinary. Yet rarely do they seem racked with self-doubt. Instead, they generally seem convinced that they are the best men (and the vast majority are, indeed, men) for their jobs—even if a large part of why they are where they are has to do with family membership, social connections, or the luck of being in the right place when a predecessor was booted out.

None of this is to say that ability, initiative, and drive have nothing to do with getting ahead in the world. They clearly do. Certainly, hard work and competence in whatever line of business in which one happens to be employed (with the possible exception of such people as Hollywood producers) are generally minimal requirements for success. But unless those traits are recognized and rewarded by one's superiors, one can have a hard time making it up the ladder. And, as Rice suggested, in corporate America and in most major law firms, those traits tend to be recognized much more easily in white men than in practically anyone else.

In *The General Managers*, an in-depth investigation of the activities and characteristics of several top executives, John Kotter, a professor at the Harvard Business School, identified different traits that the administrators had in common. The administrators were ambitious, personable, curious, and optimistic; craved power; relished achievement; and, though not brilliant, were somewhat smarter than the norm and "moderately strong analytically." Kotter also discovered that they had all benefited from what he called the "success syndrome." "The most effective GMs [general managers] had careers characterized by almost constant growth in their interpersonal and intellectual skills, in their knowledge of the business and organization, and in their relationships with relevant others. They never stagnated for significant periods of time in jobs where there were few growth possibilities. Likewise, they were seldom, if ever, moved so often or put into positions that were so rapidly changing that they simply could not learn and perform well."

Effective top executives, Kotter found, are trained, not born. They come about because companies make an investment in them, in their so-called human capital, and nurture their careers along. Any honest discussion of hiring, promotion, and merit in the workplace must, at some point, acknowledge that such investments are made for any number of reasons that may have to do with numerous factors other than the amount of raw talent these persons bring to their firms.

Certainly, as Kotter confirmed, successful executives tend to be bright, but they are not intellectually incandescent and were not at the head of the class; they are generally those who—as the Harvard admissions study indicated—are a step or two behind the academic stars. They are, to be blunt about it, more often than not, people of relatively modest intellectual endowment who are chosen for success. They have, it is to be sure, certain personal qualities that make them attractive and a certain social affinity with those in charge, and it is all the better if they share a fraternity, a social connection, or a family tree with whoever is calling the shots.

Critics of affirmative action who profess faith in a pure meritocracy ignore the reality of how the real "meritocracy" works. If all these qualified, capable, and talented minorities and women existed, they say, corporations would reward them because they would recognize that it is within their economic interest to do so. That may well be true. But it is also true that qualifications and capability, as I just mentioned, are the result of investments made in potential, and if corporations only see the potential in white men, those are the people in whom the investments are likely to be made.

A true meritocracy would do a much better job of evaluating a broader variety of people. It would not merely allow black, female, and Latino mediocrities to rise to levels that white male mediocrities have reached all along—though, one could argue, that situation might be better than what exists now. It would challenge the very way merit is generally imputed and would give people ample chances to develop and to prove themselves; in short, it would create a truly level playing field. A meritocratic workplace would also be a more democratic workplace, for it would increase access to opportunities across the board.

The irony is that much of corporate America is moving in the opposite direction. With the exception of the designated elite, workers are widely viewed as little more than controllable expenses that can easily be sacrificed in the pursuit of profitability. As Carrie Leana, a professor at the University of Pittsburgh's business school, observed: "In the current investment-mechanism model of constant restructuring, jobs are cut even when the firm is wildly profitable. The fundamental view is that people are interchangeable and the ties between them fungible." Curiously, Leana noted, this model is being imposed "at a time when experts agree that the quality of the work force is more important than ever to the success of the firm."

Do affirmative action programs change the tendency to see employees as something less than individuals? Not necessarily. But they can at least, in some limited way, get managers to focus on minority candidates for positions and promotions that they otherwise might not see.

After looking at 138 employers in the Philadelphia area, for instance, Temple University researchers Alison Konrad and Frank Linnehan found that affirmative action seemed to have a measurable effect on promotions. The study, published in the *Academy of Management Journal*, discovered that though universities and businesses with "identity-conscious" personnel practices had essentially the same proportion of minority employees as did firms without such programs, they had more persons of color represented in management. If the objective was to see more minorities and women in management, Konrad and Linnehan concluded, affirmative action was an important tool. They also found, however, a great deal of resistance across the board to the very idea that gender or ethnicity should play any role in hiring or promotions. Many of the companies had established affirmative action programs only because they wanted to get governmental contracts or feared governmental scrutiny of their employment practices. The reluctance was reflected in Konrad and Linnehan's findings, for although companies with special programs were more likely to promote minorities to management, they did not seem appreciably more likely to promote them to the highest levels.

Some time ago I had lunch with a man who was heir to substantial wealth and had a high position in the family business. He dreamed of making the enterprise even greater, with the help of a large and loyal team of people he could depend on. He floated the idea, rather tentatively, that I might perhaps be a member of that team and wanted to know whether I found the thought appealing.

I gave something less than a forthright answer as I attempted to draw him out on precisely what it was he had in mind. He refused to be pinned down, but assured me that the specific job was not important—the implication being that even if the position was less than I had hoped for, the possibility of being part of a great enterprise and down the line maybe having a top position in it was something to be coveted.

Easy enough for him to say, I found myself thinking. He knew perfectly well that his future was assured; he could afford not to care about job titles and specific responsibilities. But for me, the matter was not nearly so simple.

I was not a member of his family, and it was not conceivable that I ever would be. Though he liked me and I liked him, we were not exactly talking about an equal partnership. I had no guarantee that the possibilities he alluded to would ever materialize. A fact of corporate life, of course, is that nobody who doesn't come in with an ironclad contract (and at a high level) is guaranteed much of anything. But another fact of *my* life has to do with race. As much as I might wish to, I could not pretend that my color was irrelevant or that he viewed me just as he would a white man with the same skills and intellect. He—or his top lieutenants, certainly—would factor in the question of race whenever they got around to considering what to do with me. Part of my credentials, in other words, was my color, but it was also part of my liability, for, if nothing else, it made me stand out as someone different from the stereotype of the high-powered corporate executive. It engendered expectations, concerns, and preconceptions that a white skin wouldn't. Not to recognize that fact would not only have been naive, it would have been to deny my previous experience.

In the absence of some specific guarantees, I suspected that the odds of a black man rising to the top of such a white structure were not high. Certainly, none had done so up to that point, and I was not prepared to gamble my career on testing the proposition. I also told myself that, race aside, I wasn't exactly sold on the career path he apparently had in mind. Still, I wondered whether I would have found the prospect more tempting if I was white.

I, of course, could not know, for if I was white, I would not have been *me*. I would not have had my personal history; I would not have grown up where I had grown up or been shaped by the same kinds of experiences. If I was white, maybe the idea of being part of his family, at least part of his corporate family, would have seemed infinitely more plausible.

At no point during that lunch did either of us explicitly bring up the question of affirmative action or even of race; yet we both knew that racial issues were lurking nearby. The notion that they would not have been lurking if it was not for the existence of affirmative action—that removing affirmative action from the table somehow renders institutions nonracialist—is one I find curiously benighted. Perhaps it is because I have run into too many people who profess to be color blind leading segregated lives, or maybe it is just that I have too often seen race rise out of the blue in places where it simply doesn't belong.

A few years ago, after taking over as editorial-page honcho of the *Daily News*, I spent some time going through the papers and memorandums of some of my predecessors. One memo stood out. In effect, it laid down a policy that no more than one opinion column by a person of color was to run on any single day. The writer apparently reasoned that *Daily News* readers could only take so many minority opinions at one time—irrespective of what those opinions happened to be or whether they were even in agreement. Clearly the editor had some notion that all minority columnists were interchangeable, and I suspect that notion had absolutely nothing to do with the existence of affirmative action.

Even the very debate over ending affirmative action underscores how fixated Americans are on race. For though affirmative action programs were instituted specifically to address discrimination against blacks, numerous other ethnic groups and white women subsequently stepped under its umbrella. Yet blacks still bear a disproportionate amount of the stigma.

As Katherine Spillar, national coordinator of the Feminist Majority Foundation, told *Working Woman* magazine, "Women are being left out of the debate." The editors of the magazine agreed: "Indeed, to read the newspapers, listen to the broadcasts and hear the politicians and pundits pontificate, you'd think affirmative action was literally a black-and-white issue. The debate is nearly always framed in terms of race; when women are mentioned, it seems an afterthought." The *Working Woman* special report on affirmative action also cited a 1995 study by Alfred Blumrosen, a professor at Rutgers University Law School and consultant to the Labor Department, suggesting that an "estimated six million women wouldn't have the jobs they have today were it not for the inroads made by affirmative action."

When I asked Custred, coauthor of the California Civil Rights Initiative, why—despite the fact that many people thought white women had been the primary beneficiaries of affirmative action—white women rarely seemed the subject of the affirmative action discussions, he said that the talk shows didn't seem interested. "It's a no go; they won't talk about it." In addition, said Custred, "women don't necessarily see themselves as that disadvantaged." They also may have husbands or sons whom they feel are being discriminated against because of affirmative action, he added, which presumably would make them less likely to speak out in favor of such policies. Tom Wood, coauthor of the initiative, suggested that many white women were just as upset about affirmative action as were white men. A woman who was active in the National Organization for Women had called him, he said, to complain that her son had been turned down for medical school (presumably because of affirmative action) even though he had excellent grades.

Constance Rice thinks that politics is a large part of the reason why the affirmative action debate focuses so much on blacks. As long as foes of affirmative action can keep a black face—not a white woman's face—on the issue, she believes, the opponents have a good chance of winning. In fact, politics (and political ambition) explains a lot not only about why blacks—as opposed to other beneficiaries—have been made the public face of affirmative action, but also about why the affirmative action debate has heated up so much in the past few years. The essential appeal of the anti–affirmative action cause is that it allows one to reach out, with a wink, to certain white voters without actually crossing the line into demagoguery. California Governor Pete Wilson, who signed an executive order banning certain affirmative action programs and filed suit against some more, clearly saw the issue as a way—albeit one that turned out to be less than successful—to distinguish himself in a crowded presidential field. Louisiana Governor Mike Foster, who signed an executive order outlawing state affirmative programs as his first official act, was apparently seeking to ingratiate himself among his white constituents. In Foster's case, it may have worked better than he wished, or at least garnered support from an embarrassing quarter. When local NAACP leaders staged a rally on the steps of the state capitol to protest Foster's order, they found themselves pitted against a much smaller rally led by the National Association for the Advancement of White People (founded by former Ku Klux Klan leader David Duke). According to a report in the New Orleans *Times-Picayune*, "The crowd cheered wildly, waving American flags and hoisting 'Duke for Senate' and 'End Affirmative Action' signs" as speakers denounced policies that discriminate against whites.

In his 1995 speech on affirmative action, President Bill Clinton explained the appeal of the issue this way: "If you say now you're against affirmative action because the government is using its power or the private sector is using its power to help minorities at the expense of the majority, that gives you a way of explaining away the economic distress that a majority of Americans honestly feel. It gives you a way of turning their resentment against the minorities or against a particular government program instead of having an honest debate about how we all got into the fix we are in and what we are all going to do together to get out of it."

Even if Americans were not feeling economically distressed, affirmative action would be a magnet for resentment. It simply strikes too many people as wrong, and the longer it exists, the more irritated about it people seem to become. As Mamphela Ramphele, chancellor of the University of Cape Town, asserted, "No society can sustain indefinite affirmative action programs without creating permanent cleavages between citizens." For that reason alone, much of the machinery of affirmative action is likely to be doomed. The battle raging now is, in fact, largely over just how much of it will remain.

When I invited University of Pennsylvania sociologist Elijah Anderson to speculate on the future of affirmative action, he gave a somewhat unexpected reply. Affirmative action, he observed, is, in many ways "a form of reparation. . . . It really was above and beyond the call of duty. It was a step away from business as usual. And if you believe in the idea that this is an egalitarian society, an equal opportunity society . . . then affirmative action makes no sense—for any group. But of course, many blacks have a hard time believing that and if you look at the situation that existed [prior to the civil rights era] it was clear that blacks were living in a separate world." Without affirmative action, Anderson believes, many blacks who are now in mainstream organizations would still be back in that separate world. Nonetheless, he added, "Affirmative action was one day bound to self-destruct." And that self-destruction, he suggested, is now taking place.

One problem, as Rice sees it, is that affirmative action has not been given much of a chance to work. "The thing of it is we've only been doing it for about ten years. They fought it for twenty." Another problem, she believes, is that the opponents of affirmative action don't have any better idea: "I don't have any problem looking at other systems that check . . . bias. But I don't know any of them that are gender blind and color blind. The only thing that I know that works is something that white America doesn't want to do: full integration."

Americans are, indeed, in the habit of vigorously resisting civil rights initiatives and then pronouncing them failures. And affirmative action is no exception. Indeed, though affirmative action always had fairly limited goals, it is being blamed for some huge failures. Yet it's worth keeping in mind that affirmative action was never meant to be an all-purpose civil rights program. It was not intended to clean up the slums, end joblessness, or integrate America's neighborhoods, although all of those things need desperately to be done. As South African scholar Julio Faundez observed, "Affirmative action should not be seen as a substitute for [general] social policy." That it has failed single-handedly to bring about racial equality is not so much a sign of its failure as of the unrealistic expectations that surrounded it. The frequent criticism, for instance, that affirmative action disproportionately helps those who are middle class is a bit absurd on reflection, since programs that, in large measure, attempt to help people obtain promotions and contracts are not going to be aimed, by necessity, at the hard-core unemployed. The criticism is not unlike condemning a program to train editors because it "disproportionately" helps those who can read. The misperception comes about from assuming that any plan to assist minorities, including affirmative action, must be fundamentally a poverty program. That assumption is seriously flawed. You fight poverty by fighting poverty, not by eliminating programs and policies that attempt to foster the careers of (and end discrimination against) potential black and brown CEOs. The problem is not that affirmative action helps too many of those who are middle class, but that there are so few effective initiatives that elevate the poor. Yet the widespread disappointment in (and resentment of) affirmative action is not likely to vanish—and surely not from pointing out that some of the disenchantment is not based on logic—for, by its very nature, affirmative action (or at least the activities carried out in its name that single out some groups at the expense of others) is polarizing. And that polarization was bound at some point to threaten the viability of affirmative action. Still, any funeral is premature.

It is true that much of the apparatus of affirmative action is crumbling. Certainly, many of the more objectionable forms (call it bad affirmative action) are either being weakened or eliminated. Race norming, the practice of segregating test scores for prospective governmental employees (so that blacks competed only against other blacks, Latinos against other Latinos, and whites against whites), was eliminated in 1991. Minority set-aside programs have been sharply restricted. Diversity programs in many corporations have been defanged. Indeed, the *Wall Street Journal* reported in September 1996 that affirmative action had become so benign that opposition among white males had dropped, in a single year, from 67 percent to 52 percent in a *Wall Street Journal*/NBC poll. What has changed, explained the *Journal*, "is that the rise of women and minorities in some companies has slowed or even halted. Companies are soft-pedaling or scaling back diversity programs in response to white male backlash. A changing political climate, including recent Supreme Court decisions limiting the use of affirmative action in education, is convincing many white men that the high-water mark of affirmative action has passed." Still, affirmative action is far from dead. Indeed, the milder (and therefore least threatening) forms seem to be growing ever more entrenched. For one thing, affirmative action's advocates have made their point: It is simply bad management to exclude and demoralize the quickest-growing segments of the workforce. And the business-as-usual approach, benign indifference, doesn't seem to work very well.

Even Wood acknowledged that some form of affirmative action is necessary: "The problem is not so much intentional discrimination; the problem is with patterns and practices of discrimination that are often not intentional and not conscious. The example I often use is the guy who recruits people on the basis of who he meets at his golf course or his country club on a Saturday afternoon. He might not be a bigoted person at all; he just has this kind of lazy practice of recruiting people; and it gives you a biased sample of the qualified work force. . . . So we have to have very effective affirmative action, nondiscrimination policies to counteract that."

Some opponents of affirmative action have taken Wood's thought one step further. In a March 1995 op-ed article for the *New*

York Times, author Shelby Steele argued for stiffer penalties for discrimination. "To my mind," wrote Steele,

> there is only one way to moral authority for those of us who want affirmative action done away with: to ask that discrimination by race, gender or ethnicity be a criminal offense, not just civil. If someone can go to jail for stealing my car stereo, he ought to do considerably more time for stifling my livelihood and well-being by discriminating against me. . . . Ending affirmative action must involve more than bringing down an icon. It must also involve an extension of democratic principles to what might be an extreme degree in a racially homogeneous society. But in a society like ours, discrimination is the greatest and most disruptive social evil. In a multiracial democracy of individuals, you have to make it a felony.

A year later, *Wall Street Journal* editorial writer Hugh Pearson cited New Jersey state senator Gordon MacInnes's observation that "Republicans—who worship an unfettered marketplace—display no enthusiasm for fighting racial discrimination, which so clearly distorts free markets." Those words moved Pearson to make an observation of his own: "No matter how much capital becomes available in our economy, discrimination against African-Americans will continue to be a major problem without tougher penalties on those who practice it." They also moved Pearson to ask a series of conservatives, including several Republican presidential candidates and the chairman of the Center for New Black Leadership, their views on tougher antidiscrimination laws.

Of those who responded, wrote Pearson, none came up with much of an answer, with the exception of Steve Forbes, who had just bowed out of the presidential race. "The problem is enforcing laws, not creating new ones. We should debate how to put teeth into those laws if they don't have any teeth to begin with," Forbes said.

I thought Pearson's inquiry was intriguing enough to ask my researcher to see if he could get any better answers. After several weeks, he reported that he had not had much success. Politicians Pat Buchanan, Jack Kemp, and Bill Bennett did not respond. Forbes's communications director sent a somewhat modified answer: "The key is enforcing what is on the books now. If it appears in certain sectors that stiffer penalties are called for, they should be enacted." Bob Dole's office wouldn't give a specific reply, but sent a *Wall Street Journal* op-ed article by Dole and Congressman J. C. Watts, Jr., that urged the recruitment of "qualified women and minorities" and conscientious enforcement of current laws. The Center for New Black Leadership directed us to a letter in the *Wall Street Journal* from its chairman, Glenn Loury. The letter questioned Pearson's ethics and denounced "the victim mentality" and "the spiritual malaise afflicting our civic life." Loury also vigorously tore into Steele's proposal, contending that it would present "a nearly prohibitive evidentiary burden" for most plaintiffs. "The idea of sending entrepreneurs off to the hoosegow for failing to realize the speculative diversity projections of Federal Reserve or EEOC computer models should cause even Mr. Pearson to blush," Loury scoffed.

The upshot of it all seemed to be that for all their antagonism to affirmative action, conservatives—as Pearson indicated—don't seem to have any fresh or better ideas. Instead, many argue, in effect, that simply eliminating affirmative action programs—at least the kinds they don't like—would be enough of a solution.

One problem, as I noted previously, is that affirmative action means so many different things. But if we use the broad definition formulated earlier—programs or policies that, in the interest of equity and/or heterogeneity, consciously take race, ethnicity, or gender into account—we seem to be stuck with it for the moment. The alternative, unfortunately, seems not to be race neutrality but a recurring form of blindness—not to color, but to competence in those who are neither white nor male. Management in many corporations has recognized that and implemented policies to correct for it.

Unfortunately, correcting for a problem is not the same as eliminating it. Moreover, the corrective measures, as I discussed, introduce new tensions, new inequities, and new rumblings of discontent. That is the curse not only of affirmative action, but of any policy that aims to make people do "what is right" when they are naturally disposed not to.

Advocates of affirmative action may take a small measure of

comfort in the fact that at least some part of their message has gotten through, that society recognizes, if only dimly, that apartheid—corporate or otherwise—is no longer an option. But that small de facto victory for the affirmative action side is hardly a cause for celebration, for, among other things, the war over so-called preferences has made it clear that affirmative action does not make anyone happy. It doesn't necessarily lead either to meaningful inclusion or parity, and it certainly doesn't lead to racial harmony. At best, it gives us something to fight about and try to make work as we grapple with an unsettling, but ultimately unavoidable, question: Given the ambivalence of the American commitment to complete racial equality, are we truly capable of coming up with anything better?

CHAPTER 7

Looking into and behind the color-blind mind

As Georgetown law professor Charles R. Lawrence III sees it, affirmative action had one huge, unfortunate unanticipated result: It made people insist that America is color-blind. Justice John Marshall Harlan's famous endorsement of a "color–blind" Constitution provided the pretext, but it was the backlash against affirmative action that provided the impetus. That political and legal opposition transformed color blindness "from prescriptive ideal into a condition of societal denial," Lawrence argued in the *Boston College Third World Law Journal*: "'Our Constitution is color-blind' becomes 'We are a color-blind society.'"

Lawrence believes that such an assertion is ludicrous: "The [Supreme Court] Justices deny their own life experiences in clubs, communities and jobs where blacks are rarely seen. And if these realities are brought to their attention they say, 'but this is not evidence,' or 'this is economics, not race,' or 'this is protected racist speech, not conduct,' or 'it is not racism when white contractors hire their friends and all of their friends just happen to be white,' or 'maybe black folks don't like contracting work.' And then they say to those who seek affirmative remedies for this discrimination, *'You must be a racist if you don't believe we are a color-blind society.'"*

The professor has a point. The legal battle over affirmative action has indeed produced some peculiar arguments—and some mind-boggling instances of denial. Justice Harlan, for sure, would have been astounded to hear that the equal-protection clause of the Fourteenth Amendment is now seen, in some quarters, as virtually the only thing protecting white men from being replaced at work and at school by persons of color. Yet to understand American racial denial, it's necessary to go much further back than the recent rash of affirmative action cases, and even further back than *Plessy v. Ferguson* (1896).

America came into existence as a divided personality—a nation that celebrated freedom and proclaimed the equality of man, yet tolerated race-based slavery and offered naturalization only to persons who were free and white. Even in the aftermath of the Civil War, when the nation finally acknowledged that blacks were fully human, too, Americans struggled to find a way to embrace simultaneously the warring gods of social justice and injustice. Justice Joseph Bradley's insistence that before the Civil War, "free colored people" enjoyed "all the essential rights of life, liberty and property the same as white citizens," is a reflection of the need—both legal and psychological—to locate a justification for inequality within an argument for equality. That has been America's dilemma from the beginning.

That said, there is something new about the current racial intercourse. It is not just that there is a "full-fledged raging sense of victimhood on the part of the white community," as affirmative action advocate Constance Rice put it. It is that undergirding that sense of victimhood is a widespread conviction among whites that being black in today's United States has some substantial legal, educational, and financial advantages over being white. This is not to say that whites suddenly believe it is better to be black than to be white. One's life, after all, is more than the sum total of one's economic and educational opportunities, and not many whites—including those who believe blacks and Latinos are taking *their* jobs—would willingly change their lot for that of blacks. Many do believe, however, that racism (at least, the kind that hurts blacks more than whites) is pretty much dead and that black folks (those who are willing to work hard, at any rate) have it pretty good—maybe better than they deserve and certainly much better than plenty of whites—and that America provides blacks with all the opportunities they need. We are witnessing, in short, the death of white guilt, as well as of the notion that whites have much to do with the circumstance in which poor minorities find themselves.

Dinesh D'Souza is not alone in his belief that racism—meaning white racism—has effectively ended. In *Paved with Good Intentions*, Jared Taylor presented one example after another of opportunities and advantages available to blacks to support his case that blacks face little discrimination from whites and concluded that, if anything, black racism is a greater problem than white racism: "Doctrine holds that white society is seething with hatred for blacks. The very reverse is true. With the best of intentions and for the best of reasons, America has done everything within its power to encourage blacks to hate whites." At another point, Taylor compared the plight of Asians to that of blacks and asked, "If white racism were blighting the lives of blacks. . . . [s]hould it not be a terrible obstacle for Asians as well?" And at yet another point, he demanded to know, "When the occasional ragtag band of placard-waving Ku Kluxers is outnumbered, not only by hecklers but also by police sent to protect them from outraged citizens, can white racism really be the crippling evil it is made out to be?"

In *A Nation of Victims*, Charles Sykes made largely the same argument. After citing statistics indicating a decline in the prejudice of whites and an increase in the earnings of blacks, Sykes suggested that far too much emphasis is given to racism in analyzing social, economic, educational, and political trends. The investment in racism, he concluded, "was apparently too great for it to slip quietly into obscurity."

Without question, many white Americans agree with Sykes and company that it is time to put the charge of racism to rest; that for all intents and purposes, equality of opportunity has been achieved; and that, indeed, the balance may have tilted a bit too much in the favor of minorities. "Majorities of whites are convinced that blacks have equal opportunities to whites to achieve a quality education, obtain skilled jobs, get the same pay for the same work, find decent housing where they want to live, have equal justice under the law, obtain credit and mortgages, and achieve equal promotions into managerial jobs," reported pollster Louis Harris in 1994. "Similar majorities or pluralities share the same view about Latinos and Asians. Whites are convinced that minorities by and large have equal opportunities," he stated. People of color, discovered Harris, sharply reject that assessment. Eighty percent of blacks, 60 percent of Latinos, and 57 percent of Asians said they were not "given opportunities equal to whites," according to the study commissioned by the National Conference (formerly the National Conference of Christians and Jews).

When my researcher, Paul Rogers, asked Harris what he made of those numbers, Harris offered a sobering assessment. In the 1960s when polling for *Newsweek*, Harris said, he had also found racial differences in perceptions. Nonetheless, "blacks were sanguinely optimistic, and I was puzzled over that because they obviously were living in rather awful conditions." Eventually, he concluded that the optimism stemmed from at least two things—the very human need to "hope against hope" and an "enormous faith that government somehow was going to help them."

Today, despite the progress of the last several decades, Harris finds optimism a lot harder to sustain. Minorities have become convinced that "government has turned against them. There's real bitterness, cynicism, and indeed a deep desire for change as a consequence, but also alienation."

Much of the problem, in Harris's eyes, has to do with whites who, while acknowledging the existence of discrimination, think things are basically fine. The conflicting sentiments translate into an attitudinal gulf wider than any he has previously seen: "Back in the sixties and seventies, whites recognized that there was widespread discrimination that hadn't been attended to. Now . . . an ominous number of whites have a view that somehow race relations are behind us, somehow whatever [needed to be done] has been done and it's probably worked. . . . What you get is a complete insensitivity on the part of a majority of whites as to what minorities think of them and what the problems confronting minorities . . . are."

"When we measured minority stereotypes of whites, it was staggering," Harris noted. "We found six in ten who felt that whites are not willing to share the good things of society with minorities; we found seven in ten who felt that whites were completely insensitive to the aspirations of minorities." He suspects that whites may know that many blacks are critical of them, "but I think they don't realize that Latinos and Asians are as well. The fact that majorities [of persons of color]—sixty percent and upwards—are critical means that whites are viewed as basically trying to throttle minorities."

Harris prays that the obliviousness of whites will not last: "Somebody's got to hit the whites with a two-by-four to wake them up. . . . They see no crisis, yet there is a crisis." Persons of color, Harris stated, "must change their outlook, too. They must restore their faith in government as a vehicle for positive change." When pressed, Harris made clear that the "two-by-four" he had in mind was not a riot or some kind of racial apocalypse, but better media coverage, more responsible public debates, and more complete integration in the workplace: "If blacks can get to hold equal positions to whites and they work side by side, that's the fastest way to get rid of [racism]," he said. "You deal with people as human beings. That's what color blindness is all about."

That certainly was the dream—and not just Thurgood Marshall's—in the wake of the Supreme Court decision in the case of *Brown v. Board of Education of Topeka* in 1954. Yet, in subsequent decades, as integration has increased, so has the gulf about which Harris is so concerned. Given that, Harris's hope for a recommitment to the old liberal agenda seems to be anchored much more firmly in his heart than in his data. The very progress that has allowed blacks to make one breakthrough after another has also fostered the conviction that enough has been done or, at least, has made people extremely doubtful that discrimination is the root of the problem. In addition, as Lawrence suggested, the existence of affirmative action has made it possible for many people to accept what appears to be a contradictory set of beliefs.

On the one hand, for instance, whites say that minorities enjoy equal opportunities, but on the other hand, they say that a lot of discrimination still exists. Such conflicting sentiments make a certain amount of sense if one believes that even though discrimination against persons of color continues, "reverse discrimination" (that is, affirmative action) has more than evened the score.

To be sure, the public opinion surveys on race are rich with inconsistent sentiments. Two-thirds of whites claim that they favor "full integration," but significantly fewer—57 percent—believe that it's wrong "to have two Americas—one of privileged whites and the other of racial minorities who are treated like second-class citizens." The numbers become even more confusing and contradictory if one looks beyond the Harris poll. Two-thirds of whites told Harris's interviewers that they were willing to "give a top priority, including commitment of more government money, to making sure that people of color get the opportunities to let them become part of the mainstream of American life." Yet a 1996 survey by the Joint Center for Political and Economic Studies found that only 5.6 percent of Americans thought that race relations was among the three most important problems facing the country. (Among blacks, the proportion who believed that race relations is important was several times higher than among whites.)

Polls—particularly those that touch on sensitive social issues, especially race—must always be taken with more than a grain of salt, since the respondents don't necessarily tell what they believe, but what they think it is acceptable to admit. Still, I think that, at a minimum, the responses suggest two things: that though most people will readily profess commitment to fighting racial inequality, it is generally a rather low priority and that huge numbers of Americans (probably more than those who admit it to pollsters) think it is perfectly all right to have a country comprised of "privileged whites" and second-class minorities.

How could such a notion flourish at the very time that paeans to color blindness have become commonplace? It is partly because the subtext of *The Bell Curve* has been taken to heart. If blacks and Latinos are doing poorly, many people believe, that is because of something lacking in *them*. *They* simply aren't smart enough, or motivated enough, or diligent enough to do any better. It is also because Americans are giving up the conceit that the United States is a classless society, that we all—except perhaps for such people as the Kennedys, Carnegies, and Mellons—belong to the solid middle class. Such a notion necessarily becomes harder to hold on to when millions of people await pink slips and watch their economic security vanish as even mediocre corporate CEOs live like potentates of mid-level nation-states and major movie stars collect tens of millions of dollars for a few months of make-believe work. And giving up on classlessness necessarily implies also giving up a certain amount of faith in the goal of actual equality.

In addition, as I suggested earlier, the very civil rights breakthroughs that have made blacks' success in the mainstream possible have provided a certain cover for more subtle forms of prejudice. They have also provided a justification for the most flagrant forms of bigotry—a justification that says, in effect, "See, even when *you people* are given all the opportunities, you still screw up." Not that blatant bigotry has ever needed much of a reason to flourish.

For as long as I have been writing for publication, I have been receiving letters—usually single-spaced or crudely written and often illiterate—that attempt to explain why blacks or minorities in general are not doing as well as whites. I am never sure what the writers hope to accomplish by contacting me, but they have done a fairly good job of showing me the value—to them, at least—of racism. It seems that the writers are so insecure and their lives are so miserable that without some group to hate, they would have little choice but to hate themselves.

One missive I received recently made the following points:

> I know of five women, all of them white, who were assaulted and or robbed by niggers. And that is the only epithet for you people. . . . The only whites who do not know that blacks are dangerous are the liberal Jews you work for. . . . Black men are garbage and should be exterminated. The women have the foulest mouths I have ever heard. . . . If black people had the same intellectual and cultural development as whites, Haiti would be rich as Holland. . . . Is there a world-renowned university in any country in Africa to rival Oxford, the Sorbonne, Cambridge or Harvard? . . . I would say we are not racist enough because racism in these times means self-preservation. I never want to live anywhere near black people or even see them.

The letter rambles on—often incoherently—in much the same vein. Having received scores of similar letters through the years that, if nothing else, provide a glimpse into some particularly dark American souls, I accept the fact that blithering racists are alive and kicking. I know, and have known since childhood—growing up at a time and in a city where bigotry was often defiantly on display—that race-obsessed fanatics (such as my chess-playing, neo-Nazi high school classmate) exist in numbers larger than most Americans would be comfortable admitting. Yet I also believe that they are dying out, at least as a substantial force in American life. Not that rabid white supremacists or racist jerks will suddenly wither away. Some will always be around. Indeed, even as I write, the local newspapers are reporting a story of an off-duty New York City policeman who, according to witnesses (he denies the account), in a drink-enhanced rage, shouted racial epithets and, as he or one of his party held off onlookers with drawn guns, the other nearly bludgeoned a young black man to death with a tempered steel club. The man's crime, say the stories, was being in the company of a white woman. Such intermittent idiocy notwithstanding, the day when ranting racists could command the political center and dictate the fate of nonwhite Americans is gone, I suspect forever.

My biggest fear, to put it another way, is not that the Ku Klux Klan will invade my home or that some white mob will lynch me—though I recognize that some sick individuals (some, unfortunately, who are licensed to carry guns) remain capable of doing pretty much anything. I have the luxury, however, as do most Americans of color, of being more concerned about much less blatant forms of prejudice—the effects of which are unlikely to be the target of public service announcements or to evoke headlines in the morning papers or, for that matter, to elicit much concern from whites. In fact, in the current climate, when brazen displays of racism are relatively rare, focusing on racial problems strikes many whites as an unproductive and disagreeable exercise. The very subject makes many people uncomfortable. And those who raise it are apt to find themselves treated as if they had let loose a fart. Bill Bradley, the former basketball great and U.S. senator, confided that sometimes when he addresses racial issues he can feel the audience's annoyance. "I mean, I can see it in a room, when I'm talking about this. I can see white faces, when I start talking say, 'I like this guy *except now*,' or I can see black faces saying 'What right does he have to be saying this? He's not us.'"

As the Pulitzer Prize-winning series of articles in the *Akron Beacon Journal* observed: When it comes to race, "many whites are tired of hearing about it. Most blacks wish it would go away. All seem powerless to move it." It is a topic, as the *Akron Beacon Journal* noted, that "the typical white American will go to great lengths simply to avoid."

Two reasons are obvious. After centuries of greater or lesser racial turmoil, Americans are not terribly optimistic that the problem has a solution; also, and perhaps more to the point, discussions about race have a way of deteriorating into efforts to assign blame, and the search for villains, more often than not, ends at white America's doorstep.

When Duke University administrator Susan Wasiolek (see Chapter 4) compared being called a racist to being accused of child molestation or wife battering, she was not only noting how strong the social censure has become against certain forms of racism, but about how difficult it is to have a reasonable discussion about race, how easily even the most innocent comment is taken as evidence of racism, and why the incentive is so strong to tune out and shut up.

"So many of us feel as if we've worked hard to create more equity, to create more opportunity, I mean I guess we want to feel that we're good people," she told me. "We want to feel that we're working towards improving the situation. And to be called racist means that we've failed . . . that we're not good, that we're evil, that the lives we are leading . . . are not noble ones. . . . Some people would suggest that maybe we're fearful of it because it hits home, and I'm not suggesting to you that I don't have my prejudices and my biases. I know that I do. But that word has a life all to itself."

Part of the problem, Wasiolek believes, is that words, in these times, are often given connotations and a political context that the speaker never intended. She recalled a presentation she recently delivered that touched on the issue of intimate partners of the same sex. At one point, she outlined some of the difficulties, as a matter of university policy, of treating life partners as the exact equivalent of spouses. Certain members of the audience blew up in anger. The explosive and acrimonious reaction, focusing primarily on her use of language, stunned her. "It took my breath away," Wasiolek recalled.

Society's taboos about racism are even stronger than those around homophobia and sexism, Wasiolek thinks, so talking about racism often is simply "not worth the risk. I'm better off keeping my mouth shut than I am potentially compromising my reputation." Students, she has observed, seem to have the same fear. Though many have strong feelings about such issues as affirmative action, their feelings are often internalized—at least in interracial conversations. "Even [among] those students who are living close to each other, side by side in the same room," Wasiolek has found a lot of fear and distrust. "And yet this is supposed to be an environment where students can talk, where dialogue is important, where [there can be] an open exchange of ideas that are different." Instead, there is discomfort and defensiveness, which are unlikely to induce the sort of self-reflection that can lead people to question long-held assumptions, preconceptions, or prejudices.

Wasiolek, who grew up in Charlotte when busing was at its peak and who attended Duke in the 1970s, said she once believed that integration, the simple process of people living next door to (and interacting with) each other, would allow those of different races to see how much they have in common. But on college campuses, where people from different racial groups generally do live in close proximity, she has not seen anything approaching color blindness develop.

Indeed, what often passes for color blindness is the kind of silence Wasiolek alluded to, a silence that stems from apprehension about openly acknowledging one's recognition of race. In large measure, Janet Schofield's work at the "Wexler" Middle School (see Chapter 4) was an examination of a culture that was trying to adhere to that particular form of color blindness—a kind of willful and bogus denial of color that she ultimately concluded did more harm than good.

In her essay, "Causes and Consequences of the Colorblind Perspective," Schofield observed that the teachers were so determined to make desegregation work—and so afraid of being thought to be prejudiced—that they refused to see racial issues even when these issues were conspicuously relevant. Some claimed, as I noted previously, that they never noticed the race or ethnicity of their students; all insisted that they treated their students as individuals and simply did not take race into account. They also maintained that their young charges were equally color-blind—apparently on the assumption that if the children didn't learn about race in school, they would not learn about it anywhere else.

When researchers observed and talked to the students, however, they got quite a different picture. They noticed, for instance, that when eating lunch in the cafeteria, children of different races rarely sat together. During one seventh-grade lunch period, of over two hundred children, only six sat next to someone from a different racial group. When a white girl was asked why, she replied, "'Cause the white kids have white friends and the black kids have black friends." Asked whether she could think of a lot of white kids who had a lot of black friends, or vice versa, she answered, "Not really." At another point, a white student told an observer, "You know, it just wasn't fair the way they set up this class. There are sixteen black kids and only nine white kids. I can't learn in here. . . . [The black kids] copy and pick on you. It just isn't fair."

The suspension rate for blacks was roughly four times what it was for whites at the school, but the teachers refused to entertain the thought that any racial factors could be at work. They also saw no reason to object to textbooks that had pictures only of whites, reasoning that, since race did not matter, it was not important to have books that showed blacks participating in American society.

Over and over, the attempt to ignore race only exaggerated its significance. The avoidance of racially sensitive topics even affected the teachers' lessons on ancient Rome; the teachers simply omitted any mention of slavery. Even in noting that George Washington Carver was a great American, they thought it was important not to point out that he was black. "In the best of worlds, there would be no need to make such mention, because children would have no preconceptions that famous people are generally white," commented Schofield. "However, in a school where one white child was surprised to learn from a member of our research team that Martin Luther King was black, not white, it would seem reasonable to argue that highlighting the accomplishments of black Americans and making sure that students did not assume famous figures are white is a reasonable practice."

Schofield compared the teachers' behavior to that exhibited by certain people on encountering someone with a visible physical handicap; they pretend not to notice that the handicap exists and hope, thereby, to minimize discomfort. Schofield concluded that though the "colorblind perspective" might "ease initial tensions and minimize the frequency of overt conflict," it did so at a high price, for it also "could foster phenomena like the taboo against ever mentioning race or connected issues and the refusal to recognize and deal with the existence of intergroup tensions. Thus, it fosters an environment in which aversive racists, who are basically well-intentioned, are prone to act in a discriminatory manner." The attitude, in other words, made biased behavior easier to get away with because racism couldn't even be considered its source.

John Dovidio, a psychology professor and expert on race relations at Colgate University, believes that this subtle discrimination, practiced by people who don't believe they are prejudiced—which he calls "aversive racism"—is replacing blatant racism. The theory, he explains, is "based on the assumption that a lot of the bias and discrimination that occurs, among whites towards blacks in particular, occurs unintentionally and unconsciously." In other words, discrimination takes place primarily in situations where it can be rationalized on the basis of something other than bigotry.

An employer, for instance, may be inclined to reject a black aspirant in favor of a white person, but instead of seeing the decision as having anything to do with race, the employer may decide that the black applicant's education is not in the right field. "So that white employer leaves with a clear conscience [certain that] no bias occurred because it was rationalizable," Dovidio said. He continued:

> Now that same black person goes for another interview and is competing against a white person with a different employer and what is most likely to happen, according to the research we've done, is that the second employer will make a decision to choose the white person over the black person, but that employer will justify it on the basis of some factor other than race that may be totally different than the first one. So you're groping for reasons to justify behavior that is unconsciously discriminatory. So employer number two says, "Well maybe what we need is someone who is more outgoing, who will interact with our clientele better."

In such circumstances, Dovidio noted, the white employers will be totally convinced that no discrimination is taking place, but the black applicant will see just the opposite. "What that means is that people of color will have a tendency to see racism in many places, almost everywhere, because you can't trust what somebody says. And white people tend to see it nowhere because they only discriminate when they can justify it on the basis of some factor other than race. And so the dialogue begins with miscommunication. It starts with different perceptions, but usually quickly escalates to distrust because . . . if a black person says, 'What's going on here is racism and discrimination,' . . . whites will respond and say, 'No it isn't.'"

It is thinking similar to the thinking that guided Wexler's teachers and Dovidio's hypothetical employers that allows editors with essentially all-white staffs to deny that they make any distinctions based on color and to defend their hiring choices as examples of a meritocracy—even when their writers come up with stories that effectively eliminate just about everyone who is not white. It is, in short, the kind of thinking that allows discrimination without regret because it blinds people to their own race-based assumptions. Unfortunately, feigning color blindness does not ensure that one will see blacks and whites as equals; it only allows certain racial issues to be swept under the carpet.

Brazil, for instance, has long touted itself as something of a color-blind paradise—a "racial democracy" where color, while noticed, has no specific significance. Eugene Robinson, formerly the *Washington Post* correspondent in South America, wrestled with the question of color blindness from the Brazilian perspective in a 1995 article in the *Post* entitled "Over the Brazilian Rainbow: In This Multi-Hued Society, the Color Line Is a State of Mind."

Robinson's curiosity was piqued by the club scene in Rio de Janeiro. After a night of dancing and listening to music, he returned to his hotel, determined to figure out what it was about Brazilian nightlife that fascinated him so. "I realized that I had been in the midst of an interracial crowd that didn't really feel like an interracial crowd, at least not like one in the United States. For someone who grew up in the still-segregated South in the late 1950s and early 1960s, this was not an everyday feeling. This was remarkable."

During the next four years, wrote Robinson, he returned to Brazil many times in his quest for understanding. "I learned that there are indeed problems of racial discrimination in Brazil, in many ways much worse than in the United States. I learned that Brazilians see race in a way that remains problematic for me, with an emphasis on gradations of skin color. At the same time I learned that the remarkable feeling I felt in the Salgueiro dance hall was something real, something replicable, something in fact fairly common in Brazil—and something that now, being back home, I miss."

Not once, wrote Robinson, in all his visits "did I go into a setting where ordinary working-class Brazilians lived or worked and see evidence of racial separation or racial friction. I saw it among upper-class whites, who often kept to themselves and looked down on everyone else, but not elsewhere in society."

Robinson is only one in a long line of journalists and scholars who have grappled with Brazilian color blindness. Virtually all have concluded that despite the lack of overt racial hostility and the real ease of interracial relations, the huge importance given "gradation of skin color" makes the country very much a pigmentocracy.

In June 1978, on the occasion of the ninetieth anniversary of the abolition of slavery in Brazil, David Vidal, then the *New York Times* correspondent in Rio de Janeiro, observed: "Brazilian blacks are prominent in music, entertainment and sports but are totally excluded from the decision-making centers of the most African nation outside Africa. Their participation in politics is insignificant, considering their numbers, and their absence from fields requiring contact with the public—tourism, public relations, banks and first-class bars and restaurants—is evident." Nonetheless Brazil, he noted, "represents itself as a multiracial democracy from which other countries with racial problems might well learn." In truth, "there is no doubt that relations between the races here are warm by comparison with other countries and notably devoid of tension," Vidal concluded. "But four generations after abolition, the vast majority of Brazilian blacks remain at the very bottom of the economic and social pyramid."

More than a decade later, historian Sam Adamo made much the same observation in *Modern Brazil*. Blacks and mulattoes, he noted, "find themselves locked into poor-paying, low-status jobs that offer little promise of upward mobility. Since educational and occupational barriers to nonwhites' social mobility have not changed appreciably since slavery was abolished in 1888, it is logical to conclude that racism and discrimination play prominent roles in keeping blacks and mulattoes disproportionately represented among the lower classes." In 1996 a reporter for the *Wall Street Journal* made essentially the same point: "Today, nearly 40% of nonwhites have four years or less of schooling. The illiteracy rate of black Brazilians is twice that of whites. The income of whites, on average, more than double that of blacks. Blacks are almost invisible in the professions."

How this situation came to be is a familiar story. By delving into personnel, union, naval, and penitentiary records, Adamo found that in the half century following the abolition of slavery, blacks and mulattoes were systematically discriminated against in the job market. White immigrants with no better education or skills were more likely to be hired and were promoted more quickly. The result was a huge discrepancy in access to education and good jobs that continues to this day. Despite the "official myth of racial democracy . . . public acceptance of the myth is dwindling," he concluded.

Marvin Harris, author of *Patterns of Race in the Americas,* also found Brazilian racial classifications to be anything but neutral. He enumerated forty different racial types—*braco, preto, moreno claro, moreno escuro,* and so on—and stated that even Brazilians are incapable of telling the difference among many of them. Another survey counted 143 different words used to describe Brazilian racial types. Though the distinctions are sometimes less than clear, the basic message is unmistakable: Light is better, and white is best. The categories, however, are not inflexible. "Money whitens," in the Brazilian scheme, so, as Harris noted, "the richer a dark man gets the lighter will be the racial category to which he is assigned by his friends, relatives and business associates." By the same token, poverty darkens, so extremely poor—and poorly educated—"browns" may find themselves classified among "blacks." "Color is one of the criteria of class identity; but it is not the only criterion," Harris concluded.

That is a crucial point—and one that Robinson alluded to with his reference to "upper-class whites." Latin Americans have never pretended to be above distinctions based on class. Indeed, in many circles, being from the "right" family and having attended the "right" school are critically important credentials. Consequently, proponents of color blindness say, in effect, "Sure, we may discriminate on the basis of class, but we are not racists. It is just that so few blacks or mulattoes or Indians have the proper class credentials." The statement ignores the reality, however, that a large part of the class credential is racial—that dark skin, in the absence of some substantial mitigating factors, is a marker for lower class and that white skin, in the absence of some sign of social and educational shortcomings, accords one higher status. The fact that class can trump race in such a convoluted configuration of status hardly means that race is no longer relevant, or, as some people are growing fond of saying in the United States, "We no longer really have a race problem, just a class problem."

Signs are emerging that many Brazilians—particularly Afro-Brazilians—no longer believe in the notion of Brazilian color blindness. In November 1995, several thousand black Brazilians marched on the nation's capitol to demand an end to racism and discrimination. The demonstration took place on the tercentennial of the death of Zumbi dos Palmares, a rebel slave leader revered by many Afro-Brazilians.

Several Brazilian cities, under pressure from Afro-Brazilians, have moved to end what the Associated Press dubbed "elevator apartheid"—the practice of relegating blacks to service elevators whether or not they are service people (the presumption being that, in the absence of strong evidence to the contrary, black skin was a pretty good indicator of lower-class status). "I always felt I was being treated like the garbage I was forced to stand next to," Gildaci Dantas de Jesus, a black woman and president of the São Paulo Domestic Workers Union, told the Associated Press correspondent. De Jesus successfully led the battle in São Paulo that resulted in a 1996 ordinance prohibiting discrimination—owing to race, sex, color, origin, social class, age, physical deformity, or disease—in the city's elevators. In recent years, several Afro-Brazilians have urged adoption of some form of affirmative action. And Brazil's president, Fernando Henrique Cardoso, a sociologist with an interest in racial issues, named a commission in 1996 to explore what sorts of compensatory programs might work.

Brazil is not the only country to be caught with its racial hypocrisy showing. In much of Latin America—particularly in places with a visibly multicolored racial mix—people see themselves as paragons of racial virtue, far above the kind of prejudice and interracial friction that is common in the United States. And, as Robinson intimated, they are not totally mistaken; in many places south of the U.S. border, as was noted earlier, there is an ease in human interracial interactions that the United States is nowhere close to achieving. It is that very comfort, the unself-conscious intercourse, that allows the myth of nonracialism to thrive.

Also, as Marvin Harris suggested, race is not nearly as fixed in much of Latin America as it is in the United States. Whereas black Americans don't have the option of changing their race (unless they are light enough to "pass"), "black" Brazilians or Dominicans do. They may not be able to become "white," but they can become something other than black. That ability to climb a step or two higher in the racial hierarchy, to creep across racial boundaries (in contrast to the United States, where race is pretty much fixed at birth), not only can defuse racial resentments, but can make organizing around racial categories virtually impossible. Moreover, in parts of Latin America, members of different "races" often belong to the same family and may even have the same birth parents. Family ties, in short, make free-flowing racial animosity of the U.S. variety virtually unthinkable in Latin America, for few people, if forced to choose, would side with their race against members of their family.

Sociologist Samuel Betances made a telling point. For all the words they use to describe race, Latin Americans initially had nothing that remotely approximated "nigger." *Mayate,* he noted, is the closest Hispanics have come, and it arose from "conflicts of dealing with turf" *in the United States*. When Betances, a principal with the Chicago-based consulting firm of Sounder, Betances and Associates and a professor at Northeastern Illinois University, was asked to investigate the term, he came up with the following:

> *[Mayate]* has origins in the description of an insect/beetle type animal which is black in color and is said to feed on animal and human excrement. It has worked itself into the vocabulary of Latinos who, with malice or without thought and/or knowledge of how demeaning the term is, describe African Americans with it. In essence it is as close to the derogatory term "nigger" as Hispanics can get. There is no literal translation from English into Spanish for the insulting word

> "nigger." In the word "*mayate*" Latinos have become creative in finding their own cultural term to insult African Americans if they choose to do so.

Mayate, Betances noted, "has been transplanted from the Southwest to the Northwest and Midwest. There the term has been slightly modified and the word is spelled '*moyeto*.' The term '*moyeto*' has emerged and found currency amongst youth in the *barrios* when they refer disparagingly to African–Americans." Playwright Dolores Prida believes *moyeto* may be older than Betances suggests, having interviewed elderly Puerto Ricans who recall the term from childhood. Wherever the word originated, however, Betances's essential observation is correct: Racism in Latin America has generally not been quite as ugly as in the United States.

Vidal (who is now with the Council on Foreign Relations) has spent much of his life bounding between the United States and South America, between Anglo and Latin conceptions of race. As a person of Puerto Rican and Dominican extraction who—in the United States at least—is considered black, he has always been acutely aware that race matters considerably more than either Latinos or Anglo-Americans often wish to admit. The difference, he suggested, is in how actively or passively the racial agenda is pursued.

"Here (in America) everybody is aware of the thing I call the active paradigm," observed Vidal. The entire society, in other words, reinforces the notion, often bluntly, that racial differences count. With rigidly segregated neighborhoods and racially circumscribed social networks at every socioeconomic level, there is no avoiding the fact that racial differences are considered important, that racism exists. In much of Latin America, "you can get by with no knowledge that it exists, but if you look a little deeper, you will find it; [but] the society is not actively sustaining it, and in fact, may deny its existence." Much like the teachers in the "Wexler" school, they have ended racism by the simple act of deciding not to recognize it. Dealing with discrimination in the face of such denial can be especially frustrating, for the people who practice it, as one scholar pointed out, aren't even aware enough to be embarrassed by it.

My wife, Lee Llambelis, for example, who spent an undergraduate semester studying in Bogotá, Colombia, felt "unwelcome" during most of her time there. The treatment she and her white Georgetown classmate received could not have been more different. "In school the Colombian students were not friendly to me; they were friendly to Carol. There were endless comments about my unruly hair. And there was always commentary as to how dark I was, always a reference to my skin color, and how my skin color was the same as their maid's, or how I resembled their maid. It wasn't meant as a compliment," recalled Lee, whose Puerto Rican features show conspicuous evidence of her African and Taino ancestors.

A member of a prominent Colombian family ran the student exchange program, and one day (perhaps in the mistaken hope that Lee could somehow intervene), she pulled Lee aside to discuss a major impending problem. Georgetown was planning to send an African American female student, and the program director was finding it impossible to get a family to agree to take the student. She was furious—not with her bigoted friends, but with Georgetown officials, whose stupidity in trying to place a black student with a good, upper-class Colombian family seemed, to her, unforgivable.

Stephanie Bell-Rose, now an official with the Andrew Mellon Foundation, had a similarly eye-opening experience in South America. Bell-Rose, who is a black native of New York, won a fellowship to work in a poor area of Venezuela, where she found herself among people who looked very much like the black folks back home. She quickly realized that most were in dire economic straits, in large measure, she concluded, because of discrimination. Yet, when she tried to get them to focus on the discrimination that was clearly apparent to her, they simply tuned her out: "They did not identify personally with any sense of African heritage, or with any kind of deprivation experienced as a result of that [heritage]."

In Peru the color distinctions are, by United States standards, offensively blatant. Black Peruvians, as *New York Times* correspondent Calvin Sims noted, are sought out as paid pallbearers at the funerals of the Peruvian gentry, as doormen at fancy hotels, as maids and as butlers, but are denied positions of prestige and power. In shops and restaurants, reported Sims, blacks frequently wait while whites are served before them. In the streets, "they are frequently called derogatory names like 'son of coal' or 'smokeball.' At job interviews, they say, they are often told that their experience and references are excellent but that the owners are looking to hire people with 'good presence'—a euphemism for someone who is white."

In many Latin American countries those of very visible Indian ancestry are treated nearly as scornfully as blacks, with only whites (a more elastic category than in the United States) accorded a full measure of respect. Anyone who has spent time in Guatemala, for instance, cannot help but notice that the *indígenas* are widely presumed to be childlike (albeit colorful) dunces and are burdened with other stereotypes just as unflattering as those bestowed on blacks in the Old South. The situation in Mexico and Colombia is not much better. A Colombian woman who considers herself Indian confided to me that, when she was a child, her father's approach to building up her confidence in her abilities was to remind her that her mother was partially white. Ironically, even as such attitudes flourish, so does the belief that Latin America is somehow beyond the problem of race.

In the course of researching this book and concluding that the notion of color blindness that is gaining popularity in the United States resembles a model with which Latin America is intimately familiar, I decided it would be useful to explore ideas of race and color blindness with a group of Latin American scholars. I ended up in Puerto Rico for several reasons—some having to do with personal connections and convenience, but mostly because Puerto Rico lies at the intersection of the United States and Latin America. Although Puerto Rico has its own Latin conception of race and Puerto Ricans typically think of their island as a kind of color-blind Shangri-la, Puerto Rico also has close ties—political; legal; and, in many cases, familial—to the United States and has been witness to the raging debate about race in America. Puerto Rican scholars would find it easier than intellectuals in, say, Venezuela, Colombia, Panama, or Brazil, I assumed, to make sense not only of their own feelings about race but of the feelings of people in the United States.

Emilio Pantojas, director of the Center for Social Research at the University of Puerto in Rio Piedras, and Marya Muñoz Vázquez, a member of the psychology faculty, were good enough to pull together what amounted to an ad hoc focus group of more than a dozen people who were interested—in many cases for obvious personal reasons—in racial issues. In response to my questions, they opened up a window into their lives, allowing me to glimpse a spectrum of their disappointments and their dreams.

After thirty years at the *San Juan Star*, the island's largest English-language newspaper, Eneid Routté-Gómez abruptly resigned. She was fed up, she said, with being the paper's sole black journalist (a dubious distinction she had held for most of her time at the paper) and with dealing with, among other things, people's astonishment that a black person would be working in such a place and at such a capacity. She found herself on guard even at the most commonplace events. At ritzy parties, for instance, "I was always the only black person there. I would say, 'Well, let me keep my hands down; otherwise they'll put a tray in it.'"

Initially, Routté-Gómez had believed that things one day would be better. Some years ago, after participating in a several-weeks-long multicultural management training program at the University of Missouri, she returned recharged and thought that perhaps a management opportunity would come her way, but no such job opened up. Much of the next ten years she had spent wondering why it had not and ultimately decided that she could no longer be patient "because I had no future at the paper, no future at all." So at the age of fifty, she quit. "Of course, everybody thinks I retired. But quitting and retiring are two different things. I decided to *quit*. I said I've had enough."

Routté-Gómez had learned, through her years of reporting, that she is not alone in her frustration. At times, she would interview prominent blacks, and when the business was done and her notepad was put away, they would tell her stories of their own anxieties and humiliations. "A lot of black people find that when you're in those types of circles, the pressures are heavy."

One continuing source of aggravation for people like Routté-Gómez is the widespread, if unconscious, assumption that blacks are not authentically Puerto Rican—that they are outsiders, excluded from the mainstream, much as many blacks feel in the United States. It is an issue that the black Puerto Ricans I spoke with returned to time and again. Palmira Ríos, for instance, found that her very identity—as a Puerto Rican—is subject to constant and subtle challenges. In public, many people assume that the professor of public administration at the University of Puerto Rico is North American and therefore will address her in English. It is as if they cannot acknowledge that she is both black and Puerto Rican. Isabelo Zenón Cruz, another professor at the university and the author of an exhaustive two-volume study on blacks in Puerto Rican culture, is convinced that Puerto Rico is far from coming to terms with the extent of its racial diversity. In *Narciso descubre su trasero: El negro en la cultura puertorriqueña* (Narcissus Discovers His Rear End: The Negro in Puerto Rican Culture), Zenón Cruz observed that the Puerto Rican society sends a simple and devastating message: "Whites are Puerto Rican; blacks are merely in Puerto Rico." More than two decades after the production of his groundbreaking masterwork—exploring how Puerto Rican poets, lyricists, folklorists, historians, and other shapers and definers of culture marginalized, erased, or distorted the role of black Puerto Ricans—he believes that Puerto Rico remains far from recognizing the blackness in its midst. Indeed, the phenomenon goes beyond nonrecognition: Blacks are simply expunged from many spheres of public life. "Glance at the newspapers and look at the images presented. The ads for the expensive *urbanización* developments always have whites in them. They never put blacks in any of those ads. The people are always white," commented Zenón Cruz. Ríos made essentially the same observation: "With respect to the private sector, it's outrageous. You don't find black people in any kind of decision-making positions, even clerical positions. There's this notion that people don't want to be served by black people, and there is really no way to redress that."

After all these years, Routté-Gómez has still not grown accustomed to the exclusion that comes with black skin. "When I go to these places like the Senate, I always say, 'I don't see anybody who looks like me here. *Where are they*?'"

Ray Petty, a white American and a professor of education at Inter-American University in Ponce, had the same question. "I look around at my colleagues at the university and there are no black faces on the faculty, or one or two out of one hundred and fifty. . . . *Why?* If you talk to white Puerto Ricans, there is no racism. But go to any hospital and see how many black doctors you'll find. There are some, but not in anywhere near the numbers that blacks are represented in the general population."

That after seven years on the island, Petty remains perplexed by its racial contradictions is certainly not his fault, for looking at Latin American race relations through North American eyes can be like looking into a crazily contorting fun house mirror. In the same way that the fat become thin and the tall become short in that mirror, North America's segregation becomes Latin America's racial rainbow, the angry racial politics of the North becomes the color-blind complacency of the South, the American precedence of race over class becomes the Latin precedence of class over race, America's racial allegiances become Puerto Rico's racial denial, and what is black in one place becomes white in another. As psychologist Antonio Díaz–Royo told journalist Routté-Gómez: "Over there one drop of black blood makes you black. Here, one drop of white blood makes you white." Yet, appearances—as those just mentioned attest—can be confoundingly deceptive.

Mayra Santos, a professor of Hispanic studies at the University of Puerto Rico, described the Puerto Rican paradigm as "forced integrationist racism," compared to the "forced separation racism" in the United States. "We are forced to integrate under this thing called Puerto Rican but then, of course, there are some that are more Puerto Rican than others. At the same time that you get included, you get erased."

The erasure of black identity takes places in many ways, including the very act of racial classification. Many Puerto Ricans, for instance, will go to absurd lengths to avoid using "black" as a racial designation. "Me and other persons with skin even darker, they call *trigueño* (wheat colored). I tell people, I am not *trigueño*, I am black," remarked Zenón Cruz, whose dark brown complexion would, in the United States, leave him no alternative but to be "black." Ada Verdejo Carrión, a schoolteacher from Carolina, Puerto Rico, likewise refuses to accept what she considers a denial of her racial reality. "For me, the fundamental issue is identity." So she insists on being identified as black—not as some in-between hue or even as a "person of color." "I can deal with that phrase in the States," she said. "I understand the mentality of the movement of people of color in the U.S. as a form of uniting." But she realizes that in Puerto Rico the phrase takes on a different connotation; it is a way of "denying one's blackness," a way of saying, *"No te digo negro porque te ofendo*" ("I don't call you black because that would offend you").

Their insistence on a black identity makes Zenón Cruz and Verdejo Carrión somewhat unusual because in Puerto Rico, perhaps more so than in the United States, color is an index of status, and blackness is firmly associated with the status of a peasant. So to rise above such a status is, in a sense, to rise above being black.

Santos recalled a conversation with a white friend who had grown up in a *caserío* (a public housing project). The friend, who had light skin and blue eyes, turned to her and remarked, "'*¿Nena, qué te pasa?* I'm blacker than you.' And he was, because of the race/class thing. . . . A person that is very, very fair-skinned can consider themselves black if they live in a project."

Ríos finds it sad—if inevitable—that such attitudes motivate a huge number of people with unmistakable black ancestry to deny their African heritage or to minimize their blackness and instead stress their Taino Indian pedigree as an explanation for their color. Her parents, she recalled, accepted their blackness and tried to inculcate some measure of racial pride: "I always remember when I was a kid and Sidney Poitier won the Oscar." Though she normally went to the movies in street clothes, when Poitier's film came to town, her parents dressed the entire family up and took them to the movie theater. "It was a very subtle manifesting of pride and identification."

The link between color and class has obvious consequences for professional mobility. Verdejo Carrión observed that teaching is an area in which black professionals can get hired with relative ease: "They need teachers, so they cannot start asking how many white teachers do you have or black teachers do you have." But moving up is another matter. Though a lot of the black teachers have graduate degrees, including Ph.D.s, few are to be found in the upper echelons of public education or in the universities. "Why do they not reach the universities?" Verdejo Carrión wondered.

Black teachers are also constrained in terms of what they can teach. "There is this frame of mind that you are not for the sciences," she said. "You are not for mathematics. You are only for cultural work. I believe that teachers are one of the perpetrators of racism."

Santos wondered whether she had personally become an object of such racism. "I am facing something very weird in my department," she confided. "Even though I have received a promotion and now I am an associate professor, I am not allowed to teach in graduate school—which means it is more difficult for me to get the next promotion—because people have problems with my style, my *professional* style." She thought, however, that the real problem might have more to do with her race; yet, when she asked for an explanation, race never came up, at least not directly. Instead, she was told, via the grapevine, that she talked too much to the students and moved her butt too much: "They won't tell me directly, so I can't prove this. They tell other people." But when she would ask for a clear description of her presumed deficiencies or for help in overcoming whatever her problems might be, "They [would] say, 'You're taking this too far. This is a small criticism. You *do* have a big butt.'"

Routté-Gómez believes that what keeps most blacks in low-status positions in Puerto Rico is not malice but a widespread and unthinking acceptance of stereotypes and of the premise that blacks belong at the bottom of the hierarchy. She recalled at one point, in her capacity as a reporter, being invited to the home of a distinguished family who had produced many female physicians. "And they had this [black] lady in the kitchen who had been their housekeeper for many, many years. They were very proud, she was *'de la familia.'* When I walked in, she was so happy to see me because I was sitting in the living room. And I said to myself, 'If this person is *a member of the family*, why didn't they encourage her to get an education?'" She assumed that her hosts would never understand that race was part of the reason, that they were simply incapable of seeing the woman as anything other than a servant.

Verdejo Carrión has also found that, as reluctant as they are to admit racism, many Puerto Ricans practice it with abandon. As a child, she was occasionally kicked out of friends' homes because of her color, and she has noticed that, in public, black Puerto Ricans are often spoken down to because they are assumed to be stupid. She has also noticed that when blacks appear in television roles or in advertisements, they are generally in stereotypical or demeaning roles—in ways that would be inconceivable on the mainland. One actress, for instance, was called *"una negra sucia* (a dirty black woman)" on television.

Yet fighting discrimination in a culture that generally doesn't acknowledge it is not an easy task. Indeed, many of my newfound confidants seemed to long for some of the toughness—and comparative candor—of the United States when it came to dealing with racial issues. As Ríos observed, although the Puerto Rican "Constitution, the legal system, formally prohibits racism or racial discrimination, in practice nothing has been done to enforce the laws." And since the census in Puerto Rico does not ask about race, researchers are handicapped in trying to determine or document its impact.

Ríos thinks it is unfortunate that affirmative action was never implemented in Puerto Rico; even though she is fully aware of its many shortcomings, she also believes it has value. Having been a member of hiring committees and gone through the employment process herself, she has seen how widely discrimination is practiced: "You realize all the nuances and the cultural practices that enable someone to discriminate and try to cover [it] up."

She acknowledges that making affirmative action work in a place like Puerto Rico could be extremely difficult. For one thing, there is the basic question of whom it would affect. "People would say, 'Well, you don't know [who is] white or black,' or '[What do you do with] those who self-identify themselves as mixed?'"

The disinclination of so many people to identify with blackness has implications that go far beyond the issue of affirmative action. Among other things, it diminishes the willingness—or ability—of Afro–Puerto Ricans to embrace each other. One thing that haunts Routté-Gómez is that in all the years she worked at the *Star*, no group of blacks ever came and said, "We support you" or asked how they could help. "It was very hard." She concluded that blacks have to support each other, that blacks have to make it clear that black people of intellectual accomplishment exist and that blacks are not merely singers, ball players, boxers, and prisoners. "We have to change the social perception of black."

Zenón Cruz remembered an encounter from years ago that brought home to him how eager some black Puerto Ricans are to have that perception changed. "When a local man from the neighborhood who was black heard that I was going to the university, he celebrated that accomplishment as if I had been his son. I asked myself, 'What's the big deal? Why is he so happy that I'm going to college?' Now I understand. He felt so much pride in me. . . . In my house we would sell bootlegged rum, and I was one of the ones who would carry it. The man pulled me aside and told me, 'Listen. Don't risk your future.' It was as if he felt somewhat redeemed by me. It was solidarity. It was as if he was saying, 'I didn't have an opportunity to [be a success] but here is someone who's one of us who is going to make it.'"

One day, during an idle conversation, Zenón recalled, he told the man he was proud to be black. "And [the man] responded, 'Are you sure?' If you had an opportunity to make yourself anew, would you choose to be black?' At that time, I would have said, 'No.' I didn't answer him, but at that time, with all the garbage I had endured as a result of being black, I would have chosen to be white."

Over the course of several hours, many other anecdotes and opinions poured out, and although there was minor disagreement on a few questions (on whether it is possible for someone who is black to reach the highest levels of Puerto Rican society, for instance), the group essentially declared with one voice that color blindness, as practiced in Puerto Rico and, by extension, elsewhere in Latin America, is a psychological cover for hypocrisy and that it was certainly not a model to which the United States should aspire.

Katia Fébrissy, a native of Guadeloupe and an exchange student from Paris, said that her experiences in Puerto Rico had helped her decide that she would most likely continue her graduate studies in Europe. Puerto Rico, she stated, is, racially just too difficult to navigate; though race was a subject "not to be dealt with" on the island, it nonetheless was a constant and unpleasant intrusion in daily life.

Psychologist Marya Muñoz Vázquez noted that blacks are not the only Puerto Ricans who are wrestling with racial issues; because she is white and tall, she is often assumed to be from elsewhere. "I had the experience of being told I didn't look Puerto Rican, and it was said as if it was meant to be a compliment. . . . Like I should be thanking them for that compliment."

Muñoz Vásquez gave me a paper from one of her students who had conducted interviews in Loíza, a black community several miles outside San Juan. Included among those interviewed was a girl of thirteen who said she dreamed of getting married in a couple of years and having many children. Her hope was that even though they would be black, they would be born and die "*sin recibir el desprecio de ser negros* (without being scorned for being black)." The girl added that she counted herself fortunate, for since she lived in a black town, she did not have to suffer the disrespect of whites. She asked the interviewer whether she understood and then answered her own question. The interviewer, she said, could not possibly understand because to do so she would have to be black.

Nonetheless, as Zenón Cruz observed, some black Puerto Ricans are speaking out—and increasingly through the use of lawsuits. Indeed, his own cousin won a $10,000 settlement from a high-class restaurant after he was refused table service. And in January 1996, the San Juan Superior Court ruled in favor of an employee of the Travelers Insurance Company who had complained of racial harassment on the job.

The employee, Zaida Morris Andino, claimed that her boss had subjected her to almost constant humiliation. In one instance, a supervisor told Morris Andino—who then wore an Afro—to straighten her "bad hair" in order to make a better impression on the public. At another point, her boss demanded that Morris Andino remove a second earring worn in the "vulgar" style common to blacks. She criticized Morris Andino—the only black employee in her area—for wearing jeans, although others wore jeans without censure. She loudly admonished Morris Andino at a party for employees, telling her, among other things, that her husband had left her because she was a "*pendeja*" (a vulgarity most politely translated as "good-for-nothing"). As a result of such steady abuse, Morris Andino said she had suffered from a variety of physical ailments, including depression, insomnia, and anxiety.

The ruling—which opened with a quote from author and philosopher Eugenio María de Hostos ("Men's spirits have no color") and concluded with the words of Martin Luther King, Jr. ("The Negro today is not struggling for some abstract rights, but for concrete and prompt improvement in his way of life")—found the company liable for creating a "hostile, abusive, intimidating and offensive" work environment. It also urged the government to pass specific legislation to protect against the kind of "racial harassment" that Morris Andino had experienced.

In some respects, the Latin American and U.S. models are not all that dissimilar; each, in its own way, finds great significance in race, and each, again in its own way, makes honest racial dialogue difficult. Each has opened up a gulf between the perceptions of those who are considered white and those who are not. Moreover, racial attitudes and racial issues in the United States and Latin America seem to be converging in certain respects.

J. Michael Turner, associate professor of Latin American and African history at Hunter College in New York and a former program officer of the Ford Foundation in Rio de Janeiro, noted that in Brazil there is a fledgling debate about affirmative action that is fueled by a "growing protest movement among black Brazilians as they become more politically aware of racism and discrimination in their own country and abroad." Some black Brazilians even look with envy at the United States and its relative clarity of racial definitions. As one black Brazilian told a reporter for the *Miami Herald*: "In the United States, black is black and white is white. There is open enmity, which makes everything much easier."

Enmity, of course, is not a requirement for addressing serious racial matters, and the current president, as noted earlier, has signaled his willingness to bring the issues out of the closet. Cardoso has openly spoken out against discrimination and caused something of a ruckus by announcing he was less than 100 percent white. Ironically, at the very time that some Latin Americans are demanding that their societies come out of racial denial, many Americans, as Louis Harris's statistics attest, have concluded that discrimination is no longer a serious problem or, at least, that it no longer seriously affects nonwhites' prospects in life. The United States, of course, is not South America; it remains far too segregated for the Latin form of denial to have any plausibility. By the same token, it is inconceivable that some of Latin America's more humiliating forms of discrimination (including the practice of complimenting people by pretending that they are a lighter color) would be widely emulated or tolerated today in the United States. Nonetheless, Latin America stands as an object lesson of the folly of pretending that a society is color blind in its allocation of opportunity when it is not. The danger is that inequality becomes even more entrenched because there is so little willingness to deal with its causes.

Obviously, opportunities for blacks and other persons of color in the United States have opened up significantly in the past few decades. For those who are gifted enough, well educated enough, or simply lucky enough, more doors are open than ever before. It is far past time for racism to cease being the all-purpose excuse for lack of achievement. Yet it is clear to anyone who takes the time to notice that many of those doors swing much more easily for some groups of people than for others.

That it is possible, in light of such evidence of discrimination, to talk seriously about the "end of racism" is a reflection of the fact that racism, in many minds, is equated with lynchings, beating blacks with hoses, and refusing black people service at lunch counters. It is about separate drinking fountains for blacks and whites, restrictive covenants, and openly calling black people "niggers." It is the systematic and brutal denial of basic human rights and dignity that characterized Jim Crow and whose very memory distresses many Americans who lived through it. Compared to such outrages, some of the racial problems of today may seem trivial or just outright silly. Yes, many blacks still live in ghettos, but the government is no longer forcing them to stay there. Who cares, in the scheme of things, if blacks are not welcome in every community or in every charmed social circle they may wish to enter? And how important can it be that corporations don't have many persons of color as senior executives?

If you believe that the natural state of the world or, at least, of American society is for whites to be on top and for most blacks to be on or near the bottom, concern with such things as the dearth of high-ranking minority executives may seem awfully tiresome. In the same way that many Brazilians cannot understand the fuss about the exclusion of Afro-Brazilians from the circle of the Brazilian aristocracy, many North Americans cannot conceive of a U.S. elite that is anything other than white.

Several years ago, a friend who had taken a job as a business reporter in a large northeastern city, called to talk about her new beat. Her newspaper had sent her to cover a meeting of many of the city's top business people. As she looked around the room filled with people, the realization had slowly sunk in that she—an Asian American—was the only nonwhite professional present and that she was there only because she was a member of the press. She had not realized previously just how white the business world was, she told me, a hint of disappointment in her voice. That experience, unfortunately, is not unusual for any nonwhite person who spends time wandering around the upper tiers of the mainstream business world.

Shortly after *The Rage of a Privileged Class* was published, *Forbes* invited me to speak at its annual symposium—the main purpose of which is to give executives who are important to *Forbes* the opportunity to rub elbows with the magazine's editors and top brass and to thrash out some important issues of the day. The event that year was at a resort in Scottsdale, Arizona, and the main speaker was Margaret Thatcher, with lesser lights scattered throughout the program. The crowd was pretty much what I had expected, meaning that it was virtually all-white. One black couple spotted my wife and me and, like soldiers who had recognized a friendly face behind enemy lines, promptly made their way over.

What stood out for me from that symposium, however, was not the crowd or the quasi-academic conversation, but a chance encounter in a corridor with a sales executive and his wife. The wife was a homemaker and the executive was a corporate functionary of no obvious distinction. In the course of the conversation, it became clear that they were tickled to be rubbing shoulders with the important people *Forbes* had assembled; they apparently took their own presence there as a sign that they had arrived socially. At one point, the wife, beaming brightly, told me she had enjoyed my comments and then added, "It must really be unusual for you to be among the elite."

I found the statement both amusing and appalling. I remember wondering just what elite she thought herself to be a part of. Nonetheless, trying to sound more good-tempered than I felt, I smiled and told her that I suspected I spent a good deal more time with the "elite" than she. The husband, apparently embarrassed, grinned sheepishly, and the couple continued on their way. But long after they had gone, I found myself reflecting on that woman's view of society, on the way she automatically assumed that being black meant that one spent little time in what she imagined to be the elite world.

Color blindness, in some sense, may be the only antidote to such assumptions—if color blindness is defined as refusing to typecast, hobble, or restrict individuals on the basis of race. The problem is that the types of color blindness that seem to come most easily do not accomplish that goal at all. If Schofield's work and the Latin American experience are any indication, color blindness, as it is most commonly practiced, is not a racial equalizer but a silencer—a way of quashing questions about the continuing racial stratification of the society and a way of feeling good about the fact that the world of elites remains so predominantly white. It becomes, in short, a way of justifying the very inequality for which it claims to be the antidote.

When asked how well the philosophy of color blindness had worked in Brazil, Turner gave an appropriately neutral answer: "Of course, that depends on who you talk to. If you talk to white Brazilians, they would say, 'It has worked very well. Thank you very much.' They don't see that there's a problem and are really irritated to be told that there is one; whereas, if you talk to Afro-Brazilians, their opinion is very different."

Much the same could be said about the incipient color blindness in the United States; the perceptual gulf that Louis Harris sees in his surveys is evidence of that. It is also evidence that race continues to play a clear role in how we see the world and that, laudable though the ideal of color blindness may be, we have not yet embraced the reality.

Still, the dream of a color-blind America endures, apparently nowhere more so than on the Supreme Court, which has rendered a series of decisions declaring that racial distinctions, without a powerfully compelling reason, are an abomination. Clarence Thomas has been particularly adamant on that point, and the majority of his colleagues have consistently agreed, which casts a shadow not only over affirmative action but over the Voting Rights Act of 1965.

In the pre–Voting Rights Act South, a series of stratagems—poll taxes, white primaries, literacy tests, intimidation, and murder—kept the registration of black voters low and made black officeholders scarce. A 1944 Supreme Court decision outlawed the whites-only primary, but it took the Voting Rights Act (passed in the wake of the Southern Christian Leadership Conference's Selma campaign, a milestone in the modern civil rights movement and among the defining events of Martin Luther King, Jr.'s life) to turn the black vote into a significant force. The act and its subsequent amendments did more than simply eliminate invidious and conspicuous barriers against blacks voting; it empowered the Justice Department to monitor and counter the myriad efforts made by southern whites to disenfranchise blacks.

From the vantage point of today's more racially blasé times, it's easy to forget how unrelenting and blatant that resistance was. In 1966, Mississippi's state legislature decreed that members of the board of supervisors and the school board would be elected at-large instead of from individual districts, so that whites, voting as a bloc, could prevent blacks from getting elected. Other states threw up similar roadblocks. There seemed to be no conceivable, effective color-blind remedy. So in desperation and in response to such shenanigans—and with the backing of Congress and the Supreme Court—the Justice Department began to foster the creation of so-called majority-minority districts.

The results were spectacular. As Chandler Davidson and Bernard Grofman documented in *Quiet Revolution in the South,* the number of black U.S. representatives and state legislators went from 2 in 1964 to 160 in 1990. Had it not been for the Voting Rights Act, the authors argued, the increase would have been significantly smaller. Nonetheless, the Supreme Court has lately become uncomfortable with the fact that race played such a prominent role in the drawing of the districts from which so many blacks have won office, and it is around these districts that the Court has made its stand for color blindness.

Two predominantly black congressional districts, drawn after the 1990 census, sent the first two blacks to Congress from North Carolina since the Reconstruction era. The districts were challenged by white voters, who argued that they were a violation of the Constitution. The Supreme Court agreed. Sandra Day O'Connor, writing for the majority, declared that racial gerrymandering "reinforces racial stereotypes" and threatens "to carry us further from the goal of a political system in which race no longer matters—a goal that the 14th and 15th amendments embody—and to which the nation continues to aspire."

O'Connor was particularly disturbed by the districts' "bizarre" shapes (one snaked along an interstate for much of its 170-mile length) and left open the possibility that a more compact district might withstand Court scrutiny. That hope was crushed by a 1995 ruling that invalidated a more typically shaped district in Georgia. The Supreme Court emphasized the point with a 1996 decision, discarding "majority-minority" districts in North Carolina and Texas on the basis that race had played too large a role in their formation. The Supreme Court majority apparently believes that, given the opportunity, the electorate may turn out to be much more color blind than Justice Department officials think.

Gary Franks, a black Republican congressman who was elected from a district in Connecticut that is 90 percent white, agrees with the Court. In his book, *Searching for the Promised Land*, he wrote at length about his ongoing battle with the Congressional Black Caucus over the question of color-coded districts. To the anger and consternation of the Caucus's leaders, he consistently took to the House floor to oppose the Voting Rights Act. Franks pointed to himself as Exhibit A in his case for color-blind districting. He offered his electoral victory as proof that whites will vote for blacks with a nonpolarizing agenda: "If you represent what the voters really want, they will elect you whether you are black, brown, yellow, white, or any other color. The idea that only blacks could represent blacks and only whites could represent whites seemed an anathema to basic American principles."

Franks does indeed offer a provocative challenge to conventional wisdom, as well as to those who claim that Americans have largely overcome our history, that voters these days have more important things than race to think about when they cast their votes. Still, Franks's personal triumph notwithstanding, many experts on the Voting Rights Act are doubtful his theory is correct. In the eight southern states that have been most affected by the Voting Rights Act, Davidson and Grofman found an "almost perfect correlation" between majority-black districts and the election of blacks to office. A study by Grofman and political scientist Lisa Handley concluded: "In the majority of southern states, not a single majority-white district elected a black legislator." The evidence simply did not support the assumption, said the authors, that most whites, left to their own devices, will ignore color when they step into the voting booth.

Richard Pildes, an expert on the Voting Rights Act at the University of Michigan law school, was equally pessimistic. He cited statistics indicating that the odds of a majority-white district electing a black representative were less than 1 percent, regardless of the district's median family income, educational level, or the geographic region in which it was located. "The arguments that Blacks need not run in 'safe' minority districts to be elected, that White voters increasingly support Black politicians, that racial-bloc voting is now unusual—all turn out to be among the great myths currently distorting public discussion," he wrote in a 1994 article in the *Harvard Law Review.*

In the aftermath of the Supreme Court's redistricting decisions, advocates for minority voters were demoralized and perplexed. Brenda Wright, director of the voting rights project of the Lawyers' Committee for Civil Rights Under Law, thought it absurd to blame polarized voting on the laws crafted to combat it. "We tried to ignore racially polarized voting patterns for a hundred years in North Carolina," she said, with the result that no blacks could get elected. Only after blacks gained office through running in predominantly black districts, she stated—and whites realized that blacks could do a good job—did some of the racially polarized bloc voting begin to break down.

Theodore Shaw, of the NAACP Legal Defense and Educational Fund, acknowledged the possibility that things could improve. "Certainly, we have the opportunity for white voters to change their conduct, to change their patterns, and [if that occurred] no one would be happier than I." The Supreme Court may well ensure that Shaw will get his wish, for it seems hell-bent on testing the country, on seeing if America will become, to paraphrase George Bizos, the South African barrister, the color-blind state whose role we are playing.

Voters' color blindness is, without question, a beautiful dream, and there are a handful of exceptions to the rule that make it believable—but only if one assumes that our destiny is in the exceptions and that Americans have grown enough in the past few years (or will grow enough in the next few) to render our racial history irrelevant.

CHAPTER 8

Twelve steps toward a race-neutral nation

In *The Fire Next Time*, James Baldwin offered an eloquent and urgent plea: "If we—and now I mean the relatively conscious whites and the relatively conscious blacks, who must, like lovers, insist on, or create, the consciousness of the others—do not falter in our duty now, we may be able, handful that we are, to end the racial nightmare, and achieve our country, and change the history of the world."

For people who cling to the dream of a bias-free society and believe in the power of words, in people's endless capacity for enlightenment, Baldwin's prayer resounds like an anthem, defining the challenge that still lies before us. Indeed, in some quarters, the message (albeit in a more multiethnic version) seems even more urgent now than it did some three decades ago when Baldwin first set down those words.

Civil rights advocate Constance Rice remains a believer, yet she finds herself worrying about the growth of intolerance. She recalled attending a showing of a popular movie with an audience comprised largely of black and Latino youths. At one point a Korean grocer appeared on the screen and was shot in the head. What followed left her dumbfounded.

"Both sides of the aisle cheered. My spine went cold." The incident not only horrified Rice, it convinced her—much as Baldwin was convinced—that something tragic is in the offing unless Americans learn to connect with one another and talk about race in an intelligent way. "We can make a choice that this experiment's over and we're going to go our separate ways . . . or we can start having this discussion," she said.

Writing in the *Washington Post* in May 1995, author Julius Lester observed, "America has never had an open and honest discussion about its racial dilemma. We—blacks and whites—argue, accuse, attack, mistrust, disparage, but we do not often make the effort to see with the other's eyes. We do not make ourselves available for the grace that would allow us to modify or even discard ideas and opinions that no longer work and may even be hurtful. The aborted nomination in 1993 of Lani Guinier for assistant attorney general for civil rights was a missed opportunity for the nation to begin a discussion on race."

Not that *beginning* a discussion has been the problem. The difficulty is in *having* a discussion that doesn't suffer either from platitudinous timidity or mindless enmity. Participants tend either to be as shy as uptight parents talking to children about sex or as combative as drunken brawlers on a Saturday night. In either case, the cause of constructive dialogue is doomed.

Lani Guinier believes that Americans are capable of doing better. When she and I met for coffee in November 1995, Guinier and Susan Sturm, also a professor at the University of Pennsylvania law school, were planning a project called Commonplace. They had already attracted seed money from the Ford Foundation. Their hope was to make Commonplace, which would promote and research interracial dialogue in the Pennsylvania area, into an archetype for a new national conversation.

Guinier's experience in the spotlight brought home just how difficult having an intelligent discussion about racial issues can be. "I was grossly mischaracterized and misrepresented," an experience that was particularly frustrating because she was not given the opportunity to defend herself or, as she put it, "to speak in my own voice." Even before that trial by the media, Guinier was intrigued by the thought of elevating the national conversation about race—"That's why I was interested in the job of assistant attorney general for civil rights in the first place"—but since then, the commitment has taken on the intensity of a crusade.

While she was being "demonized," Guinier said, she was also discovering that many people were interested in what she had to say. "I also think that people respected the fact that I choose to treat the experience as a survivor and not a victim. . . . So I think in some sense it energized me and made me more optimistic." She realized that people, certainly those who came out to hear her, were hungering for new ideas.

Her experience also drove home, among other things, the drawbacks of a sound-bite culture. Part of the problem, Guinier concluded, is that public discourse is usually less about reaching a consensus than about scoring points. "The way we talk to each other in public is very much structured as a fight. The metaphor is war. . . . It's very 'us' versus 'them.'" And when the subject is race, things can quickly get ugly. It is important, Guinier decided, to create an atmosphere in which people are comfortable enough to be honest, for she has discovered, much like Susan Wasiolek at Duke University and James Johnson at the University of North Carolina at Chapel Hill, that, even on a college campus, race can be an intimidating subject that frightens into silence those who should be learning from one another. She recalled a conversation with a white male student who approached her shortly after the O. J. Simpson verdict and confided that he was afraid to speak his mind. He feared that people would be offended. She interpreted his confession as a plea for "guidance on how to engage."

Getting beyond the polarization and the combative chatter, Guinier believes, requires something more sophisticated than the typical town hall meeting in which people of different races come together and either proclaim their love for all humanity or shout at one another.

She envisioned initially putting together small focus groups that would meet periodically for several weeks. "We're talking about fifteen people getting practice talking to each other. It has to be in a safe space where people feel that if they say something that is offensive that whoever is offended will tell them. . . . It has to be a [forum] in which there is some effort at structuring participation so it is equal, so that everyone feels empowered to talk, where there's a focus on listening not just talking."

Guinier also envisioned some Commonplace participants going beyond talking and working together in problem-solving exercises that have nothing explicitly to do with race. The objective would be to get them working as mixed-race teams and, in so doing, to provide them with hands-on experience in interracial cooperation. Eventually, she hoped to have the interactions culminate with town hall meetings—but only after those taking part had already practiced talking across racial lines and had developed "a sense of community and common language and understanding" in small groups.

The goal, said Guinier, "is to create a portable methodology that other people—not us—can use in their own communities; and it is also to create some media visibility for this process so that other people know that there is a new way of doing this, or a different way of doing this. And they can then seek to replicate it in their own communities. It's essentially a bottom-up approach to public conversation" and "can be a model for other people who want to work through hard problems."

Guinier is not alone in taking up the cause of interracial dialogue. The Houston-based Center for the Healing of Racism attempts to foster interracial communication through a multiweek discussion series called "Dialogue: Racism." For many years, the National Conference has sponsored Anytown USA, summer camps (located in twenty-six states in 1996) that try to teach teenagers how to deal with prejudice and other potentially divisive issues. The National Coalition of Advocates for Students studies and promotes intergroup-relations projects in schools across the country.

But even though I am a grand admirer of Guinier, I find myself wondering whether her dream—and other efforts such as hers—will ultimately fall victim to American indifference. A meaningful national dialogue, after all, requires a lot of work and a willingness to engage around a subject that most Americans seem to find unsettling, if not outright unpleasant. Consequently, such discourse, when it does take place—at least at anything more than a superficial level—tends to be among what I call empathic elites: those "relatively conscious" souls who already are disposed to reach out to each other and to try to understand perspectives that differ from their own. Most people don't fall into that category—not under normal circumstances, at any rate. Sure, when a race riot is raging in the background or when a huge controversy erupts on some divisive political issue or hate crime, there is a rush to comprehend the racial currents swirling beneath the surface. In more normal times, however, most people are ill disposed to do the hard work or face the hard issues that honest dialogue requires. And that is not only the case in the United States. Latin Americans, as I noted in Chapter 7, tend to deny that race is much of an issue. And even South Africans, whose history forces them to acknowledge the damage done by apartheid, are not terribly interested in reopening racism-infested wounds.

When I was in South Africa in 1996, Louis Farrakhan, the head of the Nation of Islam, had recently visited the country. Though Bonganjalo Goba, head of South Africa's Institute for Multi-Party Democracy, made it clear that he did not agree with the minister's sometimes venomous rhetoric, he nonetheless called Farrakhan's visit a "breath of fresh air." It was refreshing, he said, just to hear someone talk openly about race. "We can't talk like that because that would be viewed as racist," Goba said. "In South Africa, we have underplayed ethnic identities because we are moving to be a nonracial democracy." The reality, he added, is that ethnic rivalries will persist for quite some time, as will feelings of racial alienation: "As long as the economy is perceived to be in the hands of whites, there will be tension in this country."

Ran Greenstein, a sociologist at the University of the Witwatersrand, found the lack of racial candor striking. Instead, everyone declares himself or herself to be against apartheid and denies that racial differences are important. "Granted, there are no legal political distinctions on the basis of race," Greenstein said, "but there is a contradiction in it. On one hand, [political leaders] say they make no distinctions because of race. On the other, they say there is this 'legacy of racial discrimination you need to reverse.'" The new South Africa is "not like one big happy family. Race matters a great deal and I think it will continue to matter"; and to the extent that an official policy of nonracialism "makes organizations and individuals feel they don't have to do anything else, it's a problem."

In many respects, South Africa has no choice but to deal with the racism previously embedded in the very structure of the government. Civil servants are still predominantly Afrikaner. The economic hierarchy is racially skewed. And many families continue to cope with the pain and death inflicted by agents of the state on the thousands of people who stood up to apartheid. The Truth and Reconciliation Commission, chaired by Archbishop Desmond Tutu, was created as a way of responding to that pain—through creating a record of the evil that was perpetrated, making some sort of amends to affected families, and providing amnesty for those who confess their sins, in essence, by instituting a national dialogue that will help put the past to rest.

"We cannot talk about reconciliation and forgiveness without facing the pain" observed Brigalia Bam, of the South African Council of Churches. "Those who say, 'Let's forget the past. Let's not talk about the past'" are, in her eyes, being unrealistic. Yet the exercise of reexamining past incidents will itself inevitably create new divisions: "How do you relate to a colleague in your job situation who says, 'I'm sorry I killed [someone] but I was instructed to do it?'" Bam wonders about how she will respond if she is asked to forgive and accept those who bombed her former headquarters building in 1988. "We lost everything.'"

During a recent visit to Germany, where Bam attended a commemoration for Holocaust victims, she found herself reflecting on the fact that so many families were still in pain, even family members a generation or two removed from the horror. "And I thought to myself, 'We are really in for something in this country.'" She also recalled a visit to the Robben Island prison. "My brother was on Robben Island for ten years. He went there as a student. . . . I returned last year and when I saw the quarry where they put these people for ten, twenty years, my own anger was just too much. And I said, 'We expect people who have lost their husbands, their sons [to forgive], and it's a very hard thing.'"

Because such abuses are an elemental part of South Africa's history, Bam believes that the country faces a difficult task forging a nonracial future. "It will be much, much harder for us. Laws don't change attitudes. We are inheriting not only attitudes as you have in the United States, we are inheriting a national ideology, structures that were so much in place for years and years." Also, she said, just as many whites are finding it difficult to accept blacks as equals, "I think some of us [blacks] are also going through very difficult times in accepting whites, because of the pain that they subjected us to. . . . We talk of the rainbow nation because we have to create an image for the world . . . because we have been shameful, a shameful country, . . . but to heal people and to heal nations is not easy. The healing process has got to take place in the world from generation to generation."

Nelson Mandela clearly has done much, in a short time, to ease that process—reaching out to his onetime tormentors with dignity and grace. Despite having spent a quarter of a century in jail for no reason other than fighting the madness of apartheid, he shows not even a hint of bitterness. He appears, instead, to be the soul of generosity—radiating all the benevolent goodwill of an earthbound saint. It is a state he apparently attained in prison, as he explained in his autobiography, *Long Walk to Freedom*:

> It was during those long and lonely years [in prison] that my hunger for the freedom of my own people became a hunger for the freedom of all people, white and black. I knew as well as I knew anything that the oppressor must be liberated just as surely as the oppressed. A man who takes away another man's freedom is a prisoner of hatred, he is locked behind the bars of prejudice and narrow-mindedness. I am not truly free if I am taking away someone else's freedom, just as surely as I am not free when my freedom is taken from me. The oppressed and the oppressor alike are robbed of their humanity.

That creed apparently has allowed him to wrap in forgiveness those who imprisoned him. Yet Mandela, in the end, is only a man; he cannot wipe away the legacy of a history of racial oppression. Much bitterness, as Bam suggested, remains, as do deep economic and educational disparities. And full-blown healing may well be impossible as long as such inequality lingers, as long as so many people still live in dwellings of cardboard and tin with no guarantees of a cheerier future. Indeed, the very ability to imagine a significantly brighter future has been damaged by the deprivation that is endemic among black South Africans.

Jos Kuper, director of Marketing and Media Research, a Johannesburg-based polling and market research firm, confided that her firm was engaged, not long ago, to explore the aspirations of blacks in South Africa. One of the questions her colleagues tested with respondents was, "What would you do with a million rand?" The researchers immediately realized that the question made people extremely uncomfortable. If the respondents answered at all, they would focus on basic things—running water, a roof over their heads, husbands who would bring home money. The question, Kuper decided, was causing too much distress to justify its use in a research project, and she abandoned that line of inquiry. The possibility of moving out of the present class structure, she conjectured, was so remote for the impoverished people they were querying that they could not even comprehend the question.

"[Black South] African households, on average, earn approximately 2.3 times less than coloured, 4.5 times less than Indian and 6.2 times less than white households. Africans have nearly twice the unemployment rate of coloureds, more than three times the unemployment rate of Indians and nearly 10 times the unemployment rate of whites," observed Valerie Moller, of the University of Natal's Center for Social and Development Studies, in an article entitled "Waiting for Utopia" in the journal *Indicator SA*. Though whites make up roughly 13 percent of the population, they earn more than 60 percent of the nation's total income. Of 41 countries tabulated by the World Bank's *World Development Report*, none had a higher degree of income inequality than South Africa. Brazil came in second.

Largely as a result of apartheid-era policies (such as those prohibiting blacks from owning land or engaging in many forms of commerce), the distribution of accumulated wealth is also lopsided. Nearly 90 percent of the land under private control "has been and is still in the hands of whites," noted Bam, who sees such disparities as a potential source of continuing conflict. "We have to answer for the sins of our fathers; there is no way we can escape that—especially if those sins have put us in positions of privilege and wealth. We can't say we are not responsible and still enjoy certain things in our lives because of what we inherited from those people."

Similar arguments have been made about the distribution of wealth in the United States. *Black Wealth/White Wealth*, a 1995 book by sociologists Melvin Oliver and Tom Shapiro, pointed out that nearly two-thirds of black households have no financial assets and that even most black middle-class families are living on the financial edge. Though middle-class blacks earn seventy cents for every dollar earned by middle-class whites, "they possess only fifteen cents for every dollar of wealth held by middle-class whites," Oliver and Shapiro noted. "For the most part, the economic foundation of the black middle class lacks one of the pillars that provide stability and security to middle class whites—assets. The black middle class is precarious and fragile with insubstantial wealth resources. This analysis means it is entirely premature to celebrate the rise of the black middle class." The authors went on to call for, among other things, consideration of racial reparations and "a national conversation that realistically interprets our present dilemmas as a legacy of the past that if not addressed will forever distort the American Dream."

Oliver and Shapiro admitted that they were uncertain about whether "racial reparations are the—political or economic—choice that America should make at this historical juncture," since such reparations may "inflame more racial antagonism than they extinguish." But they argued that a debate over the issue is necessary, even as they expressed fear that reparations, if granted, may become a "payoff for silence." White America will say, in effect, "Okay. You have been wronged. My family didn't do it, but some amends are in order. Let's pay it. But in return, we will hear no more about racial inequality and racism. Everything is now colorblind and fair. The social programs that were supposed to help you because you were disadvantaged are now over. No more!!"

The odds are that their fear about a payoff will never be realized; a bill for racial reparations has about as much chance of getting through the U.S. Congress as does legislation mandating a huge payment to the descendants of the seventeenth-century Iroquois and Mohegans whose ancestors were conned out of Manhattan by Peter Minuit. As Mamphela Ramphele, vice chancellor of the University of Cape Town, argued, correcting for past wrongs has its limits. Eventually, one "may have to make peace with the past." A national debate on reparations would inevitably degenerate into a loud version of the old argument in which blacks try to put a current price on slavery and whites deny any responsibility for it having taken place—much less any obligation to pay off blacks who never suffered slavery, who weren't even alive when it was practiced.

Still, Oliver and Shapiro and Bam made an important point: The past fundamentally shaped not only today's distribution of wealth but the very structure of today's society. To pretend otherwise is simply to ignore reality and as pointless as it is to pretend that American racial attitudes, rooted so firmly in the past, have suddenly blown away like so much tumbleweed. There is a danger, however, in dwelling too long on the past; it can distract one from taking advantage of the opportunities in the present. It is not that past, per se, that is the issue. It is that serious problems, rooted in the racial sins of the past, linger with us today; hence the problems are that success in today's world remains color coded, that poverty and educational disadvantage are not equal-opportunity villains, that slums are much more likely to house blacks than whites, and that slums—for that matter—exist at all.

A national conversation on such issues is probably long overdue. Indeed, what quickly becomes clear, once one plunges into these matters, is that more than one conversation is in order. A colloquy on prejudice, discrimination, and the state of race relations inevitably leads to a discussion about economic and educational inequality and to another about crime and the criminal justice system and to still others about the breakdown of families, the death of aspiration, the prospect of ending urban apartheid. For even if racial attitudes were to magically change, so that people attributed no more importance to race than to the size of one's ears, there would still be pressing problems related to race. Such things as slums, crime, and substandard schools would still be more prevalent among one group than another. Part of the reason, as Oliver and Shapiro made clear, is that people of different races don't have the same economic resources. (Nor, for that matter, have we shared the same frustrations or been blessed with the same expectations.) To say that racially stratified slums would exist even if racism disappeared, however, is not the same as saying (as D'Souza and company do) that race is no longer a serious problem; rather, it is to acknowledge that race is not the *only* problem.

A growing body of work (including the research of Claude Steele, Joe Feagin, and Melvin Sikes, as well as my own *The Rage of a Privileged Class*) is showing that even well-educated, middle-class blacks face hurdles in life that comparably situated whites do not. Certainly, enough money can insulate one from most of life's unpleasantness. And surely, poverty concerns (meaning issues of survival) are more important than racial concerns (meaning issues of privilege and comfort). Yet it is shortsighted, at best, to use one to deny the importance of the other, for ideally we would want to solve both problems. Certainly, if we could ever get past the confusion of race (or mitigate its polarizing effects), we could see and presumably deal with our other social problems much more clearly. Whether we will do so anytime soon is an open question.

Kuper is one of many South Africans who believe that, as serious as the racial problems are in their country, they will be more easily solved there than in the United States. "My view is that we have suffered such a sense of shame—from those who felt it was immoral to those who were isolated from sports, in terms of sanctions and access; when they traveled outside they were vilified. A huge [sense] of relief has settled over this country since the election." Robin Richards, a graduate student at the University of Natal in Durban, explained his confidence in South Africa's potential by saying, "We are now part of the bigger world. It's an incentive to try to get things right. We don't want to be isolated again."

Haydn Osborn, general manager of Zizamele, a Durban-based organization that teaches carpentry and construction skills to blacks from the townships, sees a big difference in attitudes since the end of apartheid: "I know people who have had Damascus-type experiences. People seem to have had a real change of heart." He has even noticed, he said, changes in himself: "I still think in terms of black and white. I still catch myself having racist thoughts," he confided. But because he is now more aware, he can at least reject such thoughts when they appear.

Another white South African made a similar observation. His in-laws, he noted, were about as racist as anyone could be; when they realized a black-dominated government was coming into power, they had assumed that things would fall apart. Yet, he had noticed that they recently stopped using racial slurs and rarely spoke negatively of blacks. He believes their change in attitude has to do with the changes in their own lives. They run a small business that serves local people, and suddenly half their clients are black and the local officials who make decisions regarding their livelihood are also black. Such things, he concluded, change people's attitudes quickly.

South Africans have no choice but to try to "get things right," to continue striving to end their own peculiar version of the racial nightmare, for they either will "achieve" (as Baldwin would put it) their country or will perish. They will either keep alive the dream of an inclusive democracy or watch their boundless potential vanish in a whirling cesspool of racial and ethnic rivalries.

The United States—historically, demographically, and psychologically—is a very different place from South Africa. Our situation—at least in the minds of the general public, as Louis Harris's research made clear—is not nearly as urgent. We are less convinced that we—black, white, brown, and Asian Americans—share a common destiny. Many of us are quite comfortable proclaiming, as do many Latin Americans, that the problem is not with us or with our opportunity structure, but with those who insist on talking about race.

The comforting possibility is that George Bizos may be right: People may, in large measure, end up assuming the role they are playing. Recent U.S. history certainly offers some hope. When, primarily as a result of the civil rights movement, the most virulent forms of racism became socially unacceptable, those who wished to be in the mainstream largely abandoned it. They did not necessarily stop harboring bigoted thoughts or even engaging in bigoted behavior, but they realized that a line had been drawn that could not be crossed lightly. And many not only acted the part but transcended their former selves and became, in a word, better. The ranks of the "relatively conscious" have grown larger than in Baldwin's day—if a measure of that consciousness is taken to be acceptance of the proposition that decency and respect cannot be denied on the basis of race or ethnicity. And their ranks are likely to swell even more—if only because more people of different races are interacting as peers than at any previous point in U.S. history.

Research psychologist John Dovidio argued that simply getting whites and people of color to cooperate—either on their jobs or elsewhere—may go a long way toward erasing prejudice and helping people to see through each other's eyes. "People have a tendency to categorize others. . . . When we categorize someone as a member of our own group we tend to value them more highly. We tend to deal with them more as individuals. We tend to remember and process more fully and deeply things that they say. And when someone is categorized as a member of some other group, we tend to see that group as pretty homogeneous." Once people are categorized on the basis of race, other attributes have a way of becoming much less important.

In his experiments, Dovidio has put people of different races together as teams and then observed the results. "What we find is, particularly if they're competing against another group, [that] the salient category is not black versus white, but it's 'we' versus 'they.' . . . Athletic teams often have very positive race relations because the categories there are not black and white, but there's a team: our team against another team."

Dealing with prejudice indirectly, Dovidio believes, is sometimes the only way, for in today's world, those who are prejudiced tend to say they are not. So instead of demanding that people stop being prejudiced, Dovidio simply tries, in his research, to get individuals from groups that normally wouldn't have much in common to join forces on joint projects. He may initially divide people into two groups and give them tasks that force them to work collectively as one group. Those who work together end up much more warmly disposed toward one another than they were in the beginning. "What it does is it forces the people within a group to begin to share the same perspective," said Dovidio, who believes that the effects may last much longer than the experiments. "If you create the right foundation, it can change the course of subsequent relationships in a dramatic way."

But even as the number of interracial interactions and team efforts increases, racial polarization of some sort is likely to be with us for a long time. Despite the fact that amity and tolerance have grown in certain sectors, prejudice lurks in every crevice of American life. What if the hope of a transcendent dialogue, of a new social consensus on racial equality, is nothing but a pipe dream? The future may very well imitate the past—meaning that we may continue to muddle along, seriously seeking interracial understanding only in times of crisis, and even then finding it difficult to see beyond stereotypes and skin color.

If that is, in fact, the future, how are we to approach it? If the "relatively conscious" are incapable of spreading consciousness much beyond their own circle, what hope is there of us *achieving* our country? Those who wish to thrive in this society, at least if they are persons of color, have little alternative but to accept the possibility that race will continue to divide us—and, in spite of that, if we are to prevail, to resolve not to be defeated by bigotry, either of the brutally conspicuous or of the subtle and totally unintended variety. It means that we must accept the fact that life is far from fair and refuse to allow life's unfairness to become an excuse for failure, self-destruction, or paralysis. It means that we must tune out the voices that say achievement is for others and that counsel defeat and despair as shields against disappointment. It means, in short, that we must come up with a strategy that racism and other people's low expectations cannot easily derail.

In *Paved with Good Intentions*, a book devoted largely to accusing blacks of being more racist than whites, Jared Taylor made a relevant, if not a tactful, point. Blacks, he wrote, "must learn, just as Asians have, that whites can thwart them only if they permit themselves to be thwarted, and that society can help them only if they are able to help themselves."

Bernard Anderson, the assistant secretary of labor, would not disagree with that point. When we spoke in early 1996, he was working with a colleague on a book entitled *Soul in Management*. The book, which details the experiences of black professionals in big American companies, assumes that racism is a fact of corporate life. "It's there. You know it's there. But if you want a career in these institutions, if you don't want to become an entrepreneur, then you're going to have to deal with it. . . . You have to be shrewd. You've got to get around it. You can't complain about it, because complaining is not going to change it."

Sharon Collins, a sociologist at the University of Illinois and author of the forthcoming *Black Corporate Executives: The Making and Breaking of a Black Middle Class*, likewise argues that black managers simply can't afford to assume that their employers are looking out for their best interests, so they must make it a point to look out for their own. Among other things, she counsels black professionals and aspiring executives to eschew "soft" areas where their contributions cannot be measured, but to seek out work that will allow them to show that they can shine. She also advises them to be prepared "to move up on the open market rather than stick around and make a lifelong commitment to a company," to "be aggressive, proactive, and entrepreneurial rather than conform to the old models of a 'team player' and 'company man.'" In addition, she contends, they must forge interracial political coalitions within their companies, as well as develop constituencies outside, particularly in black communities, to guard against becoming isolated and therefore vulnerable to corporate sabotage.

This is not to say that the only way for persons of color to survive is to approach the so-called mainstream world as if they were entering a war zone; it is instead to say that it is only prudent to proceed as if discrimination is a real and ongoing possibility. The fact is, however, that in any number of ways, American society is considerably more open and more hospitable to minorities than it was a few generations ago. Those who are strong, determined, and intelligent can generally find a path to survival and perhaps even success, although the journey may not be easy. For some, particularly those who are young, it may mean fending off the temptations and terrors of the streets. For those who have already survived the passage into adulthood, it may mean coping with (and not being immobilized by) the fact that competence alone is no guarantee of recognition, acceptance, or success.

Forecasting the future of a society is inevitably a risky proposition, and I would not be so foolish or so pessimistic as to proclaim that the race-related problems the United States faces today will always be with us. Indeed, one thing that is virtually certain is that many of the particulars will change.

America is in the midst of a seismic shift in racial composition, and our racial definitions are not likely to survive it intact. Whether or not the government sanctions a multiracial category or declares

Latino to be a race, Americans have no choice but to acknowledge that the racial mix is becoming more complex—and individuals less subject to pigeonholing—than ever before in the country's history. That demographic transformation, at the least, provides an opportunity to ask whether as we change the meaning of race, we can also render it less important.

A number of analysts, as I noted earlier, claim that we have already done so—that if it was not for those noisy group-rights people, we could pretty much put the issue of race behind us. I don't happen to be convinced, but I find the prospect a tantalizing possibility—enough so that it should be put to the test. I, for one, would find it fascinating, for instance, if the foes of the Voting Rights Act really put their theories into practice and took it upon themselves to recruit scores of accomplished people of color from around the country to run in what are now considered "white" districts and monitor the presumably color-blind results. I would find it even more exciting if those who are so adamantly opposed to affirmative action in college admissions would organize efforts to upgrade the schools and the level of instruction in every slum in America, so those who are black and brown and poor would be better prepared to compete on an equal footing with the middle-class, white children who find it so easy to belittle their achievements.

But whether or not the prophets of the color-blind state are willing to put their speculations to the test, I believe that Americans of goodwill, and certainly those who count themselves among the "relatively conscious," have a responsibility in this increasingly racially ambiguous age to ask what kind of future we want to make. Are we at all serious when we talk about a society in which people are no longer judged by the color of their skin? After conducting some sixty-five interviews for *Black, White, Other,* Lise Funderburg apparently felt we are not. She became convinced, she wrote, "that the pressures in our country to separate black and white—and to make biracial people choose one over the other—are epidemic." Yet—and one must inject a *yet* because the other side of the coin is impossible to ignore—more than ever before, people are crossing racial lines to find friends, colleagues, and spouses. Many are trying, as best they can, to tune out the racial craziness all around as they search for a way out of the continuing American nightmare.

Given that, I think we have to ask the question—if only as an experiment in thought: What would it take to create a society that is truly race neutral? Do we have the vaguest idea how we would go about trying to create such a place?

The short answer, I suspect, is no, otherwise we would probably be much further along the way than we are. Still, I believe we can at least sketch some ideas of what needs to happen to get us there, of what sort of things we should be thinking about beyond such platitudes as "let's just love one another," which is the verbal equivalent of throwing up our hands in noble resignation. Why not instead conjure up a vision of a possible future—rooted not in dreams of some benevolent deity ushering in an era of universal brotherhood, but in recognition of the fact that our racial problem can only be solved by attacking its myriad components. Enumerating steps our society could take toward racial sanity is obviously not the same as putting America's racial goblins to rest. It is, however, a necessary prelude to moving the dialogue beyond the realm of reassuring yet empty platitudes.

So what would some of those steps be?

1. **We must stop expecting time to solve the problem for us.**

In the 1967 film *Guess Who's Coming to Dinner*, there is a scene in which Sidney Poitier (who plays a physician in his thirties who is in love with a young white woman) turns, in a fit of rage, to the actor playing his father. Only when the older generation is dead and gone, Poitier declares, will prejudice wither away. The sobering realization is that Poitier is now older than his movie-land father was then, and the problem, obviously, is still with us.

Nonetheless, many people assume that there is magic in the passage of years. "Eventually white Americans will be ready for a black in this position," they may say at one point. "Yes, inner-city conditions are bad, but eventually they will be better," they will say at another.

In his 1965 interview in *Playboy*, Martin Luther King, Jr., pointed out the absurdity in such an attitude. "Where progress for the Negro in America is concerned, there is a tragic misconception of time among whites," he said. "They seem to cherish a strange, irrational notion that something in the very flow of time will cure all ills. In truth, time itself is only neutral. Increasingly, I feel that time has been used destructively by people of ill will much more than it has been constructively by those of good will."

Time doesn't heal all wounds; it certainly doesn't solve all problems. It is often merely an excuse for allowing them to fester. Our problems, including our racial problems, belong to us—not to our descendants.

2. **We must recognize that ending hate is the beginning, not the end, of our mission.**

Occasionally, I turn on my television and am greeted by some celebrity exhorting me to stop "the hate," or words to that effect. I always wonder about the target audience for that particular broadside. I suspect that it is aimed mostly at people who don't hate anyone—perhaps as a reminder of our virtue. I certainly can't imagine a card-carrying member of the local Nazi group or the Ku Klux Klan getting so fired up by the message that he turns to the television and exclaims, "Yes, you're right. I must immediately stop the hate."

The fact is that stopping the hate does little to bring people of different races or ethnic groups together. Certainly, it's better than stoking hate, but discrimination and stereotyping are not primarily the result of hatred. They never have been. Slave owners, for the most part, did not hate their slaves. They simply didn't see them as full human beings, and they certainly did not consider them equals. Tolerance and even affection often come in the same package as prejudice. Thus, if we tell ourselves that the only problem is hate, we avoid facing the reality—as has much of Latin America—that it is mostly nice, nonhating people (such as those who boasted to Eneid Routté-Gómez, in Chapter 7, about the not-quite-equal housekeeper who was *"de la familia"*) who perpetuate racial inequality.

3. **We must accept the fact that equality is not a halfway proposition.**

For as long as the idea of equal treatment has been around, Americans have been trying to figure out a way to accomplish it short of *really* accomplishing it. Booker T. Washington's most famous speech, delivered at the Atlanta Exposition in 1895, was calculated to reassure the nervous and non-integration-minded on that point: "In all things that are purely social we can be as separate as the fingers, yet one as the hand in all things essential to mutual progress."

Several months later, John Marshall Harlan's famous dissent in *Plessy v. Ferguson* pointed out that equal treatment did not necessarily mean equality: "The white race deems itself to be the dominant race in this country. And . . . will continue to be for all time, if it remains true to its great heritage, and holds fast to the principles of constitutional liberty."

This century has seen huge changes in the status of black Americans. It has also seen the growth of largely segregated school systems, the development and maintenance of segregated neighborhoods, and the congealing of the assumption that blacks and whites belong to fundamentally different communities. The mistake was in the notion that social, economic, and political equality are not interrelated, that it was possible to go on living in largely segregated neighborhoods, socialize in largely segregated circles, and even attend segregated places of worship and yet somehow have a workplace and a polity where race ceased to be a factor. As long as we cling to the notion that equality is fine in some spheres and not in others, we will be clinging to a lie.

4. **We must end American apartheid.**

Martin Luther King, Jr., recognized from the beginning that America's racial problem cannot be divorced from the conditions in which so many blacks live. In an interview in 1967, he observed, "Some ninety-two percent of the Negroes of the United States find themselves living in cities, and they find themselves in a triple ghetto in these cities on the whole: a ghetto of race, a ghetto of poverty, and a ghetto of human misery." Such circumstances, he noted, breed lack of opportunity and despair.

Hundreds of scholars and activists since then have confirmed King's observation. In *American Apartheid,* for instance, sociologists Douglas Massey and Nancy Denton concluded: "For America, the failure to end segregation will perpetuate a bitter dilemma that has long divided the nation. If segregation is permitted to continue, poverty will inevitably deepen and become more persistent within a large share of the black community, crime and drugs will become more fully rooted, and social institutions will fragment further under the weight of deteriorating conditions. As racial inequality sharpens, white fears will grow, racial prejudices will be reinforced, and hostility toward blacks will increase, making the problems of racial justice and equal opportunity even more insoluble."

In investigating why residents of Brooklyn's Red Hook neighborhood had such a hard time getting jobs even though several employers were located in the area, social scientists Philip Kasinitz and Jan Rosenberg concluded that racial discrimination against blacks and Puerto Ricans was only part of the problem. The very neighborhood itself, an isolated urban slum, was seen as so undesirable that anyone who lived there had a rough time getting work. "In Red Hook, being a member of a stigmatized race, living in a stigmatized place, and not having sufficient diversity of social connections all come together to block residents' access to jobs, even—perhaps particularly—to those located virtually on their door steps," Kasinitz and Rosenberg concluded.

Much the same could be said about countless ghettos across America in which blacks and some Latinos are housed. And America seems less than eager to change that circumstance. As I write this chapter, the Chicago newspapers are running stories of a conflict in the Northwest Side community of Hiawatha Park. Many residents in that white working-class area are up in arms about a proposal by the Habitat Company to place a small building for low-income residents in their neighborhood. A *Chicago Tribune* article by Flynn McRoberts reported:

> In the spring of 1966, Martin Luther King Jr. waged his campaign for civil rights and open housing from a three-flat building on Chicago's West Side. He and the marchers he led were met with taunts and bottles.
>
> Three decades later, another Chicago three–flat is at the center of a fight over fair housing for minorities. This time, those opposed to the idea have set the bottles aside, but the message is the same: We don't want you here. . . .

> Walking among the more than 200 people who turned out Tuesday night in a gym at Hiawatha Park, one could sense the venom and the desperation.
>
> "They don't work, they don't pay taxes!" one woman yelled. . . .
>
> "Where are you going to go?" [a] city worker asked. "Wherever you go, they're going to follow you."
>
> The evening was filled with talk of imperiled property values, of how a poor family "getting something for nothing" had no right to live in the same neighborhood as someone working three jobs to pay a mortgage.
>
> It absolutely is not, the residents insisted, an issue of racism.
>
> But all the talk of property values and other concerns usually comes with the words "these people." After some prodding, one lifelong Hiawatha Park resident offered his translation. "When they say 'they,' they mean blacks.

In analyzing 1990 census data, University of Chicago sociologist Martha Van Haitsma discovered that roughly 60 percent of black Chicagoans lived in census tracts that were 95 percent or more black. In contrast, only .5 percent of Chicago's Mexicans and Mexican Americans lived in areas 95 percent or more Mexican—and none lived in census tracts in which 99 percent of the population was of Mexican descent. The extreme isolation of the black population made it easy for non-blacks to feel both psychological and political estrangement. Cross-racial political coalitions would be difficult, surmised Van Haitsma, "as long as poor blacks remain so incredibly segregated that any policies that affect a black neighborhood are confined to blacks."

Chicago is not, in all respects, typical. A 1996 study by University of Michigan demographers William Frey and Reynolds Farley found that in certain areas with fast-growing Latino and Asian populations, black segregation seemed to be declining a bit—even as segregation of Asians and Latinos was growing. Nonetheless, blacks remain, by far, the most segregated minority group in America.

Americans have paid much homage of late to King's dream of a society where people would be judged only by the content of their character—even as they have yanked children out of schools when a delicate racial balance "tipped," or planted themselves in neighborhoods determinedly monochromatic, or fought programs that would provide housing for poor blacks outside of the slums. There is something fundamentally incongruous in the idea of judging people by the content of their character and yet consigning so many Americans at birth to communities in which they are written off even before their character has been shaped.

5. **We must recognize that race relations is not a zero-sum game.**

The stubborn survival of segregation is both a reflection and a result of the tendency of many Americans to assume that the problems of one race have little impact on another. Whites can look upon a distant black community and conclude, as Van Haitsma puts it, that if blacks suffer "they are the only ones who suffer." John Marshall Harlan was right, however, when he argued a century ago that the "destinies of the . . . races, in this country, are indissolubly linked." The notion that "mainstream" America can completely shut itself off from the problems wreaking havoc in its ghettos is a dangerous myth. As NAACP head Kweisi Mfume told journalist Michel Marriott, "You can't create within a subculture a people that you have written off and expect that you will never encounter them."

The presumption that America is a zero-sum society, that if one race advances another must regress, is every bit as wrongheaded. Yet it accounts, in large measure, for the shrill and often illogical reaction to programs that aim to improve life for minorities—and most especially to affirmative action. Zero-sum thinking even explains some of the hostility that periodically surfaces within and between members of so-called minority groups. *Can only one person of color rise within a given organization?* One hopes not. *Does an increase in Latino clout portend a decline in blacks' well-being?* It shouldn't, though people often act as if it does. Undoubtedly, in some circumstances, the zero-sum model makes sense. There are times when one individual's success only comes at the price of another's. But the larger truth of any society is that the fates of its members are interconnected. Ideally, we can all progress together. Unfortunately, we have too often reveled in political rhetoric that puts across the opposite message; and we have too often rewarded politicians who, through their demagoguery, exploit our anxiety and insecurities—as opposed to those politicians who demonstrate the willingness and ability to harness our faith in each other and in ourselves.

6. **We must replace a presumption that minorities will fail with an expectation of their success.**

When doing research with young drug dealers in California, anthropologist John Ogbu found himself both impressed and immensely saddened. "Those guys have a sense of the economy. They have talents that could be used on Wall Street," he remarked. "They have intelligence—but not the belief that they can succeed in the mainstream." Somewhere along the line, probably long before they became drug dealers, that belief had been wrenched out of them.

Creating an atmosphere in which people learn they cannot achieve is tantamount to creating failure. "There is no defense or security for any of us except in the development of the highest intelligence of all," declared Booker T. Washington in the famous speech that made his reputation. America has been much too efficient at creating factories for failure. There is no reason why we can't do better at creating laboratories for success.

The various academic programs that do wonders with "at-risk" youths share a rock-hard belief in the ability of the young people in their care. These programs manage to create an atmosphere in which the "success syndrome" can thrive. Much like the general managers in John Kotter's study, *The General Managers* (discussed in Chapter 6), the more fortunate young scholars are challenged and supported at crucial junctures in their development.

One reason why theories about the heritability of intelligence are so appealing is that many people like to consider merit a fixed quality: Either you have it or you don't; either you are born talented or you are not. The real world is not so simple. How well you do in life and how good you are at a job depend greatly on what opportunities you were offered and what challenges were provided. Instead of focusing so much attention on whether people with less merit are getting various slots, we should be focusing (through the sorts of enrichment programs noted previously and, more broadly, by making achievement a priority in communities where it is generally discouraged) on how to widen—and reward—the pool of meritorious people.

7. **We must stop playing the blame game.**

Too often America's racial debate is sidetracked by a search for racial scapegoats. And more often than not, those scapegoats end up being the people on the other side of the debate. "It's your fault because you're a racist." "No, it's your fault because you expect something for nothing." "It's white skin privilege." "It's reverse racism." "If white people weren't so self-centered. . ." "If black people weren't so crime-prone . . ." And on and on it goes.

American culture, with its bellicose talk-show hosts and pugnacious politicians, rewards those who cast aspersions at the top of their lungs. And American law, with its concept of damages and reparations, encourages the practice of allocating blame. Although denying the past is dishonest and even sometimes maddening, obsessing about past wrongs is ultimately futile.

Certainly, loudmouths will always be among us and will continue to say obnoxious and foolish things, but it would be wonderful if more opinion leaders who engage in what passes for public discourse would recognize an obvious reality: It hardly matters who is responsible for things being screwed up; the only relevant question is, "How do we make them better?"

8. **We must do a better job at leveling the playing field.**

As long as roughly a third of black Americans sit on the bottom of the nation's economic pyramid and have little chance of moving up, the United States will have a serious racial problem on its hands. There is simply no way around that cold reality. As Latin Americans are realizing, it is rather pointless to say that the problem is class, not race, if race and class are tightly linked.

During the past several decades, Americans have witnessed an esoteric debate over whether society must provide equality of opportunity to minorities or somehow ensure equality of result. It is, however, something of a phony debate, for the two concepts are not altogether separate things. If America was, in fact, providing equality of opportunity, then we would certainly have something closer to equality of racial result than we do at present. The problem is that equality of opportunity has generally been defined quite narrowly—such as simply letting blacks and whites take the same test, or apply for the same job. Yet as Oliver and Shapiro made clear, equality of opportunity is meaningless when inherited wealth is such a large determinant of what schools one attends (and even whether one goes to school), what neighborhoods one can live in, and what influences and contacts one is exposed to.

Most blacks, Oliver and Shapiro pointed out, have virtually no wealth—even if they do earn a decent income. A mere two thousand dollars in financial assets, according to their calculations, is sufficient to put one among the wealthiest one-fifth of black households. Whites with equal educational levels to blacks typically have five to ten times as much wealth, they estimated, largely because whites are much more likely than blacks to inherit or receive gifts of substantial unearned assets. This disparity is a direct result of Jim Crow practices and discriminatory laws and policies that prevented most blacks, until recently, from amassing much of anything that could be passed on to their children.

Clearly, at this juncture, America is not about to adopt any scheme (justifiable though it may be) to redistribute resources materially. What Americans must do, however, if we are at all serious about equality of opportunity, is to make it easier for those without substantial resources to have secure housing outside urban ghettos, to receive a high-quality education, and to have access to decent jobs.

In *When Work Disappears,* William Julius Wilson made the startling point: that for the first time in this century most adults in America's inner ghettos are without work. Joblessness, in and of itself, is bad enough; but as Wilson made clear, it also fuels a host of other ills—including crime, family dissolution, and despair. To talk about economic equality without also talking about jobs for those in America's most distressed communities is to talk nonsense. Similarly, a theoretical commitment to equal educational opportunity is meaningless without a genuine commitment to ensuring that all Americans can receive a good education.

Foes of academic affirmative action inevitably point to how poorly prepared some students of color are for a college education. They tend to be silent when it comes to offering support for programs that could boost those students' achievement long before they knock at the university door. Their silence is not only socially irresponsible, it is unconscionable.

9. **We must become serious about fighting discrimination.**

It's impossible to ensure access to better jobs and better housing without actively taking on the residual discrimination in our society. Shelby Steele was right when he suggested (see Chapter 6) that discrimination is evil and that morality requires resisting it, although that is a message a lot of people would prefer not to hear.

In their rush to declare this society color blind, some Americans have leaped to the conclusion that discrimination has largely disappeared. They explain away what little discrimination they believe exists as the fault of a few isolated individuals or the result of the oversensitivity of minorities or by observing that most Americans, being decent people, would not dare to break the law by practicing discrimination. A white talk-show host on the West Coast once told me—seriously, I think—that the treatment he received when he walked around the city in blue jeans was probably no different from what a similarly dressed black man would encounter. On any given day, that may or may not be true. The point is that assuming it is true is not the same as ensuring that it is.

As Rice observed, we would not do away with the Internal Revenue Service out of an assumption that Americans, left to their own devices, generally obey the law. Instead, we empower the IRS to audit their returns, confiscate their property, and put them in jail if they don't pay the proper amount. We certainly don't leave it up to individuals who feel cheated out of their fellow citizens' tax dollars to take the delinquents to court.

Making discrimination a felony is probably not a solution, but more aggressive monitoring and prosecution—especially in housing and employment situations—would not be a bad start. Instead, many Americans seem determined to make discrimination easier to ignore. The Equal Employment Opportunity Commission is perennially underfunded and backlogged. (EEOC chairman Gilbert Casellas was so frustrated after sixteen months on his job that he bitterly complained to a *Washington Post* reporter, "Nobody gives a crap about us.") And politicians are calling for cutbacks in the use of interracial "testers" who investigate discrimination in housing markets. Just as one cannot get beyond race by treating different races differently, one cannot get beyond discrimination by refusing to acknowledge it. One can get beyond discrimination only by fighting it vigorously wherever it is found.

10. **We must keep the conversation going.**

Dialogue clearly is no cure-all for racial estrangement. Conversations, as opposed to confrontations, about race are inevitably aimed at a select few—those who are "relatively conscious," those who make up the empathic elite. Many (probably most) Americans have virtually no interest in race until a racial situation explodes in their backyard. Yet, limited as the audience may be, the ongoing discourse is crucial. It gives those who are sincerely interested in examining their attitudes and behavior an opportunity to do so, and, in some instances, can even lead to change, assuming that individuals are willing to do so.

During the 1996 Democratic Convention, Bill Bradley presided over an "UnConvention" that focused on interracial communication. The meeting, sponsored by the Human Relations Foundation of Chicago, featured several big-name authors, including Toni Morrison, Cornel West, Bharati Mukherjee, and David Henry Hwang. Bradley reasoned that writers, particularly those who cross racial lines in their fiction, might be able to help people to see the world through the eyes of another race. He also hoped the event would attract enough attention to serve as an inspiration to President Clinton, and to persuade him of the importance of speaking more regularly on racial issues. The president of the United States has a mighty microphone, said Bradley. "Why not take this microphone and take people on a journey toward racial healing."

Although the UnConvention drew a crowd of enthusiastic Chicagoans, it did not attract much attention from the media or from delegates to the DNC. Yet when I spoke with Bradley the following day, he refused to believe the news media's indifference was indicative of the feelings of ordinary people. Many Americans, he argued, were eager for an in-depth conversation exploring racial issues. One can only hope that he is right; for dialogue at its best, as Lester suggested, can provide the wisdom and grace that enable us to focus on useful strategies and to discard those that are not. It clarifies issues that, sooner or later, will become important to everyone; it defines the goals that the nation must strive to reach—even those goals that seem impossible or currently unachievable.

As Baldwin observed: "[In] our time, as in every time, the impossible is the least that one can demand—and one is, after all, emboldened by the spectacle of human history in general, and American Negro history in particular, for it testifies to nothing less than the perpetual achievement of the impossible."

11. **We must seize opportunities for interracial collaboration.**

Dovidio has an irrefutable point: Even those who have no interest in talking about the so-called *racial situation*, can, through the process of working with (and having to depend on) people of other races, begin to see beyond skin color. Conversation, in short, has its limits. Only through doing things together—things that typically have nothing specifically to do with race—will people succeed in breaking down racial barriers.

The Changing Relations Project, a Ford Foundation-funded effort to promote cooperation among immigrants and established residents, examined relations among various groups in six U.S. communities and concluded that successful efforts rarely had an explicitly racial agenda. "When groups come together to participate in a shared task, the inspiration is usually a desire to improve specific community conditions—to secure better social services or housing, or to battle neighborhood crime and deterioration. The groups are not searching consciously for cross-cultural means to improve an abstract sense of 'quality of life.' Rather . . . they are struggling together over a loss of control in the face of dramatic changes in their standard of living. Shared activities reduce tension and competition and build bonds of trust among groups," the board's report concluded.

"If you can establish a sense of groupness, of being on the same team even artificially and temporarily, that begins to create a foundation on which people can have more personal, deeper discussions and understanding," observed Dovidio.

Those who are truly concerned about bridging the racial ravine cannot afford to ignore that insight. Facing common problems as community groups, as work colleagues, or as classmates can provide a focus and reduce self-conscious awkwardness in a way that simple conversation cannot.

12. **We must stop looking for one solution to all our racial problems.**

Meetings on racial justice often resemble nothing so much as a bazaar filled with peddlers offering the all-purpose answer. "What we need is a national dialogue," says one person. "No, we need more entrepreneurship," says another. "No, we need to talk about integration." "What we really need is self-help." "Well, what about education?" "If we could just get rid of affirmative action . . ." "No, it's values. What we need to do is restore spirituality and high moral values to our communities." "You're wrong, we need to focus on stopping the hate." "No, we need to save the children."

The reality is that the problem has no single or simple solution. If there is one answer, it lies in recognizing how complex the issue has become and in not using that complexity as an excuse for inaction. In short, if we are to achieve our country, we must attack the enemy on many fronts.

It is too much to dream that all the points just discussed will have relevance to every reader. I hope, however, that they will provide a useful framework for those who are searching for a sense of the possible and grappling with the difficult question, "Where do we go from here?" I hope as well that these points, and the rest of this book, will help to spark a more honest racial debate—one that acknowledges real problems for what they are but that also illuminates the fact that, intractable as those problems may seem, they are not unsolvable.

During an interview, Louis Harris recalled that early in his career, he confided his interest in race to Paul Lazarsfeld, and the great sociologist replied, "'Good luck. By the time you're an old man, you'll still be working hard on it and not sure how much visible progress there is.'" Having worked in the field for most of his life, Harris said, "I can say that's true, but having said that, I don't give up, and I [still] think, 'By God, it's going to change.'"

Martin Luther King, Jr., had pretty much the same attitude. In his final Christmas Eve sermon—delivered at Ebenezer Baptist Church in 1967—he recalled his most famous speech:

> In 1963, on a sweltering August afternoon, we stood in Washington, D.C. and talked to the nation about many things. Toward the end of that afternoon, I tried to talk . . . about a dream that I had, and I must confess to you today that not long after talking about that dream, I started seeing it turn into a nightmare. I remember the first time I saw that dream turn into a nightmare, just a few weeks after I had talked about it. It was when four beautiful, unoffending, innocent Negro girls were murdered in a church in Birmingham, Alabama. I watched that dream turn into a nightmare as I moved through the ghettos of the nation and saw my black brothers and sisters perishing on a lonely island of poverty in the midst of a vast ocean of material prosperity, and I saw the nation doing nothing to grapple with the Negroes' problem of poverty. . . . I am personally the victim of deferred dreams, of blasted hopes, but in spite of that I close today by saying I still have a dream, because, you know, you can't give up in life.

In the most moving address of the 1996 Democratic National Convention, the Rev. Jesse Jackson preached a parable of faith. He spoke of the joy his father (a veteran of World War II) and other black soldiers had felt upon setting foot on U.S. soil following the war. They had celebrated on the train that was to take them home, exulting in their victory, as they proclaimed to one another: "The Germans said we were inferior, but we beat them. Our pilots from Tuskegee shot them down. We won the war." Yet, as their train had proceeded South, past the Mason-Dixon line, the black veterans, in deference to Jim Crow, had to change their seats. Years later, in telling the story to Jackson, his father had tried to communicate some sense of his faith in God and country, even as he recalled the disgraceful treatment he had received. "And while he cried bitter tears, he said to me, 'Hold that Bible in one hand and the flag in the other, and you hold on.'" Later, as Jackson had looked upon his own son and namesake who was about to enter Congress, he remembered his father's humiliation: "And that day, as Jesse [Jr.] was being sworn in by Newt Gingrich, and when his hand went up heavenly [and] his [other] hand touched the Bible, I had one eye on him and one eye on that station about three blocks away, where my father had to get off the train as a veteran and sit behind Nazi war criminals. *My son* has been sworn into the U.S. Congress. It's called faith in the substance of things hoped for—and evidence of things unseen."

In the course of writing this book, I ran into Jack White, an old friend and correspondent for *Time* magazine, who inquired into my current project. When I told him I was working on a book on the subject of the "color-blind society," he shot back, "Oh. It's fiction."

White's lighthearted quip—and his was not an uncommon reaction, especially from people of color—had a serious point: that racial color blindness is a fantasy, something that exists only in the unreal world of the imagination. And certainly at this moment, one would be hard pressed to dispute the point. Yet the goal of race neutrality is one we cannot afford to abandon—not if we believe that America can achieve its potential, not if we wish to keep alive faith in the triumph of good ideas over bad.

Some years ago, in a detention center in Hong Kong filled with Vietnamese refugees, I spotted a huge cardboard replica of the Statue of Liberty. As I made my way through the center, chatting with people about their aspirations, I noticed that many of them had drawings of Lady Liberty as well. When I asked a man who had spent several years in various prisons and "reeducation" camps in Vietnam what the statue represented, he replied, with an almost beatific look on his face, "Freedom."

I was struck by the power of that statue, by its ability to inspire so much hope in people who had only the vaguest idea of what America was and a slim likelihood of ever reaching American soil. Yet the fact is that American ideals have always inspired the loftiest dreams. Liberty, justice, and equality, after all, are hardly trivial ambitions. Nor, at this point, are they subject to repudiation. They define, for us and for the world, a large part of what we claim to represent and the better part of who we are—a fantasy, rooted in audacity, hope, and the demands of morality, that we have no choice but to try to achieve.

SELECTED BIBLIOGRAPHY

Books and Monographs

Adamo, Sam. "Race and Povo." In *Modern Brazil*, edited by Michael L. Conniff and Frank D. McCann. Lincoln: University of Nebraska Press, 1989.

Bach, Robert. *Changing Relations*. New York: Ford Foundation, 1993.

Baldwin, James. *The Fire Next Time*. New York: Dial Press, 1963.

Bergmann, Barbara. *In Defense of Affirmative Action*. New York: Basic Books, 1996.

Biddle, Jeff E., and Daniel S. Hamermesh. *Beauty, Productivity and Discrimination: Lawyers' Looks and Lucre*. Cambridge, Mass.: National Bureau of Economic Research, 1995.

Bradlee, Ben. *A Good Life*. New York: Simon & Schuster, 1995.

Brodkin, Karen. "How Did Jews Become White Folks?" In *Race*, edited by Steven Gregory and Roger Sanjek. New Brunswick, N.J.: Rutgers University Press, 1994.

Cose, Ellis. *The Press*. New York: William Morrow, 1989.

———. *The Rage of a Privileged Class*. New York: HarperCollins, 1993.

Davidson, Chandler, and Bernard Grofman, eds. *Quiet Revolution in the South*. Princeton, N.J.: Princeton University Press, 1994.

Davis, F. James. *Who Is Black?* University Park: Pennsylvania State University Press, 1991.

DeMott, Benjamin. *The Trouble with Friendship*. New York: Atlantic Monthly Press, 1995.

Der, Henry. "The Asian American Factor: Victim or Shortsighted Beneficiary of Race-Conscious Remedies." In *Common Ground*, edited by Gena A. Lew. Los Angeles: Asian Pacific American Public Policy Institute, 1995.

D'Souza, Dinesh. *The End of Racism*. New York: Free Press, 1995.

Du Bois, W.E.B. "The Conservation of Races." *The Oxford W.E.B. Du Bois Reader*. Ed. Eric J. Sundquist. New York: Oxford University Press, 1996.

Duster, Troy, et al. *The Diversity Project: Final Report*. Berkeley: University of California Press, 1991.

Eastland, Terry. *Ending Affirmative Action*. New York: Basic Books, 1996.

Ebling, F. J. G. *Racial Variation in Man*. New York: John Wiley & Sons, 1975.

Ellis, Trey. "How Does It Feel to Be a Problem?" In *Speak My Name*, edited by Don Belton. Boston: Beacon Press, 1995.

Feagin, Joe R., and Melvin P. Sikes. *Living with Racism*. Boston: Beacon Press, 1994.

Franks, Gary. *Searching for the Promised Land*. New York: HarperCollins, 1996.

Friedman, Nathalie, Theresa Rogers, and Elinor Barber. *The Dilemmas of Diversity*. New York: Columbia University Press, 1992.

Funderburg, Lise. *Black, White, Other*. New York: William Morrow, 1994.

Galton, Francis. *Hereditary Genius*. 1869, 1892. Reprint, London: Macmillan, 1925.

Getler, Michael, et al. *Challenge and Change: A Report by the Task Force on the Newsroom*. Washington, D.C.: Washington Post, 1993.

Gill, Lucia, Michael Reilly, and Anne Wheelock. *Looking for America*. Vol. 1. Boston: National Coalition of Advocates for Students, 1994.

Haizlip, Shirlee. *The Sweeter the Juice*. New York: Simon & Schuster, 1994.

Harris, Marvin. *Patterns of Race in the Americas*. New York: Walker, 1964.

Herrnstein, Richard J., and Charles Murray. *The Bell Curve*. New York: Free Press, 1994.

Hirschfeld, Lawrence A. *Race in the Making*. Cambridge: MIT Press, 1996.

King, Martin Luther, Jr. *A Testament of Hope*, edited by James M. Washington. New York: HarperCollins, 1986.

Kotter, John P. *The General Managers*. New York: Free Press, 1982.

Leonard, David, et al. *The Implementation of the Karabel Report on Freshman Admissions at Berkeley: 1990–1993*. Berkeley: University of California Press, 1993.

Lipstadt, Deborah. *Denying the Holocaust*. New York: Free Press, 1993.

Lynch, Frederick R. *Invisible Victims: White Males and the Crisis of Affirmative Action*. New York: Greenwood Press, 1989.

Mandela, Nelson. *Long Walk to Freedom*. Boston: Little Brown, 1994.

Mensh, Elaine, and Henry Mensh. *The IQ Mythology*. Carbondale: Southern Illinois University Press, 1991.

Montagu, Ashley. *Man's Most Dangerous Myth: The Fallacy of Race*. 1952. Reprint, New York: Oxford University Press, 1974.

Montalvo, Frank F., "Phenotyping, Acculturation, and Biracial Assimilation of Mexican Americans." In *Empowering Hispanic Families: A Critical Issue for the '90s*, edited by Marta Sotomayor. Milwaukee: Family Service America, 1991.

Okihiro, Gary. *Margins and Mainstreams*. Seattle: University of Washington Press, 1994.

Oliver, Melvin L. and Tom Shapiro. *Black Wealth, White Wealth*. New York: Routledge, 1995.

Page, Lisa. "High Yellow White Trash." In *Skin Deep,* edited by Marita Golden and Susan Richards Shreve. New York: Doubleday, 1995.

Pompa, Delia, and Michael Reilly. *Looking for America.* Vol. 2. Boston: National Coalition of Advocates for Students, 1995.

Ramphele, Mamphela. *Towards an Equity Environment.* Rondebosch, South Africa: Institute for Democracy in South Africa, 1995.

Review of Federal Measurements of Race and Ethnicity: Hearings Before the Subcommittee on Census, Statistics and Postal Personnel. Washington, D.C.: U.S. Government Printing Office, 1994.

Ross, Thomas. *Just Stories.* Boston: Beacon Press, 1996.

Russell, Kathy, Midge Wilson, and Ronald Hall Sacks. *The Color Complex.* San Diego: Harcourt Brace Jovanovich, 1992.

Rutstein, Nathan. *Healing Racism in America.* Springfield, Mass.: Whitcomb Publishing, 1993.

Scales-Trent, Judy. *Notes of a Black White Woman.* University Park: Pennsylvania State University Press, 1995.

Schofield, Janet Ward. *Black and White in School*: New York: Praeger, 1982.

———. "Black-White Contact in Desegregated Schools." In *Contact and Conflict in Intergroup Encounters,* edited by M. Hewstone and R. Brown. Oxford, England: Basil Blackwell, 1986.

———. "Causes and Consequences of the Colorblind Perspective." In *Prejudice, Discrimination, and Racism,* edited by John F. Dovidio and Samuel L. Gaertner. Orlando, Fla.: Academic Press, 1986.

———. "Review of Research on School Desegregation's Impact on Elementary and Secondary School Students." In *Handbook of Research on Multicultural Education,* edited by J. A. Banks and C. A. McGee. New York: Macmillan, 1995.

Sowell, Thomas. *Affirmative Action Reconsidered.* Washington, D.C.: American Enterprise Institute for Public Policy Research, 1975.

Sykes, Charles J. *A Nation of Victims.* New York: St. Martin's Press, 1992.

Taylor, Jared. *Paved with Good Intentions.* New York: Carroll & Graf, 1992.

Thomas, Piri. *Down These Mean Streets.* New York: Alfred A. Knopf, 1967.

Tien, Chang-Lin. "Affirming Affirmative Action." In *Common Ground,* edited by Gena A. Lew. Los Angeles: Asian Pacific American Public Policy Institute, 1995.

Whimbey, Arthur. *Analytical Reading and Reasoning.* Cary, N.C.: Innovative Sciences, 1989.

———, Eugene Williams, and Myra J. Linden. *Keys to Quick Writing Skills.* Birmingham, Ala.: EBSCO Curriculum Materials, 1994.

Wilson, William Julius. *The Declining Significance of Race.* Chicago: University of Chicago Press, 1978.

———. *When Work Disappears.* New York: Alfred A. Knopf, 1996.

Wright, Richard. *Uncle Tom's Children.* New York: Harper & Bros., 1940.

Zack, Naomi. *Race and Mixed Race.* Philadelphia: Temple University Press, 1993.

Zenón Cruz, Isabelo. *Narciso descubre su trasero.* 2 vols. Humacao, Puerto Rico: Editorial Furidi, 1975.

Journals and Magazines

Alstyne, William Van. "Rites of Passage: Race, the Supreme Court, and the Constitution." *University of Chicago Law Review* 46 (1979): 775–810.

Andrews, Lori B., and Dorothy Nelkin. "The Bell Curve: A Statement." *Science*, January 5, 1996, 13–14.

Berkowitz, Ari. "Our Genes, Ourselves?" *BioScience* 46 (1996): 42–51.

Besharov, Douglas J., and Timothy S. Sullivan. "One Flesh." *The New Democrat*, July–August 1996, 19–21.

Biddle, Jeff E., and Daniel S. Hamermesh. "Beauty and the Labor Market." *American Economic Review* 84 (1994): 1174–94.

Bok, Derek. "Admitting Success." *New Republic*, February 4, 1985, 14–16.

Carmichael, J. W., et al. "Minorities in the Biological Sciences—The Xavier Success Story and Some Implications." *BioScience* 43 (1993): 564–69.

Cleghorn, Reese. "Taboos and Race in the Newsroom." *American Journalism Review*, November 1995, 4–5.

Dunkel, Tom, et al., "Affirmative Reaction." *Working Woman*, October 1995, 39–48.

English, Rodney K. "What are Lily-White and Read All Over?" *Folio*, August 15, 1993, 36–38.

Faundez, Julio. "Promoting Affirmative Action." *Indicator SA* 11, No. 4 (Spring 1994): 57–60.

Gilanshah, Bijan. "Multiracial Minorities: Erasing the Color Line." *Law and Inequality* 12 (1993): 183–204.

Gissler, Sig. "Newspapers' Quest for Racial Candor." *Media Studies Journal*, Summer 1994, 123–132.

Gladwell, Malcolm. "Black Like Them." *New Yorker*, April 29 and May 6, 1996, 74–81.

Gould, Stephen Jay. "The Geometer of Race." *Discover*, November 1994, 65-69.

Howard, Jeff, and Ray Hammond. "Rumors of Inferiority." *New Republic*, September 9, 1985, 17–21.

Jen, Gish. "An Ethnic Trump." *New York Times Magazine*, July 7, 1996, 50.

Johnson, James H., Jr., and Walter C. Farrell, Jr. "Race Still Matters." *Chronicle of Higher Education*, July 7, 1995, A48.

Kahlenberg, Richard. "Class, Not Race: Toward a New Affirmative Action." *Current*, September 1995, 3–8.

Kasinitz, Philip, and Jan Rosenberg. "Missing the Connection: Social Isolation and Employment on the Brooklyn Waterfront." *Social Problems* 43 (1996): 501–19.

King, Martin Luther, Jr. "Playboy Interview: Martin Luther King—Candid Conversation." *Playboy*, January 1965, 65–78.

Komaromy, Miriam, Kevin Grumbach, and Michael Drake. "The Role of Black and Hispanic Physicians in Providing Health Care for Underserved Populations." *New England Journal of Medicine* 334 (1996): 1305–14.

Konrad, Alison and Frank Linnehan. "Formalized Hiring Structures: Coordinating Equal Employment Opportunity or Concealing Organizational Practices?" *Academy of Management Journal* 38 (1995): 785–818.

LaBrecque, Ron. "Racial Resentment Hits Home." *Spectrum*, Summer 1993, 47–50.

Lawrence, Charles R., III. "The Epidemiology of Color-Blindness: Learning to Think and Talk about Race, Again." *Boston College Third World Law Journal* 15 (1995): 1–18.

Leana, Carrie. R. "Why Downsizing Won't Work." *Chicago Tribune Magazine*, April 14, 1996, 15–18.

Lemann, Nicholas. "Taking Affirmative Action Apart." *New York Times Magazine*, June 11, 1995, 36–62.

Lodge, Tom. "The South African General Elections, April 1994: Results, Analysis and Implications." *African Affairs* 94 (1995): 471–500.

Lythcott-Haimes, Julie C. "Where Do Mixed Babies Belong?" *Harvard Civil Rights–Civil Liberties Law Review* 29 (1994): 531–58.

Mbatha, Madoda. "Sharing Wealth." *Indicator SA* 11, No. 3 (Winter 1994): 43–46.

McGrath, Mike, and Andrew Whiteford. "Disparate Circumstances." *Indicator SA* 11, No. 3 (Winter 1994): 47–50.

McKinley, Colleen. "Custody Disputes Following the Dissolution of Interracial Marriages: Best Interests of the Child or Judicial Racism?" *Journal of Family Law* 19 (1980): 97–136.

Moller, Valerie. "Post-Election Euphoria." *Indicator SA* 12, No. 12 (Summer 1994): 27–32.

———. "Waiting for Utopia." *Indicator SA* 13, No. 1 (Summer 1995): 47–54.

Murray, Charles. "Affirmative Racism." *New Republic*, December 31, 1984, 18–23.

———, and Richard Herrnstein. "Race, Genes and I.Q.—An Apologia: The Case for Conservative Multiculturalism." *New Republic*, October 31, 1994, 27–38.

"The Negro in America." *Newsweek*, July 29, 1963, 15–36.

Norment, Lynn. "Am I Black, White or In Between? Is There a Plot to Create a 'Colored' Buffer Race in America?" *Ebony*, August 1995, 108–110.

Ogbu, John. "Cultural Problems in Minority Education: Their Interpretations and Consequences—Part One: Theoretical Background." *Urban Review* 27 (1995): 189–205.

———. "Racial Stratification and Education in the United States: Why Inequality Persists." *Teachers College Record* 96 (1994): 264–98.

Pildes, Richard H. "The Politics of Race." *Harvard Law Review* 108 (1995): 1359–92.

Piper, Adrian. "Passing for White, Passing for Black." *Transition: An International Review* 58 (1992): 6-32.

Pogrebin, Robin. "The Best Lawyers in New York." *New York*, March 20, 1995, 32–46.

Pollitt, Katha. "Subject to Debate: Affirmative Action." *The Nation* 260 (March 1995): 336.

Routté-Gómez, Eneid. "So, Are We Racist?" *San Juan*, December 1995–January 1996, 54–58.

Rudenstine, Neil. "The Uses of Diversity." *Harvard Magazine*, April 1996, 49–62.

Samelson, Franz. "From 'Race Psychology' to 'Studies in Prejudice': Some Observations on the Thematic Reversal in Social Psychology." *Journal of the History of the Behavioral Sciences* 14 (1978): 265–78.

Schofield, Janet Ward. "The Impact of Positively Structured Contact on Intergroup Behavior: Does It Last Under Adverse Conditions?" *Social Psychology Quarterly* 42 (1979): 280–84.

Shalit, Ruth. "Race in the Newsroom: The Washington Post in Black and White." *New Republic*, October 2, 1995, 20–37.

Shaya, Stephen B., Howard R. Petty, and Leslie Isler Petty. "A Case Study Of Supplemental Instruction in Biology Focused on At-Risk Students." *BioScience* 43 (1993): 709–11.

Shepard, Alicia C. "Too Much Too Soon?" *American Journalism Review*, December 1995, 34–38.

Steele, Claude. "Race and the Schooling of Black Americans." *Atlantic Monthly*, April 1992, 68–78.

———, and Joshua Aronson. "Stereotype Threat and the Intellectual Test Performance of African Americans." *Journal of Personality and Social Psychology* 69 (1995): 797–811.

Wanniski, Jude. "Journalists Who Accept the Findings of The Bell Curve Are 'Benevolent Racists.'" *Forbes Media Critic*, Spring 1995, 85–91.

Webb, Veronica. "Where Have All the Black Models Gone?" *Essence*, September 1996, 108.

Weber, Bruce. "Inside the Meritocracy Machine." *New York Times Magazine*, April 28, 1996, 44–59.

Whimbey, Arthur. "Mastering Reading Through Reasoning." *Journal of Reading* 29 (1986): 466–72.

Wills, Christopher. "The Skin We're In." *Discover*, November 1994, 77–81.

Wilson, William Julius. "Class Consciousness." *New York Times Book Review*, July 14, 1996, 11.

Wright, Lawrence. "One Drop of Blood." *New Yorker*, July 25, 1994, 46–55.

INDEX